12.50

THE ATTACK ON 'FEUDALISM' IN EIGHTEENTH-CENTURY FRANCE

STUDIES IN SOCIAL HISTORY

Editor: HAROLD PERKIN

Professor of Social History, University of Lancaster

Assistant Editor: ERIC J. EVANS

Lecturer in History, University of Lancaster

◆◆

For a list of books in the series see back endpaper

THE ATTACK ON 'FEUDALISM' IN EIGHTEENTH-CENTURY FRANCE

J. Q. C. Mackrell

Department of History
Westfield College, University of London

LONDON: Routledge & Kegan Paul
TORONTO: University of Toronto Press

First published 1973 in Great Britain
by Routledge & Kegan Paul Ltd
and in Canada and the United States of America
by University of Toronto Press
Toronto and Buffalo
Printed in Great Britain
by Ebenezer Baylis & Son Ltd
The Trinity Press, Worcester, and London
Copyright © J. Q. C. Mackrell 1973
No part of this book may be reproduced in
any form without permission from the
publisher, except for the quotation of brief
passages in criticism

RKP ISBN 0 7100 7583 9
UTP ISBN 0 8020 2089 5

For Alice

Contents

Acknowledgments

It was the inspiration and encouragement of Professor Cobban that enabled me to complete this study. He both showed me the possibilities of the subject, and gave me an apprenticeship in writing by his patient correction of my many drafts. If I can aspire to be a rebel among established scholars, I owe it to his example. My chief regret is that my thanks to Professor Cobban appear in a publication so long after his death.

I am also most grateful to those many friends and colleagues for whom *The Attack on 'feudalism'* has also been an attack on their patience. Professor H. Perkin deserves special thanks as the editor of the series, for his perceptiveness in seeing more clearly than myself what I was attempting to do. Professor A. Davies of the University of Swansea and Professor D. Dakin of Birkbeck College London were my indulgent examiners when an earlier version of this study was submitted as a doctoral thesis. I have tried to heed the valuable advice which they both gave me then, and am further indebted to Professor Davies for his kindly encouragement since. Professor C. N. L. Brooke of Westfield College London spared from a schedule, that others find exhausting even to contemplate, the time to give me some excellent advice about the presentation of my material. As the writing of the Introduction proved particularly difficult, I owe much to Dr J. J. Tumelty of the University of Glasgow for his kindness in helping me to clarify the logic in the argument. The meticulous reading of chapter II by Miss E. Moles of the University of Glasgow and of Dr W. A. Smeaton of University College London raised points which were important for the revision of the other chapters as well. I am further indebted to the latter for the loan of his elegantly-appointed flat in the Banff House, which made visits to the British Museum from the far North both possible and pleasurable. For Chapter IV, S. H. Johnson Esquire of the University of Glasgow allowed me to draw on his considerable specialist knowledge. Valuable suggestions for its improvement also came from both Dr F. V. Parsons of the University of Glasgow and Dr C. H. Church of the University of Lancaster. I wish to thank also Dr N. M. Sutherland of Bedford College London for her kindness in the early stages of my research in bringing to my attention many useful works. Miss J. Guyatt of Birkbeck College London, in her dual role as librarian and expert on eighteenth-century France, has been most generous with her advice.

Over the years I have imposed papers on many seminars. I am grateful especially to the members of the French Seminar of London University for much helpful and friendly criticism; valuable advice has also come from the members of Professor Hatton's Seminar in International Relations; the Seminar on the Enlightenment that was held at the School of Slavonic and East European Studies during 1971–2; and the History Staff Seminar of Dr A. G. R. Smith at Glasgow University.

I wish to stress that neither Professor Cobban, nor anyone who has been kind enough to help me, is responsible for the errors and misjudgments that remain: these are my own distinctive contribution.

This book could not have been written without financial assistance from many quarters. I am particularly grateful to the Centre National de la Recherche Scientifique for a generous *Bourse* to enable me to do research in Paris for three months. I am also grateful to the Central Research Fund of London University for paying at a critical moment the cost of a further visit of three months to use the Bibliothèque Nationale. The wide gap between these grants and my own earnings on the one hand, and the expenses of doing three years research on the other, was bridged by the generosity of my father who gave me much financial help, especially by lending me money at a time when there seemed little likelihood that it could ever be repaid. I am happy also to acknowledge a later contribution towards the cost of doing research at the British Museum from

Glasgow University, where I spent several happy years as a lecturer.

In preparing the MS. for the press I have incurred many further debts. My wife, in particular, has given me invaluable help in both typing the script and in elucidating many tough bibliographical problems. I have also received much help with the typing from my sister, Miss S. R. Colborne Mackrell, from Miss E. Hunter of the University of Glasgow and from Miss A. Freeman. The very survival of the MS. in one of its earlier versions I owe to my cousin, J. P. Dowson Esquire. When the pages cascaded onto the pavement during a rainstorm, it was he, not the distracted author, who had the presence of mind to preserve their legibility by ironing them.

During all the latter stages of the preparation of this study my wife has been a source of unfailing help and encouragement. She has been far more tolerant than I had any right to expect, of all the inconvenience and dislocation of our lives which the preparation of this MS. has brought.

Bibliographical Note

When writings are cited for the first time full bibliographical particulars are given. Thereafter, works are identified simply by the author's name, and by an abridged title in the few cases where reference has been made to more than one of his writings.

Although it is usual for scholarly works to be garnished with arcane abbreviations, such as *op. cit.*, *loc. cit.*, *idem*, *et seq.*, not to mention the repellent *id.* with its fatal fascination for certain academics, they have been omitted to avoid confusing the reader by an enigmatic brevity in a foreign tongue. Exceptions have been made for *ibid.* and *passim* which, despite their source, are useful.

The names of eighteenth-century authors give much scope to the perverse ingenuity of librarians. At the British Museum and other centres of bibliographical fashion they delight, for example, in hiding Condorcet under Caritat, Mirabeau under Riquetti and even dare to put Montesquieu under Secondat. Here the prosaic practice has been to allow each author to retain the name by which he is commonly known.

For anonymous works and those difficult to locate the reference number, at either the B.M. (British Museum) or at the B.N. (*Bibliothèque Nationale* in Paris), has been given.

I

Introduction

●◆

When 'the sleep of reason brought forth monsters' one of the first to appear was 'feudalism'. It was very characteristic of the *siècle des lumières* that it should have conceived from its own fears the monster which it then tried to slay with its reason. The hysterical tone of some of the writings on 'feudalism' itself betrays the limits of eighteenth-century rationalism. It is hardly surprising, therefore, that almost all historians, except the incurably old-fashioned Marxists, have tended to represent 'feudalism' as no more than a contemporary term of abuse. Many medievalists have long thought that feudalism was moribund, if not actually dead, by the end of the twelfth century, which would make the eighteenth-century attack on 'feudalism' six hundred years behind the times. These twentieth-century historians have the immense advantage over their predecessors, that the latter cannot answer them. It is difficult to understand, however, why eighteenth-century writers, including some of their best historians, should have expended so much energy in demolishing what was already in ruins. Their attitude only makes sense if their conception of 'feudalism' differs from that of today's historians. And it is, of course, contemporary conceptions of 'feudalism', and not the history of feudal institutions, that is the subject of this study.

Feudalism is usually defined by the latter as a form of land tenure in return for military service. According to that view, the disappearance of knight-service had removed the *raison d'être* of feudalism well before the eighteenth century. Yet, the pretence that it existed in its traditional medieval form was still maintained until the late seventeenth century. An ordinance of 1635 laid down an obligation to knight-service in the *ban* and *arrière-ban* for three months each year within the French frontiers and forty days outside them. Despite the fact that the *ban* gave fresh proof of its unreliability whenever it was summoned, it met for the last time as late as 1697.[1] Even in the eighteenth century many nobles regarded service in the army as the chief duty of their class. The very fact that feudal and seigniorial rights were condemned in some *cahiers* of 1789 on the grounds that the holders no longer performed the military service for which they had been granted, shows that the original purpose of feudal tenure had not been forgotten.

Feudal rights properly so-called were derived, therefore, from the contract under which a fief was held. With the disappearance of knight-service fiefs naturally tended to become assimilated to private property. The confusion was made all the greater by the snobbish habit of dignifying almost any landed property of the well-to-do by the name of 'fief' and by describing ordinary tenants as 'vassals'. Yet, as happened so often under the *ancien régime*, a partial collapse of the system did not lead to its replacement. Faith and Homage continued to be paid by holders of fiefs in the eighteenth century to their overlords, as in earlier times.[2] Among the most important marks of the fief were the *droits de mutation*, which consisted mainly of various types of relief, which were levied by the overlord when a fief changed hands. On *roturier*, or non-noble, property, similar rights of *lods et ventes* were claimed. The Crown itself reinforced these distinctions by levying a tax called franc-fief on *roturiers* whenever they acquired land that was classified as noble. The original purpose, a monetary compensation to the Crown when land passed into the hands of *roturiers* who were ineligible for knight-service, had, of course, disappeared much earlier. In the eighteenth century *franc-fief* was regarded as a tax on property which worked to the disadvantage of nobles, as well as of *roturiers*, by reducing the saleability of land.

The holder of a fief also owned the *directe*, or right to levy dues on lands that fell outside his personal domain, but within

[1] M. Marion, *Dictionnaire des institutions de la France aux XVIIe. et XVIIIe. siècles* (Paris: A. Picard, 1923), p. 34.

[2] *Ibid.*, p. 236.

the fief or seigneurie. The customary mark of feudal overlordship was the *cens*, which therefore retained an importance in the
eighteenth century out of all proportion to its yield, which, as
it was nearly always paid in coin, had long since been eroded by
inflation. It was sometimes replaced as the mark of overlordship
by the *champart*, which brought the seigneur much more
because it was still paid in kind. The *rente seigneuriale*, despite its
name, and also payable in kind, fell into the same category.[1]

Modern historians usually draw a distinction between 'feudal
rights' which were derived from the contract that upheld a fief
and the 'seigniorial rights' which were all those that had come
into the seigneur's hands by other means. Attempts to distinguish closely between the two, however, are far from easy,
as the Feudal Committee itself discovered during the Revolution. None the less, seigniorial rights can be classified roughly by
whether they fell on the person or on the property of the vassals –
or *censiers*, as those who paid the ubiquitous *cens*, were called.

The greatest restraint on the person of the vassal arose in
cases of personal servitude. In that condition if he left the
seigneurie the lord could exercise his *droit de poursuite*, although
the law courts in the late eighteenth century no longer upheld
him automatically. By the prohibition of *formariage* the serf was
also forbidden to marry anyone outside the seigneurie without
the lord's permission. Personal servitude was both rare and in
decline in the eighteenth century and differed, in any case, from
the serfdom of the Middle Ages. Rather commoner was mortmain which affected property. Under this tenure the *mainmortable*
enjoyed personal freedom, while being free to dispose of his
possessions only to direct descendants and then on condition that
they lived in the same household. Otherwise, everything at his
death fell forfeit to the seigneur.

The seigneur's hold over the person of a free vassal was most
complete in the case of seigniorial justice. If it were true that in
the last resort every Frenchman was a subject of the king, the
seigneur's right to have justice administered in his name
invested him with a share of the public authority for the misuse
of which he was seldom called to account. The chief advantage
of the seigniorial courts to the lord was that they gave him a

---

[1] A. Soboul, *La France à la veille de la Révolution* (Paris: Société d'Édition
d'Enseignement Supérieur, 1966), I, pp. 171 ff.

means of enforcing the payment of feudal and seigniorial dues. The right of seigniorial justice was also prized for the *droits honorifiques* which usually accompanied it. These accorded the *haut-justicier* pre-eminence in the parish church, which included the right to his own pew in the choir, to be sprinkled with holy water and incensed separately, and to be named personally in prayers of intercession. In rural communities where status counted for far more than wealth, these rights were often the cause of endless rivalries and dissensions. As it was a common maxim, however, that 'fief and justice have nothing in common' it might seem that seigniorial justice itself could be classified with complete assurance as a seigniorial, rather than feudal, right. However, even this rule did not always hold good: in some provinces the owner of a fief was assumed also to have the right of having seigniorial justice administered in his name.

Another right which the seigneur, by virtue of his power of seigniorial justice, exercised over the persons of his *censiers*, was the *corvée personnelle*, which usually entailed work on the seigneur's domain. In the Middle Ages the peasants had been *corvéables à merci*, but by the eighteenth century it was unusual for the *corvées* to account for more than twelve days of unpaid labour each year. The *corvées*, none the less, figured as a major grievance in the peasant *cahiers* of 1789.

Seigniorial taxes which bore on the property of the *censier* were often as burdensome as those which fell on his person. In some cases the same right could apply to either. There were, for instance, *corvées réelles* which were attached to land as well as *corvées personnelles*. Among the levies on property were the so-called regalian rights of the seigneur which included the *péages* and *droits de marché*. The former were tolls which were levied more or less arbitrarily and still numbered nearly 6,000 in 1770. The *droits de marché* existed under a wide variety of names, but were essentially taxes on merchandise brought to fairs and markets within the seigneurie. Along with the *péages*, they often proved remunerative to the seigneur.[1] The hunting rights of the seigneur can also be classified as arbitrary exactions on the lands of *censiers*. The *droit de chasse* itself belonged in most areas to all nobles and could wreak considerable havoc on crops. The seigneur himself usually had the right to maintain

[1] *Ibid.*, I, 176.

4

a rabbit warren and dovecot, which brought the crops of the unfortunate peasants under attack, as it were, from both land and air. Although it was beyond the ingenuity of the seigneurs to mount a water-borne attack, they did deprive the peasants of fishing rights by arrogating the *droit de pêche* to themselves or to others at what was often a lucrative rate.

The rights of banality do not fit neatly into any of the above categories. Although they took a variety of forms, the most widespread and onerous were those by which the vassal was forced to bring his corn to be ground at the lord's mill, his flour to be baked in his oven and his grapes pulped in his lord's winepress. The *banalités* were often ascribed along with other seignorial rights to the tyranny of the nobles during the Middle Ages. Yet it was often claimed with some justification that the *banalités* fulfilled an economic service in the countryside. According to this line of argument, the obligation of the peasants to use the lord's *banalités* was no more than a recompense to the seigneur for providing these services in the first place. Whatever their origin, however, the peasants in some of their *cahiers* showed that they resented the *banalités* as arbitrary exactions that lacked all justification.

None of the above rights can be termed 'feudal' without extensive qualifications. At most some contain a certain 'feudal element', while others do not possess even that. Therefore, it is easy to appreciate the impatience of medievalists with the 'feudalism' of the eighteenth century. Yet, surely contemporary writers ought not to be condemned by modern historians solely because their conception of feudalism differed from that of our medievalists. A better test is whether their ideas about the past made sense in eighteenth-century terms.

One sign that ideas are relevant to their times is the invention of a new vocabulary to express them. The fact that the word *féodalité* was itself rediscovered in the eighteenth century suggests that the attack on 'feudalism' sprang from contemporary needs.[1] Although the use of *féodalité* has been traced back to 1515,[2] it was employed rarely enough for a modern compiler to

---

[1] M. Reinhard, 'Sur l'histoire de la Révolution française: travaux récents et perspectives', *Annales. Economies. Sociétés. Civilisations,* XIV (1959), p. 569.

[2] A. Dauzat, *Dictionnaire étymologique de la langue française,* 7th ed. (Paris: Larousse, 1947), p. 319.

note its appearance in the *Coutume* of Normandy in 1599.[1] While the adverb, *féodalement*, appears in the first edition of the French Academy's *Dictionnaire* in 1694,[2] the noun *féodalité* was still too newfangled to appear in the third edition of 1718,[3] and so had official recognition deferred until the next in 1762.[4]

In the seventeenth century 'feudal' and its derivatives had been essentially legal terms. Lawyers concerned professionally to define the rights connected with a fief used 'feudal' descriptively without pejorative overtones, while, as they had no reason to refer to feudalism as a whole, the substantive was largely superfluous, which surely explains why so few of the *feudistes* in their treatises attempt to define it.[5] In the eighteenth century scholarly works still clung to the seventeenth-century juristic usage of 'feudalism'. The French Academy's *Dictionnaire* of 1762, for instance, defined 'feudalism' as 'Juristic term. Quality of fief. This word also means allegiance and homage. Feudalism is not prescriptive.'[6] if this definition is discounted because of the Academicians' well-known practice of trailing half a century behind the ideas of their time, it is notable that the authoritative *Dictionnaire de Trévoux* had described 'feudalism' in similar terms ten years earlier.[7] Even in the great *Encyclopédie* of Diderot under 'feudalism' there is no caustic criticism but only lawyers' jargon, which was indeed hardly surprising as it was written by a feudal commentator, Boucher d'Argis.[8]

Alongside the unexceptionable 'feudalism' of the lawyers there existed a looser concept of 'feudalism', which has received much criticism. For some eighteenth-century writers 'feudalism' admittedly was little more than a term of abuse. For instance the abbé Sieyès, who showed some care for accuracy in other

---

[1] A. Hatzfield and A. Darmesteter, *Dictionnaire général de la langue française du commencement du XVIIe. siècle jusqu'à nos jours*, 7th ed. (Paris: Librairie Delagrave, 1924), p. 1043.

[2] *Ibid.*, p. 1043.

[3] *Nouveau Dictionnaire de l'Académie Françoise*, 3rd ed. (Paris: J.-B. Coignard, 1718).

[4] *Dictionnaire de l'Académie Françoise*, 4th ed. (Paris: Brunet, 1762), I, p. 730.

[5] A. Soboul, 'La Révolution française et la "féodalité". Notes sur le prélèvement féodal', *Revue Historique*, CCXL (July–September 1968), p. 36, n. 3.

[6] *Dictionnaire de l'Académie Françoise* (1762), I, p. 730.

[7] *Dictionnaire universel françois et latin, vulgairement appelé Dictionnaire de Trévoux*, ed. P. C. Berthelin (Paris, 1752), III, p. 1464.

[8] D. Diderot, ed., *Encyclopédie ou dictionnaire raisonné des sciences, des arts et des métiers*, (Paris, 1751–65), VI, p. 493.

matters, in his *Qu'est-ce que le tiers état?* denigrated primogeniture as 'homage rendered to feudalism'.[1] P.-H. de Ségur's edict of 1781, in which those seeking certain commissions in the army were required to establish before the royal genealogist that they had three generations of nobility, was condemned in similar fashion by an anonymous pamphleteer as marking 'the return to barbarism and Gothic feudalism'.[2] While such pejorative uses of 'feudalism' were common, it is unfair to judge the eighteenth century on a point of history by its non-historians. Even the historians require to be read with more than usual care. Thus, Letrosne should not be convicted of ignorance because he wrote in his own day that 'feudalism exists'.[3]

He made it clear elsewhere that 'feudalism' as a system of land tenure in return for military service had ended much earlier and had, indeed, provided a perceptive historical sketch of feudalism's genesis and decline.[4] Similarly, when Perreciot headed a chapter, 'Inconvenience of feudalism: diversity of weights and measures', he was thinking of the centrifugal forces of feudalism, which he seemed to attribute to the very nature of knight-service.[5] Eighteenth-century historians and those of today differ less over the facts than in their outlook. The latter, if only because their inquiries usually concern a briefer time-span, tend to emphasize change at the expense of continuity. The eighteenth-century writer naturally saw feudal society *en bloc*, whenever he compared and contrasted it with his own. He seldom drew sharp distinctions between rights that were derived directly from the fief and those like the right to serfs or to administer justice which had grown up around it. Doubtless it was felt that, if feudalism had not given rise to all these privileges, it had at least provided the anarchical conditions in which they could flourish. Eighteenth-century historians gave to feudalism more meanings than meet with the approval of twentieth-century academics. Yet, that does not

---

[1] E.-J. Sieyès, *Qu'est-ce que le tiers état?* (n.p., 1789), p. 61 n.

[2] (Anon.), *Réformes dans l'ordre social et particulièrement dans le commerce* (n.p., n.d.), p. 18. For a discussion of the effects of the edict itself, see below, p. 45.

[3] G.-F. Letrosne, *De l'Administration provinciale, et de la réforme de l'impôt.* (Basle and Paris: P.-J. Duplain, 1788), II, p. 464.

[4] Letrosne, *De l'Administration provinciale* (1788), II, pp. 442 ff.

[5] C.-J. de Perreciot, *De l'État civil des personnes et de la condition des terres dans les Gaules, dès les temps celtiques jusqu'à la rédaction des coutumes* (Switzerland, 1786), II, p. 198.

mean that the eighteenth-century writers knew no history. They seem, however, to have felt more deeply about the past than most modern writers, which may explain why the latter find it so hard to forgive them.

Eighteenth-century conceptions of 'feudalism' cannot be understood unless they are placed in the context of contemporary historiography. It was the comte de Boulainvilliers, who rescued *féodalité* from the dry folio volumes of the lawyers and gave it back its historical meaning. Whatever the eccentricities in Boulainvilliers' ideas — and the professional historian with his deft understatements tends not to relish them — he showed considerable historical insight in his appreciation of feudalism. As a result, those who later disagreed with his views were forced to take issue with him in historical terms, which itself broadened their understanding of the past.

Boulainvilliers first seems to have stirred the interest of contemporaries when he announced provocatively, in a manuscript that was circulating at court in well-publicized secrecy about 1722,[1] that feudal government had been 'the masterpiece of the human mind'.[2] Boulainvilliers, who regretted that the French nobles had lost their former political power to the Crown, tried to show that the original Frankish rulers had been elected by fellow-nobles, to whom they had remained answerable in matters of government. The abbé Dubos countered with evidence that was designed to show that royal absolutism, far from being a recent innovation, had existed long before the nobles had usurped their power during 'the feudal anarchy'.[3] Anyone who studies Carcassonne's massive summary of the many views propounded in the controversy,[4] can hardly doubt that the reading public had at their disposal a considerable body of surprisingly well-informed writings on the genesis and decline of feudalism. The large space given to reviews of even

[1] R. Simon, *Henry de Boulainvilliers: historien, politique, philosophe, astrologue, 1658–1722* (Paris: Boivin, 1942), p. 152 n. (The careful reader will see that, unlike Mlle Simon, I have not ventured to take what might be construed as orthographical liberties with Boulainvilliers, which is the customary spelling of his name.)

[2] H. de Boulainvilliers, *État de la France* (London: T. Wood, S. Palmer and W. Roberts, 1727–8), III, p. 37.

[3] See pp. 25–7 ff.

[4] E. Carcassonne, *Montesquieu et le problème de la constitution française au XVIIIe. siècle* (Paris: PUF, 1927).

the most forbidding historical works in contemporary periodicals, which naturally had to cater to their readers' interests in
order to survive, provides proof of the public's heroic pursuit
of historical themes.[1] Some reference to the historical back-
ground is made in almost all the legal, commercial, humanitarian, and utilitarian writings that are considered in separate
chapters below.

The quality, as well as the quantity, of eighteenth-century
historiography increased enormously as a result of the debate
over the origins of feudalism. Even the most polemical of these
works were an improvement on those of seventeenth-century
historians who had so often strained after literary or edifying
effects at the expense of the truth. Eighteenth-century historians
also helped to fill a real gap in the thinking of the philosophes
who were sometimes more concerned to break with the past
than to understand it. Their own descriptions of the past, as a
time of unrelieved oppression by feudal nobles and superstitious
clerics, challenged historians to explain how such conditions
had brought forth *le siècle des lumières*. To solve the problem
which they had created so ingeniously for themselves, they
resorted to a kind of *deus ex machina* in the shape of the largely
mythical 'rise of the communes'. In the Middle Ages the towns
were supposed to have joined forced with the king against their
common enemy, the feudal nobility. Many pamphlets called for
the renewal of this victorious alliance. A strong belief in the
inevitability of human progress pervaded many writings besides
those of Turgot and Condorcet. To identify a right or practice
as a 'remnant of feudalism' was often tantamount to prophesying
its speedy demise.[2]

While the 'feudalism' of the eighteenth century almost always
bore the mark of its historiographical origins, as the century
progressed there were criticisms of 'feudalism' from many other
quarters. The first area in which 'feudalism' acquired a wider
sense was juristic writings. Although French jurists of the
eighteenth century were hardly distinguished intellectually,
under the stimulus of their enlightened contemporaries in other
fields they managed to resuscitate some of the writings of their
more able predecessors. In this sense the juristic attack on

[1] See p. 28.
[2] See pp. 43–4 ff.

'feudalism' preceded that of the historians. However, it was the latter who stimulated the former in the eighteenth century and who invested their writings with wider significance.

Eighteenth-century jurists drew much of their inspiration from Charles Du Moulin, who wrote in the sixteenth century. Du Moulin had elaborated a defence of the Crown's rights against the claims of the feudatories in which he insisted that the *complexum feudale*, or knot of feudal rights, had interposed a false hierarchy between the sovereign and his subjects. In Du Moulin's view, feudalism, by defining the status of the individual in terms of a system of land tenure, deprived him of his rights as a person. Consequently, he wished to limit the scope of all feudal rights as far as possible. His hostility to them was so great that the Latin wording of his *Traité des fiefs* has the vituperative ring of a papal encyclical.

The influence of a seventeenth-century jurist, Charles Loyseau, was particularly influential on those writings which advocated the reform of seigniorial justice. It was his principal axiom that the administration of justice was an essential right of royal sovereignty that had been impaired by feudalism, which he called 'a many-headed monster'. Loyseau's *Des Abus des, justices de village* was an important source for those eighteenth-century writers who criticized the actual workings of the seigniorial courts.[1]

The reign of Louis XIV formed a chasm between the royal jurists of the sixteenth and seventeenth centuries and their successors in the eighteenth. The jurists who had done so much to lay the foundations of royal absolutism were no longer patronized by the Crown when the goal appeared to have been reached.[2] Louis XIV and his entourage did not deign to look for justification of the French monarchy in less than messianic terms, for the propagandist use of which the court preacher was justly esteemed. The sonorous piety of Bossuet, however, was to prove a poor substitute for the astringent theorizing of the royal lawyers who were needed so badly to stiffen the resolve of the royal governments in the eighteenth century.

The French monarchy, while absolute in theory, was limited

---

[1] See p. 55 ff.

[2] W. F. Church, 'The Decline of French jurists as political theorists, 1660–1789', *French Historical Studies*, V (1967), p. 39.

in practice by the undergrowth of local and particularist and, above all, of feudal and seigniorial rights. The latter were strongly protected by the law of fiefs and by the *coutumes* of the different provinces. Most seigneurs had their own seigniorial courts in which they could enforce their claims. If they were foolish enough to lose cases in their own courts, or in those of the Crown to which they could be transferred, they could carry an appeal with every hope of success to their fellow-landlords in the local parlement. The need to limit the power of the seigneurs became increasingly urgent as the Crown sank deeper into debt during the eighteenth century. If the government were to raise more money in taxes, either the privileged had to pay a higher proportion or the government had to intervene to reduce the exactions of the seigneurs so that the peasant could afford to pay more in royal taxes. The government throughout the century did no more than toy with the problem, while this conflict of interests was even allowed to be settled triumphantly in favour of the holders of fiefs in 1776. Then, the king's great reforming minister, Turgot, had to retreat before a storm of abuse, because, among other reforming activities, he had patronized the author of *Les Inconvéniens des droits féodaux*.[1]

The Crown, which was so ready to allow its case to go by default, was supported by more stubborn friends. These, however, were no longer drawn from the jurists proper, but from the publicists and lower officials in the royal administration. The jurists themselves had long since abandoned public for private law. As he who pays the piper usually calls the tune, it was natural that interpretations of the *coutumes* and particularly of feudal law should favour the landlord and his business agent. Indeed, the legal bestsellers in the eighteenth century appear to have been the practical manuals on how to maximize profits from the legal rights that were vested in the holder of a fief. The philosophes were essentially right in believing that 'most of the jurists were utterly reactionary and must be circumvented if any significant legal reforms were to be achieved'.[2] The men who led the legal attack on feudalism, however, inevitably suffered from the fact that they were not well-versed in juristic thought. Thus, although the works of Du Moulin, Loyseau and

[1] See pp. 164–7.
[2] Church, *French Historical Studies*, V (1967), p. 28.

other leading writers of the past were reissued in the eighteenth century, there were few who were capable of fully understanding, and therefore of developing and expounding, their ideas. Yet, although the attack on 'feudalism' undoubtedly suffered from the poverty of the legal arguments at its disposal, it was an achievement that a challenge of any kind could be raised in that quarter.

Eighteenth-century writings on commerce may seem far removed from any discussion of 'feudalism'. Yet theories which defined the needs of the state in economic terms were implicitly hostile to privileges which were commonly believed to be derived from feudal times. This difference in outlook was brought into the open by the expansion of trade, which had given a new urgency to the old issue of whether nobles could engage in trade without incurring loss of status. The prejudice that high birth and commercial activity were incompatible came from the Middle Ages when society recognized a threefold division of its members into those who prayed, fought and worked. In the eighteenth century, when it was occasionally felt necessary to justify 'feudal' or seigniorial privileges, they were still represented as the compensation to the nobles for fulfilling their traditional role as the defenders of their country. Indeed, some eighteenth-century writers almost suggest that they habitually slept in chainmail waiting to be summoned to the feudal host. The gap between medieval practice and eighteenth-century conditions was devastatingly ridiculed by the abbé Coyer in his *La Noblesse Commerçante*,[1] which in 1756 precipitated heated discussion in pamphlets and periodicals. Almost from the start, the controversy widened to include the nature of contemporary society and the relative value in it of nobles and businessmen.

It may seem tempting to interpret some of the views expressed in these writings as prefiguring the triumph of capitalism over the remnants of feudalism. Anyone who could provide the Marxists with evidence to fit their theories about the French Revolution would surely be doing them a service that is long overdue. However, even the writers themselves hardly fit Marxist theory, as most did not engage in trade and therefore lacked

[1] G.-F. Coyer, *La Noblesse Commerçante* (London and Paris: Duchesne, 1756), esp. pp. 152–3.

any personal economic motive to promote it. Nor did they have any discernible effects on the habits of the trading community. Those who had made their fortunes in business seem intent throughout the century on investing their gains in social respectability by buying land and 'living nobly', or 'idly' as it is called today. As Professor Taylor has shown, almost all wealth in eighteenth-century France was used to buttress existing social status, instead of forging capitalist fortunes.[1] On the other hand those who took the lead in industrial enterprises were more often nobles than bourgeois.[2] Whatever the flaws in their reasoning, however, the Marxists have ensured that the eighteenth-century attack on 'feudalism' has been distorted by their own ideology. If eighteenth-century writers are to be understood, the Marxist connotations of 'feudalism' and their academic backlash must first be effaced from the mind of the reader.

'Humanity' was the most fashionable of all the secular virtues of the eighteenth century. Diderot's *Encyclopédie* described it as 'that sublime enthusiasm which is tormented by the sufferings of others and the need to alleviate them', and which 'would like to rush through the world abolishing slavery, superstition, vice and misfortune'.[3] It must be confessed that this ambitious programme was not achieved even in France. Although feudal and seigniorial rights were sometimes condemned as 'contrary to humanity', eighteenth-century publicists, who mainly lived in Paris, lacked enough first-hand knowledge to make their case convincing. While the same was doubtless true of serfdom, which eighteenth-century writers usually associated with 'feudalism', Voltaire, the abbé Clerget, and a few other writers succeeded in bringing home to their contemporaries some of its more inhuman features. This campaign for the abolition of serfdom is worth studying, as it is a helpful index to the growth of a social conscience in eighteenth-century France. It also provides very revealing evidence of the extent to which even a small sector of enlightened opinion could influence royal

[1] G. V. Taylor, 'Noncapitalist wealth and the origins of the French Revolution', *American Historical Review,* LXXII (1967), *passim.*

[2] G. Richard, 'La Noblesse de France et les sociétés par actions à la fin du XVIIIe siècle', *Revue d'Histoire Economique et Sociale,* XL (1962), esp. pp. 512–13.

[3] F. Brunot, *Histoire de la langue française dès origines à nos jours* (Paris: Armand Colin, 1924–53), VI, pt I, sect. 1, p. 118.

governments. Not only was serfdom abolished on Crown lands in 1779, but the royal decree itself reads as if it had been drawn up by Voltaire.[1] The scant recognition that this reform and others like the abolition of judicial torture and the conferring of civil liberties on Protestants have received in many general works, almost suggests a conspiracy of silence over the achievements of the royal administration. Perhaps some historians feel that those who lose their heads deserve to lose everything. If some of the writings on commerce suggest that eighteenth-century society was incapable of reforming itself, these reforms, particularly the abolition of serfdom, provide strong evidence to the contrary.

Finally, the remnants of feudalism were condemned on grounds of utility or practicality. Writers who were mainly allied to the physiocrats took the initiative in introducing a new criterion into the controversy over feudal rights and privileges. They shifted the whole basis of the argument when they by-passed the traditional preoccupation with 'rights' and judged the seigniorial regime by their own criterion of social usefulness. They put their chief trust in enlightened self-interest. They argued that feudal and seigniorial rights interfered with efficient farming. The peasant, in their view, had no motive to increase the yield from his land, as prosperity was a signal for the seigneur to raise his feudal and seigniorial dues. Practical in outlook, if doctrinaire in their language, these writers tried to convince the landlords that they would profit from taking a fixed rent in place of the random dues and labour services, which were often difficult to collect or enforce.

The proposals to commute feudal and seigniorial rights for a fixed rent had little success, if only because, without an agricultural revolution, the rural population in most of France would still be too poor to pay more to the seigneur, however 'physiocratically' the sums were levied. Serfdom and seigniorial justice offered more promising targets for attack. The small number of estates that were worked by serfs seemed to ensure that the institution would find few defenders. Yet, there was in fact a sullen and largely inarticulate opposition which was strong enough to deter the royal administration in 1779 from issuing more than a pathetic appeal to the seigneurs to follow the king's

[1] See p. 107.

example in abolishing serfdom on his lands. Seigniorial justice was another part of the seigniorial regime which seemed to be falling to pieces of itself. The best guarantee that really determined resistance to the abolition of the manorial courts would be lacking was that their operation had become burdensome even to the seigneurs themselves. Yet, it took until 1788 for the government to take strong measures against the seigniorial courts, and then it was only to suppress the right of criminal jurisdiction, which had already largely fallen into disuse. As these writings, particularly those on seigniorial justice, were often sensible and well-informed it would be interesting to know why they did not have more effect on an administration which was enlightened in many respects.

The abolition of feudal and seigniorial rights during the Revolution probably owed nothing to the literary attack on 'feudalism'. The real destroyers of the remnants of 'feudalism' were the peasants, who did not use arguments but seized the opportunity which the Revolution brought them to improve their lot. When communities of peasants in 1789 rose in open rebellion against feudal and seigniorial rights, they forced the deputies in Paris 'to abolish feudalism' in their decree of 4 August, as a means of pacifying the countryside. Naturally, the deputies, many of whom in all three orders owned feudal and seigniorial rights themselves, tried soon afterwards to retract what they had conceded under force. However, although Merlin de Douai and the *Comité des droits féodaux* fought a canny rearguard action, their arguments were continually overtaken by events. In the end, the revolutionaries were forced into legislation to seal beyond any doubt the peasants' determination to be rid of feudal and seigniorial rights. Their abolition, in so far as it was achieved, was settled by force, and unless the hedging of Merlin de Douai and the *Comité* count as theorizing, there was little intellectual debate.

The attack on 'feudalism' in eighteenth-century French thought is hardly worth studying, if its importance is measured in terms of political results. I hope, however, that this study will serve to throw some light on the attitude of eighteenth-century writers towards some of the social problems of their time. Too often in the past, the political writers of the century have been represented as doctrinaire theorists. Professor Gay has corrected

INTRODUCTION

this view in the case of Voltaire by showing the extent to which his political ideas were shaped by his personal concern on particular occasions, such as during the Calas Affair[1] and the levying of Machault's *vingtième*.[2] By a similar development, their attack on 'feudalism' prompted some French writers to take stock of France's liabilities from the past and possibilities for the future.

---

[1] P. Gay, *Voltaire's politics, the poet as realist* (Princeton University Press, 1959), pp. 273 ff.
[2] *Ibid.*, pp. 124 ff.

II

‘Feudalism’ in Eighteenth-century French
Historiography

By their refusal to study them, modern scholars have convinced
themselves that the historians of eighteenth-century France
possessed little originality. It is, of course, common practice to
pay tribute to the historical gifts of Montesquieu and Voltaire;
the eighteenth century is allowed a few outstanding writers.
Far rarer is it, however, to find even the suggestion that authors
such as Boulainvilliers, Dubos, Linguet and Letrosne made
important contributions to the development of historiography
in France.[1] It is impossible to study the debate over the origins
of feudalism and the descriptions of its operation and decline
without coming to appreciate the remarkable development of
historical understanding in the century. Eighteenth-century
historians are seen at their best when they are dealing with
particular problems, like those connected with the history of
feudalism. There can be no surer way of making eighteenth-
century historians appear to be abstract and doctrinaire than
for a modern historian with those qualities to study them.

Most historical writing, before it was revived in the early
eighteenth century by the debate over the origins of fiefs, had
become oppressively desultory. Mézeray, the leading French
historian of the mid-seventeenth century, seems to have no

---

[1] These authors are not mentioned, for instance, in the excellent chapters on
historiography in E. Cassirer, *The Philosophy of the Enlightenment*, trans. F. C. A.
Koelln and J. P. Pettegrove (Boston: Beacon Press, 1951), nor in N. Hampson,
The Enlightenment (Harmondsworth: Penguin Books, 1968).

criterion for separating the important from the unimportant, with the result that his *Histoire de France depuis Faramond* is often only a monumental heap of antiquarian lore. He stated in the preface that his main object was to immortalize service to the public, which he practically equated here with martial prowess.[1] Whatever the object, the result is interminable accounts of battles and warfare. This is hardly surprising, as Mézeray also says in his preface that the historian cannot omit anything without obscuring what follows,[2] which is a statement that the reader who follows his laborious year-by-year account might feel inclined to challenge. Periodically, Mézeray throws the reader some curious piece of information, such as the story of a peasant with a horn in the middle of his head, which, according to Mézeray's biographer, was designed to revive flagging interest.[3] The aptest comment on the dullness of Mézeray's *Histoire de France* was its use to lull the infant Louis XIV to sleep.[4]

Père Daniel, who was Mézeray's chief rival at the beginning of the eighteenth century, wrote the same sort of history, though, as befitted a Jesuit, less impartially and more elegantly. Voltaire describes how Madame du Châtelet, his gifted mistress, reacted to Daniel's writings: 'She could not bear those endless recitals of battles, while she searched for the history of the States General, of the parlements, of the municipal laws, of chivalry, of all our customs and above all of society, barbarous then and civilized today.'[5] To do Daniel justice, he considered that the historian should describe the customs and way of life of the people, although he warned against too deep a treatment of these matters for fear of making the account too dry and of holding up the narrative of events.[6] Style mattered so much to Daniel that he assumed a moral responsibility to interest his readers. 'May it please God', he wrote in the preface of his

[1] F. E. de Mézeray, *Histoire de France depuis Faramond jusqu'à maintenant* (Paris: M. Guillemot, 1643–51), preface (unpaginated), first page.

[2] *Ibid.*, third page.

[3] W. H. Evans, *L'Historien Mézeray et la conception de l'histoire en France au XVIIe. siècle* (Paris: J. Gamber, 1930), p. 88.

[4] G. Lacour-Gayet, *L'Education politique de Louis XIV* (Paris: Hachette, 1898), p. 112.

[5] Voltaire, *Oeuvres*, ed. L. E. D. Moland and G. Bengesco (Paris: Garnier, 1883–5), XXIV, p. 544.

[6] G. Daniel, *Histoire de la milice françoise* (1721), I, p. ii.

Histoire de France, 'that this work in which the material is so interesting, may also be as interesting in its presentation, so that it can occupy usefully many young people, and turn them away from reading so many of the books which our century has produced to the injury of religion and good morals.'[1] By the same token, many of today's historians must surely drive the young to crime! Daniel's moral concern to interest his readers was stronger than his regard for the truth. A contemporary historian quoted ironically Daniel's 'wise rule' for the historian 'not to surrender to the spirit of curiosity and research for fear of failing to substantiate his conjectures'. He commented unkindly that although Daniel dismissed as *bagatelles* the dates of events, the origins of laws and so forth, the accounts of warfare which he put in their place were hardly subjects worthy of the rhetorician.[2]

Descartes was doubtless reacting against the inaccuracies in earlier seventeenth-century historiography when, 'without any sense of irony', he 'put the historian beside the writer of historical romances'.[3] As these words imply, the inaccuracies in the works of seventeenth-century historians did not stem primarily from twisting the evidence to prove a case. Mézeray, when Historiographer Royal, had been outspoken enough about the *gabelle* and other taxes to forfeit his royal pension.[4] Although Voltaire often accuses Daniel of prejudice,[5] he says that while another historian finds ten thousand errors in his *Histoire*, the majority matter as little as the truths which he would have put in their place.[6]

Here Voltaire surely pinpoints the besetting fault of seventeenth-century historiography, which was not prejudice, but aimlessness. The truth was less often perverted than lost to sight among a welter of unimportant detail. The random facts would have made more, not less, sense had they been made to serve prejudice in a coherent fashion. This view is partly borne

[1] G. Daniel, *Histoire de France, depuis l'établissement de la monarchie françoise dans les Gaules*, 2nd ed. (Amsterdam, 1720–5), I, p. lxviii.

[2] Boulainvilliers, *État de la France*, III, pp. 8–9.

[3] L. Lévy-Bruhl, 'The Cartesian spirit and history', *Philosophy and History: essays presented to Ernst Cassirer*, ed. R. Klibansky and H. J. Paton (New York: Harper & Row, 1963), p. 192.

[4] Evans, pp. 75–6.

[5] Voltaire, *Oeuvres*, XXIX, pp. 413 ff.

[6] *Ibid.*, XIV, p. 61.

out in the century's more erudite works in which historians hotly debated such topics as the real ownership of the vase of Soissons and the still more acrimonious controversy over the hair-styles of the Merovingian kings.[1] In these circumstances the debate over the origins of fiefs served to orientate historiography around a broader and more important theme.

There had long been speculation about the origin of fiefs. Hotman in *Franco-Gallia* in the sixteenth century had outlined already in Professor Ford's words, 'the Germanist theory in all its vigor'.[2] According to this, France had originally been a free society under the aegis of the Frankish nobles who settled public affairs among themselves at the famous assemblies of the Champ de Mars. However, Hotman gave an anti-feudal twist to the theory which normally attributed the hereditary holding of fiefs to the original conquest of Gaul.[3] For Hotman claimed that fiefs became hereditary only as the concession whereby Hugues Capet shrewdly bought support from the nobles for his own usurpation of the Crown.[4] The political implications of the debate appear as early as 1664 when a group of dukes and peers commissioned Le Laboureur to provide an historical basis for their rights and privileges. He argued in his *Histoire de la pairie* that the peers as the descendants of the original tenants-in-chief of the Crown were the legatees of the political powers of the Frankish assemblies on the Champ de Mars.[5] The delay in publication until 1740, as Carcassonne suggests, seems to show that the peers had real fears of provoking retaliation from the Crown.[6]

It was the comte de Boulainvilliers who injected new life into the long-standing controversy over the origins of fiefs. The perverse eccentricity of some of his views and interests, however, have all too often been allowed to obscure his originality as an historian. Many contemporaries gave Boulainvilliers

---

[1] It is only fair to add that the length of a king's hair was interpreted as a valuable indication of his political views. Short hair was assumed to show acceptance of Roman customs and methods of government. Long hair, as today, was taken to symbolize a lingering preference for the barbarian way of life.

[2] F. L. Ford, *Robe and Sword: the regrouping of the French aristocracy after Louis XIV* (Cambridge, Mass.: Harvard University Press, 1953), p. 225.

[3] See pp. 21–3.

[4] F. Hotman, *La Gaule françoise* (Cologne: H. Bertuphe, 1574), p. 165.

[5] Carcassonne, *Montesquieu*, pp. 11–13.

[6] *Ibid.*, pp. 11–12.

chief credit for his success as an astrologer. Even the duc de
Saint-Simon felt a grudging admiration for one who, although
he was no *duc et pair*,[1] had managed to predict among other
events the exact hour of his own death.[2] For the record it
should be added that Boulainvilliers had gone astray in pre-
dicting the decease of Voltaire, who was apologizing for his
inconsiderate longevity thirty years later.[3] Along with his
astrological activities, Boulainvilliers' praise for feudalism and
support for aristocratic reaction have also failed to recommend
him to the liberals of three centuries. Voltaire is an intelligent
exception. Although he disapproved strongly of Boulainvilliers'
championship of feudal government, he still described him as
'the gentleman in the kingdom most learned in history and
most fitted to write that of France, had he not been too imbued
with a theory [*trop systématique*].'[4] Boulainvilliers' theories,
however, benefited historiography by stimulating 'enlightened'
historians to develop their case against him.

In his main aim of asserting the political claims of the
noblesse de race Boulainvilliers tried to prove two points: first,
that the true nobility was marked out historically as superior
to the rest of the nation by its racial descent and traditional way
of life; second, that the Crown's curtailment of the nobility's
rights was a violation of a still-valid Frankish constitution.

Boulainvilliers claimed that 'originally the Franks had all
been free and perfectly equal'.[5] The native Gauls, on the other

[1] Although every *pair* was a *duc*, every *duc* was not a *pair*. There were three
categories of *ducs*: at the top the *ducs et pairs* of whom there were 43 in 1789;
next the *ducs non pairs* who numbered 15; and lastly the 16 *ducs à brevet d'honneur*
who held their titles for life. The chief concern of the *ducs et pairs* was to preserve
their privileged status in the Parlement of Paris where they sat by right, unlike
the other *ducs*. The rest of their energies were expended in ensuring that they
would not share the honours of their caste with their social inferiors, especially
those of ducal rank. See M. Marion, *Dictionnaire*, arts. 'Duc', 'pairs' and 'Bonnet
(affair du)'. On the political role of the peers see the works of R. M. Mettam.

[2] Saint-Simon, *Mémoires*, ed. A. de Boislisle (Paris: Hachette, 1879–1928),
XL, p. 239.

[3] Voltaire, *Oeuvres*, XVII, p. 448.

[4] *Ibid.*, XIV, p. 45.

[5] Boulainvilliers, *État de la France*, I, 'Mémoires Historiques', p. 16.
This stress on the absolute equality of the Franks was intimately connected
with another aspect of Boulainvilliers' historical thesis: his concern to refute the
claim, which was advanced by Jean Le Laboureur in his *Histoire de la Pairie de
France et du Parlement de Paris* (London: S. Harding, 1740), that the peers, as
distinct from the nobility as a whole, were the rightful heirs to the political

hand, lacked a proper nobility, as they had been utterly debased by their subjugation at the hands of the Romans.[1] Any vestigial nobility had obviously been very adequately extirpated by the Franks themselves. These had entered Gaul with a hatred for the name, the language and the customs of the Romans.[2] The possessions of the Gauls, he said, lay at the mercy of their conquerors,[3] to whom they stood in the relation of slaves to masters.[4] As Boulainvilliers remarked drily in his account of the parlements, 'The third estate was not included then, as the people were enslaved.'[5]

Boulainvilliers also wanted to show that the rights of the nobles preceded those of the Crown. In his view, Clovis, far from being an all-powerful conqueror in his own right like Alexander the Great, entered Gaul as the elected commander of a free army.[6] The spoils and lands were, accordingly, divided equally among those who had faced a common risk and expense.[7] He said that the kings were, strictly speaking, only civil magistrates who had been chosen by the various localities to settle private disputes. It was absolutely contrary to truth and the character of the Franks, he said, that they should be called 'subjects', as they were all *Leudes,* and therefore on an equal footing.[8] That it had been the will of the nobles that prevailed, he said, was shown by the fact that all important matters of

---

powers of the early Franks. Boulainvilliers' objections are stated forcefully in his pamphlet, *Mémoire pour la noblesse de France contre les ducs et pairs* (n.p., 1717).

It is interesting to see how the *thèse nobiliaire* was split at the outset by the rival claims of the *pairs* on the one hand and of the nobles as a whole on the other. As late as 1753 Dominique Simmonel in his *Dissertation sur l'origine, les droits, et les prérogatives des pairs de France* (n.p., 1753) tried to refute the claim that the affairs of the *pairs* as a body lay outside the jurisdiction of the Paris Parlement. In it he affirms that 'Since the time when feudal government entirely ceased, it appears that the Parlement alone and without the participation of the peers has judged all these civil cases concerning the peerages' (p. 54). This split in the *thèse nobiliaire* explains some of the extreme bitterness which surfaced during and after the Revolution when the introduction of a second chamber on the lines of the British House of Lords was discussed.

[1] H. de Boulainvilliers, *Essais sur la noblesse de France, contenant une dissertation sur son origine et abaissement* (Amsterdam, 1732), pp. 14–15.

[2] *Ibid.,* p. 18.

[3] Boulainvilliers, *État de la France,* I, 'Mémoires historiques', p. 22.

[4] Boulainvilliers, *Essais sur la noblesse de France,* p. 41.

[5] Boulainvilliers, *État de la France,* III, p. 19.

[5] *Ibid.,* I, p. 15.

[6] *Ibid.,* p. 21.

[8] *Ibid.,* p. 16.

policy were settled by the General Assembly of the Franks on the Champ de Mars, where the wishes of the king were by no means always followed.[1] Finally, Boulainvilliers stressed the decentralization of local government under the Franks. The people, he says, attached themselves to the chiefs who organized their defence, instead of to remote kings whom they hardly knew. In this way, as many individual sovereignties grew up as there were groups for mutual protection.[2]

The 'Germanist thesis' which I have just outlined may seem closer to polemics than to history. Yet Boulainvilliers' case was plausibly and closely argued, and he reinforced it with the findings of seventeenth-century scholars. However, what made Boulainvilliers more than just a good historian was the way in which he treated society as a whole. His attitude emerges clearly in a letter to a friend to whom he explains his lack of sympathy for historians and their readers.[3]

Do you believe, *Mademoiselle* [he asked his correspondent] that it is very enlightening to know the date of certain events, the name of princes, their ministers, their generals and their mistresses, while remaining ignorant of the motives of their actions, of their government; if the character of each century, the opinions, behaviour, dominant ideas, in short [if] the passions which drive men, are omitted?

This attitude towards the writing of history explains why Boulainvilliers, unlike many other contemporary writers, did not treat the origins of fiefs in isolation, but on the contrary saw feudalism in the wider context of the warlike propensities of Frankish society. It was significantly not 'feudalism', but 'feudal government', that he acclaimed as 'the masterpiece of the human mind', of which the Greeks and even Aristotle had attained no conception.[4] In relating the decline of feudalism to changes in methods of warfare Boulainvilliers reached a more profound explanation of historical causation than almost any writer of the century before Montesquieu. Boulainvilliers suggested that the use of mercenaries in warfare had enabled

---

[1] *Ibid.*, pp. 46–7.
[2] Boulainvilliers, *Essais sur la noblesse de France*, pp. 109–10.
[3] Simon, p. 48.
[4] Boulainvilliers, *État de la France*, III, p. 37.

French kings to dispense with the military aid of the feudatories, who thereby lost their chief means of bringing political pressure to bear on the king. In his own words:[1]

Since that time monetary payment had become the backbone of monarchical power, and kings have come to assess the services of all their subjects as equally useful, seeing that the noble of ancient family cannot serve in any way more cheaply than the commoner. And indeed, on the contrary, the newly ennobled are richer and more in a position to give the help, which the noble of ancient family himself awaits from the sovereign's bounty. That makes him [appear] odious or importunate. From that moment the gentleman of good family ceased to be regarded as an important member of the State; neither the interests of government, nor those of the prince's private pleasures, called for his presence on any ground of usefulness. It would therefore be unreasonable for them to expect preferential treatment, if they are not distinguished by real usefulness. The decline of the ancient families . . . is therefore a consequence borne from the changes in warfare.

Boulainvilliers accepted philosophically that the fortunes of the nobility should be bound by the same rules as everyone else.[2] Instead of trying to retreat into the past, like so many other advocates of the political claims of the nobility, he seems to have hoped that the nobles would acquire wealth as a means of regaining political power. He made an eloquent plea to the Regent in a *Mémoire* that many impoverished nobles should be allowed to engage in retail trade without loss of status.[3] Thus Boulainvilliers had related feudalism and the fortunes of the nobility to the overall development of the government and economy of France. However strenuously later historians rebutted Boulainvilliers' political views, they owed him more gratitude than they cared to give for having broadened the debate over the origins of fiefs, so that historical inquiry would range over the whole history of the past.

Not the least of Boulainvilliers' services to historiography was to provoke replies from other historians. Even while his works were still only in manuscript, the lawyer Marais commented in his Journal in September 1722: 'It looks as if the authorities should act to prevent the circulation of these

[1] Boulainvilliers, *Essais sur la noblesse de France*, pp. 269–72.
[2] *Ibid.*, p. 228.
[3] See p. 79.

manuscripts which teach things that are so strange and so contrary to sovereignty, that it is almost criminal to read them.'[1] The three leading French periodicals, the *Mercure*, the *Mémoires de Trévoux* and the *Journal des Sçavans*, according to Boulainvilliers' biographer, were all full of criticism of his theories on the origins of the nobility.[2]

The abbé Dubos was Boulainvilliers' most influential critic. Montesquieu himself paid him the compliment of singling him out for attack as the foremost proponent of the *thèse royale*. He wrote in *De l'Esprit des Loix*:[3]

This work has seduced many people, because it is written with great art; because what is in doubt is continually taken for granted. . . . And, while endless erudition is placed, not within the system, but beside it, the mind is distracted by the accessories and no longer fastens on the central argument. Besides, with so much research it would be unthinkable if nothing were found; the length of the voyage creates the idea that the end has at last been reached.

It is remarkable how little Montesquieu's well-directed scorn did to undermine Dubos' influence. According to Hénault, the respected historian and *parlementaire*, the *Histoire critique de l'établissement de la monarchie françoise dans les Gaules* of Dubos had an influence in the field of historiography that was 'no less revolutionary than that of Descartes on the philosophy of the previous century'.[4] Unlike most earlier historians who so often lacked clear objectives, Dubos set as his unwavering goal the vindication of the rights of the Crown. His *Histoire* appeared at the opportune moment to blaze a trail for his readers towards a destination which both wished to reach.

Dubos opened by announcing his dissatisfaction with the accepted version of events. Recent historians, he said, had depicted the Franks before Clovis as barbarians who glorified in destroying the Roman Empire. Consequently, they were imagined to have treated the Gauls with all the harshness of ferocious conquerors towards subjugated peoples. Dubos tried

---

[1] Simon, p. 152 n.

[2] *Ibid.*, p. 62.

[3] C.-L. Montesquieu, *Oeuvres complètes publiées sous la direction de M. André Masson*, (Paris: Nagel, 1950-1), I, 'De l'Esprit des Loix', p. 344.

[4] R. Shackleton, *Montesquieu: a critical biography* (London: Oxford University Press, 1961), p. 330.

to prove, as the title of his work suggests, that the supposed disruptive conquest was really a peaceful settlement by allies of Rome. The Romans in his view used the Franks as an advance-guard to ward off the attacks of other barbarians. The Franks, he said, showed themselves to be faithful allies of Rome, as on a certain occasion when they were cut to pieces by the Vandals, while guarding the approaches from the Rhine.[1] It was typical of Dubos' mastery of the sources, which the antiquarian researches of the seventeenth century had done so much to make available, that he attributed what in his view was a misrepresentation of events to an unscholarly misreading of Frédégaire. His authority, Gregory of Tours, Dubos claimed, did not say that Childeric had attacked the Roman Empire, but on the contrary that he had defended it. Dubos argued that this error lay at the root of the view that Childeric and his son, Clovis, were the enemies of Rome.[2] Not only was there no evidence of resistance by the Gallo-Romans, but the inhabitants were glad to be ruled by the Franks.[3] Dubos supported his claim that the Gauls had not been enslaved by trying to show that the Gallic tribes had all kept their traditional dress, customs, languages, and laws.[4] He supported his case by an imaginative reconstruction of the past. Dubos stressed the small number of the invaders, and suggested that the 'military bene-fices', which had been vacated by the Romans, would have satisfied their needs, and would have removed any motive to dispossess the Gauls of their lands.[5] As a small minority among armed Gallo-Romans, he suggested, they had every need to treat the original inhabitants with consideration.[6]

Dubos' political intent was the opposite of Boulainvilliers'; he wished to show that the rights of the sovereign had preceded those of the nobles. It was basic to his argument that the settlement had been executed under the direction of a firm leader. Dubos contended that the small band of Franks would never have been successful, had they not been under strict

---

[1] J.-B. Dubos, *Histoire critique de l'établissement de la monarchie françoise dans les Gaules* (Amsterdam: Osmont, 1734), I, 'Discours Préliminaire', pp. 1–4.
[2] *Ibid.*, I, pp. 16–17.
[3] *Ibid.*, III, p. 371.
[4] *Ibid.*, p. 245.
[5] *Ibid.*, pp. 470–1.
[6] *Ibid.*, pp. 532–3.

discipline. Their survival after the conquest depended equally on their ability to work together and avoid falling out among themselves.

Dubos' conclusion was that Hugues Capet and successive French kings were under no obligation to leave the seigneurs in undisturbed possession of the rights over their fiefs, as there were no historical grounds for the claim that these were as old as the law of succession and had been erected independently of the Crown. The great kings of the Capetian dynasty, Dubos maintained, far from being tyrants, had done no more than reclaim the imprescriptible rights of the Crown and people from those who had despoiled both in the ninth and tenth centuries.[1] As the 'Roman thesis' enhanced the Crown's authority in all periods of history, including by implication the eighteenth century, it is hardly surprising that the royal censor recommended Dubos' work as 'extremely useful and even necessary'.[2] Similarly, Montesquieu, as the supporter of aristocratic reaction, condemned Dubos' ideas as amounting to 'a conspiracy against the nobility',[3] and elsewhere added unkindly that Dubos had never seen anything in his *Histoire* except a pension.[4]

Montesquieu's genius raised him above the polemical debate over the origin of fiefs. Despite his sympathies for the ideas of Boulainvilliers and dislike for those of Dubos, Montesquieu was too good an historian to apply 'the lessons of history' to his own time. In *De l'Esprit des Loix* he was surely concerned primarily with more fundamental questions of sociology and politics. As far as Montesqueu was the theorist of aristocratic reaction, he did not greatly strengthen his argument by rewriting the early history of the nobility. As Mr Shackleton has pointed out, 'It was after *De l'Esprit des Loix* had been completed according to its original design that Montesquieu decided to add to the work a discussion of feudal origins. It was a matter of pride that he should add his own decisive word to the discussion of this difficult problem.'[5] Books Thirty and Thirty-One, despite Montesquieu's valuable insight into early French history almost constitute little more than an appendix.

---

[1] Dubos, I, 'Discours Préliminaire', pp. 51–2.

[2] *Ibid.*, III, p. 552.

[3] Montesquieu, *Oeuvres*, I, 'De L'Esprit des Loix', p. 302.

[4] *Ibid.*, III, p. 234.

[5] Shackleton, p. 328.

Contemporary writers on the origins of fiefs seldom give much space to Montesquieu's ideas, compared with those of Boulainvilliers and Dubos. The last sentence in *De l'Esprit des Loix*, 'I finish the treatise on fiefs where the majority of authors have begun it',[1] explains the reason. It was of the essence of the polemical debate to use the history of feudalism as ammunition for or against the claims of the French nobility in the eighteenth century. Montesquieu, for all his aristocratic prejudice, did not reduce history to such simple terms.

Dubos and even Montesquieu were far from having the last word in the controversy over the origins of fiefs. There are scores of later works which can be classified from the summaries that are given in Carcassonne's massive *Montesquieu et le problème de la constitution française au XVIIIe. siècle*, according to whether they follow, combine, or plagiarize, the writings of Boulainvilliers on the one hand and of Dubos on the other. As late as 1788 there was yet another edition of the abbé Mably's popular *Observations sur l'histoire de France*, in which he restated the 'Germanist thesis' in his efforts to prove that the primitive French government had enjoyed a republican basis. In May 1789, when the educated public might have been expected to be more preoccupied with the meeting of the Estates General, the *Journal des Sçavans* devoted seven quarto pages to a review of Gautier de Sibert's *Considérations sur l'ancienneté de l'existence du tiers-état*.[2] The author was praised for refuting in passing 'the intolerable and almost universally rejected system of the comte de Boulainvilliers'.[3] The volume of these and other historical writings is daunting, as indeed is shown by the few references to them in modern secondary works. When Daniel Mornet examined the catalogues of private libraries which were auctioned in the second half of the eighteenth century, he found that historical works comprised over a quarter of the total.[4] A look through eighteenth-century periodicals, such as the *Journal des Sçavans*, the *Mémoires de Trévoux*, *L'Année Littéraire* and the *Journal Encyclopédique*, shows that a large amount of space was always given to reviews of historical writings, some

[1] Montesquieu, *Oeuvres*, I, 'De L'Esprit des Loix', p. 430.

[2] *Journal des Sçavans* (Paris, 1665–1792), May 1789, pp. 259–66.

[3] *Ibid.*, May 1789, p. 260.

[4] D. Mornet, 'L'Enseignement des bibliothèques privées, 1750–1780', *Revue d'Histoire Littéraire de la France*, XVII (1910), p. 457.

of which put to shame the works of later scholars for whom sources are far more accessible.

The polemical debate over the origins of fiefs naturally issued in descriptions of feudal society at work, or, more precisely, at war. As a large majority of writers followed Dubos' bias in favour of the Crown, feudal society was painted in unflattering colours. It could be argued that even in the seventeenth century feudalism had received a bad press from historians. Mézeray's account of French society under Charles Martel, for instance, is already in the best eighteenth-century tradition:[1]

> The different seigneurs, unceasingly having some quarrel among themselves, or their vassals, murdered each other at every moment; and always engaged in bloodshed and slaughter, gloried only in fighting, so that their subjects themselves becoming imbued with their taste for brutality, killed each other in defiance of law and justice. Acts of brigandage were commonplace . . . assassinations and burnings were committed everywhere, and France seemed to produce only bandits and robbers.

That Mézeray associated these atrocities with feudalism might appear to be borne out by the famous passage where he compares the government of France to that of a great fief. Yet on another occasion Mézeray seemed to favour feudalism when he wrote that 'Some districts were governed by the people, others by petty kings, and the most fortunate by a certain number of seigneurs, who had, more or less as today, vassals and seigniorial rights'.[2] Daniel, Mézeray's rival in popular esteem at the turn of the century, contributed even less towards the systematic denigration of feudalism. In a rare aside on the subject, he describes the powerful vassals of Philip I as 'more ungovernable than ever'. He added that 'they were themselves often the most blameworthy for the great disorders which were being committed throughout the kingdom'.[3] Daniel had just shown, however, that Philip's authority in France had already been undermined by his excommunication by the Pope and lack of application to government business.[4] Neither historian, therefore, made an attempt to show that political disorder was implicit in feudal government itself.

[1] Mézeray, I, p. 359.
[2] Evans, p. 167.
[3] Daniel, *Histoire de France*, II, p. 481.
[4] *Ibid.*, II, p. 480.

The shift in emphasis which brought the so-called 'feudal anarchy' into the forefront of historiography hardly lends itself to chronological treatment. It was an obvious development of Dubos' 'Roman thesis' to show how the feudal nobility had misused their ill-gotten power in the Middle Ages. A typical example is to be found in the *Journal Encyclopédique* of 1756. In this long extract from Saint-Foix's *Histoire de Paris*, the Middle Ages was described as a time when 'the seigneurs, under the pretext of protecting themselves from the incursions of brigands, fortified themselves in their châteaux, from which they attacked [and] held to ransome passers-by, pillaged merchants, and raped women, provided', the author adds with eighteenth-century fastidiousness, 'they were pretty. . . . Brigandage, abduction, rape', he said, 'could be described as "rights of the seigneur".'[1] The marquis d'Argenson in *Considérations sur le gouvernement ancien et présent de la France*, which was eagerly read in manuscript long before its publication in 1764, gave a similar picture of the past. The great vassals of the Crown, he said, 'raped women and took estates unpunished, and from this inhuman oppression are derived the rights attached to fiefs, which are so odd and which are so admired by our studious *feudistes*'.[2] According to the Burgundian antiquary, Courtépée, in a passage which was widely cited,[3] the Middle Ages was a time when, 'the nobility, galloped through the countryside, pursuing and cutting in pieces unarmed travellers and peasants'. This epidemic of violence had reached such proportions that, according to Courtépée, the number of crosses in the countryside had been increased (by whom, he does not say) so that those in danger of their lives could cling to them for safety from nobles, whose lust for blood was equalled only by their piety.[4] The marquis de Mirabeau wrote in the seventies, 'It has become obligatory in recent times to anathematize feudal

---

[1] *Journal Encyclopédique* (Liège, then Bouillon, 1756–93), vol. 8 pt 3 for 1756, p. 88.

[2] R. L. de V. d'Argenson, *Considérations sur le gouvernement ancien et présent de la France* (Amsterdam: M. M. Rey, 1764), p. 127.

[3] E.g. by P.-F. Clerget, *Le Cri de la raison, ou examen approfondi des loix et des coutumes qui tiennent dans la servitude main-mortable quinze cent mille sujets du Roi* (Besançon: Simard, 1789), p. 35; Perreciot, I, p. 458.

[4] C. Courtépée and E. Beguillet, *Description générale et particulière du duché de Bourgogne, précédée de l'abrégé historique de cette province* (Dijon: L.-N. Frantin, 1774–85), I, p. 137.

government; there is no scribbler who as much as treats its history in a date-chart, without adding his jibe'.[1] By the time of the Revolution no charge was too far-fetched to be levied against the hated feudal regime. In his very uncritical *Histoire critique de la noblesse* Dulaure quoted a peasant, whom he casually described as being one hundred and twenty years old, as saying that he had often seen a Monsieur de Bauffremont, Abbot of Clairvaux, shooting at peasants. 'This noble pastime,' he added, 'much practised in earlier times, was called "hunting the villeins".'[2] Other picturesque descriptions of the past, notably the seigneur's alleged former right to spend the first night of the marriage with his vassal's bride, which one writer aptly ascribed to 'the history of feudal delirium',[3] are considered, as far as modesty permits, in chapter V.

For many eighteenth-century anti-clericals the indiscriminate rapine of the feudal barons was childhood's innocence in comparison with the businesslike ways in which the clergy had profited from the times of 'feudal anarchy'. Ecclesiastics were credited not only with usurping feudal rights along with the nobility, but also with gaining, as donations, those of 'usurping nobles', who showed themselves to be 'as ignorant, as [they were] pious and barbarous'.[4] Voltaire, doubtless, had the same Gibbonian recipe in mind when he wrote in *l'Essai sur les moeurs* of 'those bishops and monks, everywhere at the head of the feudal government'.[5] Other authors wrote more specifically about the role of the clergy in leading their vassals to war.[6] The tide of anti-clerical feeling was so strong that the abbé Fleury, who had argued sensibly enough earlier in the century that the clergy had been drawn willy-nilly into both affairs of state and the holding of fiefs, was almost alone in his convictions.[7]

---

[1] Carcassonne, *Montesquieu*, p. 324.

[2] J.-A. Dulaure, *Histoire critique de la noblesse depuis le commencement de la monarchie jusqu'à nos jours* (Paris: Guillot, 1790), pp. 299–300.

[3] Clerget, *Le Cri de la raison*, p. 35.

[4] See (Anon.), *Considérations sur l'injustice des prétentions du clergé et de la noblesse* (n.p., 1789), pp. 7–8.

[5] Voltaire, *Oeuvres*, XIII, p. 176.

[6] See Perreciot, I, p. 59, and P.-L.-C. Gin, *Les Vrais principes du gouvernement français, démontrés par la raison et par les faits* (Geneva and Paris: Servière, 1782), p. 245.

[7] C. Fleury, J.-C. Fabre and G. P. Goujet, *Histoire Ecclésiastique* (Paris: Mariette et Guerin, 1722–04–38), XIII, p. 10.

Eighteenth-century writers persisted in believing that the clergy, far from being victims of exploitation, had thrived as exploiters.

The clergy were regarded as compromised particularly by their supposed part in extending serfdom. Serfdom on a large scale was considered to be the most sinister of all the by-products of the 'feudal anarchy'. Velly, the initiator of the *Histoire de France, depuis l'établissement de la monarchie jusqu'au règne de Louis XIV . . .*, which provided the later eighteenth century with a standard national history, gave an equally standard explanation of the increase in the number of serfs in the Middle Ages. In his view, serfdom had arisen from the attempt of the weak to save their lives by enlisting the help of a powerful protector, at the cost of surrendering to him their property and personal liberty.[1] Eighteenth-century publicists naturally made great play with the supposed disparity between Christian principles and the clergy's readiness to own serfs. In the words of one anonymous author, 'they have vassals and serfs against the express commandments of Jesus Christ'.[2] 'And what is as horrible as it is contradictory, slaves of monks,' exclaimed Voltaire,[3] in what the charitable call his campaign for the serfs of Mont Jura and the uncharitable his campaign against the Chapter of Saint Claude. Feeling was such, that it was hardly necessary for another author, Linguet, to reassure his readers that the material interests of the Church had not suffered from any religious scruples of its members. 'The purity of its morality,' he wrote, 'appeared to it during that long period to be very compatible with servitude. Its ministers accepted without even a scruple, the magnificent presents of this kind which were given through the piety of the faithful. Ecclesiastical estates, the lands of abbeys, were peopled by slaves, bought for money, who as Christians were perfectly equal to their masters, and as serfs entirely at their disposal.'[4]

[1] P.-F. Velly, C. Villaret and J.-J. Garnier, *Histoire de France, depuis l'établissement de la monarchie jusqu'au règne de Louis XIV . . .*, new ed. (Paris: Desaint, Nyonet Saillant, 1769–63–99) B.M. ref. 283,d.6, VI, p. 183.

[2] (Anon), *Considérations sur l'injustice des prétentions du clergé et de la noblesse*, p. 8.

[3] Voltaire, *Oeuvres*, XII, p. 69.

[4] S. N. H. Linguet, *Théorie des loix civiles, ou principes fundamentaux de la société* (London, 1767), II, pp. 493–4.

The charge against the clergy was far more than one of complicity alone. Clerics were often accused of exploiting the misguided piety of the laity in order to increase their material possessions, and particularly the numbers of their serfs. The clergy were supposed to have encouraged the superstitious laity to give themselves in bondage to a religious institution in this world, as a means of securing their eternal salvation. Some people, in Velly's graphic words, 'struck by some sudden stirring of misplaced devotion gave themselves, their children and all their possessions to male and female saints, whose power and influence with God they believed they had experienced'. Meanwhile, the clergy carefully made a written record of these protestations of devotion, which became legal documents that were rigorously enforced.[1] In the same vein, Perreciot, in his learned work on the condition of people and property in Gaul, headed a chapter on *Letes*, whose condition he clearly equated with that of the serfs: 'Other causes of the increase of *Letes*: ill-conceived devotion.'[2] The abbé Clerget, who succeeded Voltaire as the chief spokesman in the campaign against serf-dom, wrote about the 'demon of superstition' which dared to imitate the voice of heaven in order to preach a love of slavery and to dictate 'the impertinent formula of an extravagant devo-tion'.[3] Démeunier, in the famous *Encyclopédie Méthodique*, described, in words borrowed from Perreciot, how freemen in the Middle Ages had rushed precipitately into serfdom in search of the protection of a particular saint.[4] Such ideas were found even outside the works of popular historians and pamphleteers, with both of whom gullibility was something of an occupational hallmark. Renauldon could speak seriously in his *Traité historique et pratique des droits seigneuriaux* . . . of 'serfs through devotion'.[5] Letrosne only expressed the accepted view when he pronounced, 'superstition ended by making the debasement universal'.[6]

---

[1] Velly, VI, pp. 183–4.

[2] Perreciot, I, p. 427.

[3] Clerget, *Le Cri de la raison*, p. 41.

[4] J.-N. Démeunier, *Encyclopédie méthodique. Economie politique et diplomatique* (Paris and Liège: Panckoucke, 1784–8), III, p. 208.

[5] J. Renauldon, *Traité historique et pratique des droits seigneuriaux* (Paris: Despilly, 1765), p. 197.

[6] Letrosne, *De l'Administration provinciale* (1788), II, p. 448.

It is amusing to watch some of the anti-clerical writers catch the fanaticism of those they attacked. With more earnestness than good sense, they succeeded in digging up a religious ceremony for personal enslavement from the *Glossarium* of the seventeenth-century antiquary, Du Cange. The abbé Fleury's *Histoire Ecclésiastique* referred readers to Du Cange, and prepared the ground for later writers by generalizing freely from a few instances cited in the *Glossarium*. He retailed in touching detail how 'serfs through pious devotion' would sometimes symbolize their dedication by putting the bell-rope around their necks, by placing four *deniers* on their heads, or by laying their heads upon the altar.[1] Almost identical accounts occur in Glatigny's *Dissertation sur la servitude*, Clerget's *Le Cri de la raison* and Dulaure's *Crimes et forfaits de la noblesse et du clergé*.[2] The length to which eighteenth-century publicists would go in this way to provide an historical case against the Church bears eloquent witness to their anti-clerical feelings.

It may seem from the above descriptions of the 'feudal anarchy' that in every eighteenth-century historian there was a Hollywood director screaming to get out. Yet anyone who has survived the reading of Mézeray and Daniel can hardly help feeling that even the most lurid and unsubstantiated account of the 'feudal anarchy' marked an advance in historiography. Attention was focused on the ordinary peasant, whose fate at the hands of marauding barons and rapacious clerics, while it may arouse the mirth of today's insensitive reader, seems to have stirred the genuine concern of his eighteenth-century counterpart. At least these historians gave a wider significance to the events of the past than most of their immediate predecessors, with their interminable accounts of the private wars and intrigues of the nobility, as these affected themselves and the king. Most descriptions of the 'feudal anarchy', however imperfectly, represented society as a whole, which was an essential precondition for understanding its development.

The very gusto with which eighteenth-century historians describe the 'feudal anarchy', and its sequel, the 'rise of the

[1] Fleury, *Histoire Ecclésiastique*, XIII, p. 530.
[2] G. de Glatigny, *Oeuvres posthumes de Monsieur de ***, contenant ses harangues au Palais, ses discours académiques* (Lyons: Duplain, 1757), p. 370; Clerget, *Le Cri de la raison*, p. 41; J.-A. Dulaure, *Crimes et forfaits de la noblesse et du clergé, depuis le commencement de la monarchie jusqu'à nos jours* (Paris, n.d.), pp. 32–3.

communes', may give the reader the impression that they are as guilty as the Marxists in reducing feudalism to a timeless abstraction. In almost all the historical writings, however, the stages by which feudalism waxed and waned were well-defined. Feudalism was usually seen to start with an idyllic phase when fiefs were the recognized reward for public services and personal merit. The moment when the nobles were reputed to have profited from the weakness of the Crown, to make the tenure of their lands and offices hereditary, was taken to mark the beginning of the 'feudal anarchy'. Finally, as I will try to show shortly, the 'feudal anarchy' was supposed to have been ended through the alliance of king and communes for their mutual protection against the feudal nobility.[1]

The average historian or publicist of the eighteenth century, however, had no more understanding of the development of feudalism than his counterpart today has of the development of democracy. The theory which is carefully worked out is, doubtless, the exception in any age. One writer, however, who came near to providing an overall history of feudalism was Letrosne. By profession, he was *avocat du roi* at the *bailliage* and *présidial* of Orléans for most of his adult life.[2] Because of his occupation and his position as one of the leaders of the physiocrats, Letrosne is in danger of being written off, with less justification than most of his fellow economists, as a man of affairs who dabbled in ideas. Yet, the unprejudiced reader will almost certainly be impressed by the *Dissertation sur la féodalité*, which was published for the first time with *De l'Administration provinciale* in 1779. Letrosne distinguished three separate 'ages' in the development of feudalism. The first, which he labelled its 'origin', he described as 'a means of administration, and a way of repaying public service', when it consisted solely in fighting for the king.[3] It was during the second 'age', the 'reign' of feudalism, that in Letrosne's view it entirely changed its character. The decisive moment, he implied, was when fiefs became hereditary as a matter of course, and no longer just in exceptional cases.[4] As a result, seigneurs escaped altogether

---

[1] See pp. 39–40.

[2] L.-G. Michaud, *Biographie universelle ancienne et moderne*, new ed. (Paris: Desplaces et Michaud, 1843–65), XXIV, p. 373.

[3] Letrosne, *De l'Administration provinciale* (1788), II, pp. 442–3.

[4] *Ibid.*, pp. 445–6.

from the control of the Crown, shared its essential prerogatives, and so dismembered the very sovereignty of the king. Feudalism in this form represented what he called the new 'monstrous constitution' of the State.[1] Finally, the third age or 'decadence' of feudalism came when the kings with the help of the people regained their powers, until only the purely fiscal side of feudalism remained.[2] The fact that feudalism had no constitutional or political role in eighteenth-century France was a principal argument among writers of a utilitarian stamp, that what they dubbed the 'remnants of feudalism' should be finally abolished.[3]

Simon Linguet, perhaps, may be credited with showing equal insight into the nature of feudalism. Linguet's ideas were inevitably coloured by his stormy temperament. He succeeded in antagonizing more influential people than almost any other public figure of the time, before he met a suitably violent end at the guillotine. The only contemporary who seems to have had a kind word for him was Voltaire, who shot a brilliant epigram at him, 'il brûle, mais il éclaire'.[4] The main difficulty in interpreting Linguet's ideas is to know when he is serious. For instance, although one of Linguet's principal preoccupations appears to be the vindication of slavery, it has been suggested that he had the good sense not to mean what he said.[5] Linguet himself, however, claimed the opposite. In the *Discours Préliminaire* of his chief work, *Théorie des loix civiles*, he claimed that if he rewrote it, he would not change a single idea, but would like to develop several which he had hardly dared to disclose.[6] It, therefore, does not seem unreasonable to suppose that his ideas on the origins of society were more than the musings of a disinterested anthropologist.

According to Linguet, mankind had originally been divided into 'hunters' and 'farmers' or 'pastoralists'. He considered that it was among the hunters that society first came into being.

[1] *Ibid.*, p. 453.
[2] *Ibid.*, pp. 451–2.
[3] See p. 135.
[4] C. Monselet, *Les Originaux du siècle dernier: les oubliés et les dédaignés* (Paris: Michel-Lévy, 1864), p. 7.
[5] H. R. G. Greaves, 'The Political ideas of Linguet', *Economica*, XXVIII (March 1930), p. 49.
[6] Linguet, *Théorie des loix civiles*, I, p. 9.

These had grown accustomed to concert their actions in order to capture their prey and to divide the spoils afterwards. The farmer he describes as peaceable and in search of solitude, as he is afraid of being robbed of the fruits of his labours.[1] Thus, Linguet spoke of two different ways of life. The hunters in the nature of their occupation would go hungry from time to time, while the farmers lived in abundance. Sooner or later, he said, this difference between them would lead to a conflict. It was a foregone conclusion that the hunters could massacre the farmers with impunity.[2] The hunters, however, found it more convenient to kill off only part of the flocks of the pastoralists. To save themselves trouble they left the former owners in charge as their tenants. In order to complete their subjection, the hunters forbade them to bear arms and themselves undertook to defend them from wild animals.[3] As society grew more complex, they felt the need for laws to protect their property. So, the original dispossession of the pastoralists became the sacred title of their own property rights, while they outlawed all subsequent acts of usurpation. Such in Linguet's view was the origin of society and the source of all human laws.[4]

It hardly seems accidental that Linguet described in similar terms the origins of human society and the conditions of France under the 'feudal anarchy'. At the height of the 'feudal anarchy', according to Linguet, 'there was not a quarter of a league which lacked its château, serving as a den for a pack of furious wolves, always ready to fill the neighbourhood with murders and carnage'. He invited his readers to contemplate 'the condition of the disarmed sheep who grazed trembling in the fields, and whose ears were unceasingly assailed by the cries of these sanguinary beasts.'[5] In this piece the wolves and the sheep have surely only taken the place of the hunters and pastoralists who figured so prominently in Linguet's account of the origins of society. He developed the analogy, a little farther on, when he described how the kings regained their powers. The kings saw the need to ally with the people against the barons who oppressed them. The rulers began, in Linguet's words, 'to remove their

---

[1] *Ibid.*, pp. 278 ff.
[2] *Ibid.*, pp. 288–9.
[3] *Ibid.*, pp. 291–3.
[4] *Ibid.*, p. 298.
[5] *Ibid.*, II, p. 500.

chains, as a hunter uncouples his dogs when he finds himself near the animal which he wishes to spear'.[1] This whole elaborate analogy concerning feudal times has, indeed, all the appearance of being a development of the author's ideas about the origins of society. This view is reinforced by the reactions of contemporaries. *Théorie des loix civiles* received a chorus of criticisms from such disparate sources as the *Mercure*, the periodical of the fashionable world, and Mirabeau, the self-styled 'Friend of Man'. One writer was particularly annoyed by Linguet's comments on feudalism. In *Mes Rêves* the vicomte de Toustain asked, 'Why has he declaimed so violently against the feudal chains?' De Toustain also expressed wonder at his not knowing of 'the sweetness and tranquillity' of the serf's life at Saint-Claude.[2] As Greaves wrote in his article on him, 'Linguet's reasoning may seem over-simplified to modern ears, but there was enough truth in it to make him many a bitter enemy in his own day.'[3]

The lengths to which publicists would go to blacken the 'feudal anarchy' was itself a spur to the development of historiography. It forced on historians the need to explain how comparative sanity and order had come to prevail. Once again the inventive powers of French historians did not fail. The problems raised by the mythical 'feudal anarchy' were answered after a fashion by the equally mythical 'rise of the communes'. This idea was not entirely new. Daniel at the beginning of the eighteenth century had mentioned that Louis the Fat had granted considerable privileges to certain townships which co-operated with the Crown in maintaining order.[4] This idea, which could be thrown off casually in the course of a narrative account, played an important role in historiography when its implications were worked out later in the century.

Bréquigny in 1738 in *Recherches sur les communes* and again in *Recherches sur les bourgeoisies* was the first French historian to write at length about the communes.[5] According to Bréquigny,

[1] *Ibid.*, p. 504.

[2] J. Cruppi, *Un Avocat journaliste au XVIIIe. siècle, Linguet* (Paris: Hachette, 1895), pp. 175 ff.

[3] Greaves, p. 46.

[4] Daniel, *Histoire de France*, II, pp. 481–2.

[5] L. G. O. F. de Bréquigny, 'Recherches sur les communes' and 'Recherches sur les bourgeoisies', *Collections des meilleures dissertations, notices et traités particuliers relatifs à l'histoire de France*, ed. C. J. Leber (Paris: J.-G. Dentu, 1826–38), XX, pp. 42–144 and 145–211, respectively.

'the need to unite in self-defence against the tyranny of the seigneurs, whose manifold excesses had been carried to the most unheard of lengths, was the first cause which led the inhabitants of the towns of France to form themselves into communes'.[1] And the 'fundamental act' of the communes, he said, was the confederation of the inhabitants, united under oath against the seigneurs who oppressed them.[2] In *Recherches sur les bourgeoisies* Bréquigny described 'the decrease in feudal power' which followed the establishment of municipal liberties. For, it was by the 'fortunate resource', he wrote, of taking the towns under their protection that Louis VI and his successors were able to regain the powers of the Crown. When the king entered into partnership with the towns against the seigneurs, he claimed, the population of the countryside was attracted to the towns. As a result the seigneurs, to keep them under their jurisdiction, were forced themselves to establish municipalities in their fiefs in imitation of the sovereign.[3]

Similar ideas are to be found in many other histories. Linguet, in stressing the importance of the communes, called them the very 'foot-stool' of the throne. 'The destruction of feudal servitude', he said, using a different metaphor, 'was the jack which slowly, but with unlimited power, had raised the throne to its present position'.[4] Less important was the disagreement on the ways in which these results had come about. Some, unlike Bréquigny, considered that the seigneurs had been driven by an urgent need to raise money to sell charters to their vassals. In Saint-Foix's view the majority did so 'to equip themselves for the Crusades', or because they had been ruined by wars across the seas.[5] The marquis d'Argenson also described the nobles as being drained of their resources by the tournaments and the crusades, 'their devout acts of folly'. Louis VII, he added, encouraged the towns to buy their independence, with a consequent strengthening of royal power.[6]

---

[1] *Ibid.*, pp. 72–3.
[2] *Ibid.*, p. 87.
[3] *Ibid.*, pp. 153–5.
[4] Linguet, *Théorie des loix civiles*, II, p. 508.
[5] G.-F. Poullain de Saint-Foix, *Essais historiques sur Paris*, new ed. (London and Paris: Duchesne, 1759), II, p. 144.
[6] Argenson, pp. 141–2.

The motives of the Crown were also disputed. A few writers, notably Hénault, considered that French sovereigns had joined forces with the communes only through motives of self-interest. In his popular *Abrégé* he said that the kings had taken back step by step all the privileges which they had granted, once the towns had served their purpose of curtailing seigniorial power.[1] It was far commoner to make the less radical accusation that monarchs had been too weak in their dealings with the feudatories. In particular, Hugues Capet was blamed for the concessions with which he was supposed to have bought recognition for his own usurpation of the Crown.[2] Yet, on the whole, as some of the earlier extracts suggest, the Crown received a favourable press. The marquis d'Argenson seems to have expressed the accepted view when he said that it was the increase in the powers of the Third Estate that had enabled the Crown to curb the powers of the nobility, and drew his celebrated conclusion that democracy was as much the friend of monarchy as aristocracy was its enemy.[3]

There was a ring of historical inevitability in some accounts of the development of the communes. These were regarded as the very spearhead of the creative forces of an evolving society; the oases of sanity which, even at the height of the 'feudal anarchy', pointed towards a happier future. Thus Letrosne wrote in *De l'Administration provinciale*: 'The establishment of the communes has founded or has repeopled the towns, has created arts and industry, has civilized manners, has invited men to liberty, has changed the face of the kingdom'.[4] In Turgot's *Tableau philosophique des progrès successifs de l'esprit humain*, a lecture delivered at the Sorbonne in 1750, the towns played the chief part in his theory of the blind, but inevitable, march of human progress. 'The towns among civilized peoples,' he said, 'are by their nature the centre of commerce and the forces of society. They continued to exist, and if the character of feudal government born from the ancient customs of Germany, combined with certain fortuitous circumstances, had laid them low,

---

[1] C. J. F. Hénault, *Nouvel abrégé chronologique de l'histoire de France* (Paris: Prault, 1768), III, p. 983.

[2] See p. 20.

[3] Argenson, p. 148.

[4] Letrosne, *De l'Administration provinciale* (1788), p. 451.

it was a contradiction in the constitution of States which would disappear in the long run.'[1]

The historical determinism, which was often implicit in ideas of the rise to power of the communes and Third Estate, reached its fullest expression in the twin idea of the increasingly commercial character of the State. The spread of the communes and the growth of commerce were nearly always firmly, if indiscriminately, bracketed together by French writers. An obscure pamphleteer expressed the accepted view in these words: 'When the various charters granted to the communes had restored some of its rights to the people, commercial activity and the advance of enlightenment were the happy results.'[2] Argenson also spoke as if commerce became the chief concern of the people once they had regained their freedom.[3]

The importance attached by French writers to commerce and trade is discussed in a later chapter. My concern here is more specifically with commerce, in so far as it was regarded by some eighteenth-century writers as a factor in the historical evolution of their society. Although some contemporaries were not unaware of the contribution which mercantile rivalries had made to the wars of their century,[4] there was a widespread belief that the development of commerce had the effect of making wars increasingly anachronistic. Montesquieu said in *De l'Esprit des Loix* that commerce tended to promote peace, because nations by their commercial dealings made themselves dependent on one another.[5] It is worth quoting at some length Monsieur Vanderk père, the hero of Sedaine's popular *Le Philosophe sans le savoir*, on this point:[6]

Some bold individuals make the kings arm; war flares up; everyone is engulfed; Europe is divided. That English, Russian, or Chinese merchant, however, is no less dear to me. On the surface of the world

[1] A.-R.-J. Turgot, *Oeuvres de Turgot et documents le concernant, avec biographie et notes par Gustave Schelle* (Paris: F. Alcan, 1913–23), I, p. 230.

[2] Murat-Montferrand, *Qu'est-ce que la noblesse, et que sont ses privilèges?* (Amsterdam, 1789), pp. 24–5.

[3] Argenson, p. 144.

[4] See C.-L. Chassin (ed.), *Les Elections et les cahiers de Paris en 1789* (Paris: Jouaust et Sigaux, 1888–9), I, the *Mémoire* of the *Six Corps de Paris*, p. 24; and Démeunier, I, p. IV.

[5] Montesquieu, *Oeuvres*, I, 'De l'Esprit des Loix', p. 446.

[6] M.-J. Sedaine, *Le Philosophe sans le savoir, comédie en prose et en 5 actes*, ed. Cloudesley Brereton (London: Blackie, 1907), p. 26.

[we merchants] are so many threads of silk, which tie the nations together, and lead them towards peace through the need to trade.

Baron d'Holbach, the author of the article 'Représentants' in the
Encyclopédie, shared the same conviction that the commercial
spirit would triumph ultimately over the militarism of the
nobility. He wrote that under feudal government the nobility
and clergy had long had the exclusive right to speak in the name
of the whole nation. After giving an abridged version of the
'feudal anarchy', he went on to say that circumstances had
changed. The tyrants of the people, he claimed, perceived that
in the long term their behaviour ran counter to their interests:
'Manufactures and trade become necessities of State and require
peace; warriors are less necessary; frequent shortages and
famine have ultimately made the need felt for good farming,
which used to be upset by the bloody quarrels of some armed
brigands.'[1]

Writers who credited trade with promoting international
peace naturally saw the world as inhabited by a single community. If this view was only implied by Montesquieu, Sedaine
and in the *Encyclopédie*, it was stated unequivocally by at least
one writer, Lefèvre de Beauvray. In his *Dictionnaire social et
patriotique* he wrote: 'The world has become one large political
entity, in which the parts have the closest interactions with each
other, and receive life and impetus from the same principle.'[2]

Turgot harnessed to the same idea his belief in the inevitability of progress. Commerce, in his view, had the effect of
welding Europe into a whole which the forces of progress could
manipulate the more easily. 'Trade and politics,' he wrote,
'bring together all the parts of the globe, and the entire mass
of the human race by alternations of calm and agitation, of good
and evil, moves always, although by slow steps, towards greater
perfection.'[3]

The rather rarefied reasoning of many of these writers does
not mean that they gave no thought to the needs of society in

---

[1] Diderot (ed.), *Encyclopédie*, XIV, p. 144. (Although the article is often
attributed to Diderot himself, the author was, in fact, d'Holbach. See J. Lough,
The 'Encyclopédie' in England and other studies (Newcastle: Oriel Press, 1970),
p. 161.
[2] P. Lefèvre de Beauvray, *Dictionnaire social et patriotique* (Amsterdam, 1770),
p. 54.
[3] Turgot, *Oeuvres*, I, pp. 215–16.

their own day. Although most writers were agreed that feudalism proper was dead, many considered that the remnants of the system still did serious harm in contemporary society. In the words of the marquis d'Argenson, 'What remains is only a shadow of lordship, yet this shadow is still very harmful to the public.'[1] Filangieri wrote in *Scienza della legislatione*, which seems to have been widely read in French translation on the eve of the Revolution:[2]

I am concerned only with feudal government such as it exists among us and among several other peoples of Europe. I dare to say that despite all the changes which it has undergone, and the perceptible progress which the monarchy has made in recent times, this ancient system of [distributing] power still presents a crowd of abuses [which are] destructive of the social order.

Letrosne was more specific: 'There is nothing real in feudalism except the expenses,' he wrote.[3]

These attacks on the 'remnants of feudalism' almost invariably served as ammunition against the French nobility itself. Sieyès, for example, wrote of feudalism in *Qu'est-ce que le tiers état?*, 'It is to the odious remnants of this barbarous regime that we owe the division, still existing to France's misfortune, of three orders, [that are] enemies of one another.'[4] He returned to the same theme later in the pamphlet, when he assured his readers that 'The nobility has ceased to be that monstrous feudal reality which could wield oppression unpunished'. He warned his readers, however, that although the power of the nobility was only a shadow of its former self, they were still trying to frighten the entire nation.[5] For the anonymous author of one pamphlet it was 'feudalism which has made nobles a distinct order; it is it alone which has given [us] the present regime with all its faults'.[6] In *Crimes et forfaits de la noblesse et du clergé*, Dulaure wrote about the nobility: 'Let us overthrow this ancient

[1] Argenson, p. 119.

[2] G. Filangieri, *La Science de la législation . . . ouvrage traduit de l'italien d'après l'édition de Naples de 1784*, (Par J.-Ant. Gouvain Gallois), (Paris: Cuchet, 1786–1791), III, p. 318.

[3] A. Cobban, *The Social interpretation of the French Revolution* (Cambridge University Press, 1964), p. 36.

[4] Sieyès, p. 28.

[5] *Ibid.*, p. 40.

[6] (Anon.), *Réflexions patriotiques, sur l'arrêté de quelques nobles de Bretagne . . ., du 25 Octobre 1788* (n.p., n.d.), p. 11.

idol . . . by making known the odious origin of the heredity of fiefs and of the nobility.'[1] Similarly, Le Scène-Desmaisons considered that the very existence of the nobility had been 'excusable', up to a point, while their unjust titles had been hidden 'in the night of time'. However, he felt that after the 'abusive origin of its privileges' had been demonstrated, it was 'necessary to change the system'.[2] Publicists, such as Clicquot de Blervache, insisted that if fiefs had been originally awarded as compensation for undertaking military service, in the eighteenth century when the soldiers were paid by the king, seigneurs had no right to levy a second charge in the form of seigniorial dues.[3] These and other writings are hardly noteworthy for their profundity. It is significant, however, that they were so widely current. It was surely a sign of their influence, when the celebrated genealogist, Chérin, who had exposed the pretentions of so many *roturiers*, seemed to admit that times had changed, and that the nobility no longer had a right to be exempt from paying taxes.[4]

The case for the nobles, such as it was, tended to go by default. Those who tried to defend their privileges were in such a weak position that they could only claim that conditions had not really changed at all. Thus one writer claimed that the nobles had every right to their fiscal exemption, as they were still subject to the *ban* and *arrière-ban*, whenever the king cared to call them out.[5] No king, however, was unwise enough to do so after the late seventeenth century. The ineptitude of the defenders of privilege only goes to reinforce Brinton's claim that the French nobility had lost faith in itself as a ruling class, to the point that it was paralysed in face of revolution.[6]

---

[1] Dulaure, *Crimes et forfaits de la noblesse*, p. 2.

[2] J. Le Scène-Desmaisons, *Histoire politique de la Révolution en France, ou correspondance entre Lord D*** et Lord T**** (London, 1789), II, pp. 78–9.

[3] S. Clicquot de Blervache, *Mémoire sur les moyens d'améliorer en France la condition des laboureurs, des journaliers, des hommes de peine vivans dans les campagnes, et celle de leurs femmes et de leurs enfans* (Paris: Delalain, 1789), pp. 31–3. See also (Anon.), *Mémoire sur les rentes directes et les droits féodaux . . . par un dauphinois* (Paris, 1789), p. 33.

[4] L. N. H. Chérin, *La Noblesse considérée sous ses divers rapports dans les assemblées générales et particulières de la nation* (Paris: Boyez, 1788), pp. 27–8.

[5] F. de P. La Garde, *Traité historique de le souveraineté du roi et des droits en dépendans de commencer à l'établissement de la monarchie* (Paris: Durand, 1754), I, p. 449.

[6] C. C. Brinton, *The Lives of Talleyrand* (New York: Norton, 1937), p. 56.

The Third Estate, unlike the nobility, could derive nothing but confidence from the majority of eighteenth-century historians; the story of the past was the vindication of their rights. The rise of the communes and the advent of commerce as the dominant political power seemed to imply that irresistible forces were conspiring to secure victory for the people. It is, of course, impossible to say if the exultant tone of many pamphleteers was more than a reflection of the improved economic, and therefore also social and political, standing of the Third Estate. At all events, judging by the number of historical writings in their favour, there were many *roturiers* who liked to be justified in historical terms. This seems to be borne out by the reactions, among pamphleteers to P.-H. de Ségur's edict of 1781, in which it was laid down that the possession of three generations of nobility was a requirement for the acquisition of certain commissions in the army. Until recently, historians have interpreted this edict as an instrument of the 'aristocratic reaction', which is itself now being called in doubt. Professor Gruder has shown in an important work that the edict was intended less as a blow against the status of commoners than as a means of promoting professionalism in the army by reducing the sale of commissions, in order to allow more appointments of the better trained and motivated. The career prospects of the majority of officers who came from the provincial nobility, she contends, were threatened more by the court nobility than by the bourgeoisie. The latter when they were career officers of long standing may even have benefited from the edict.[1] When the edict is seen in this light, the outcry against it is all the more significant, as it seems to show that even a slight threat to the social standing of *roturiers* was enough to arouse keen resentment on the eve of the Revolution. The *avocats* of the Parlement of Brittany, for instance, declared the edict in their *Mémoire* to be 'one of the greatest outrages to the French people since the foundation of the monarchy'.[2] The author of *Réformes dans l'ordre social* described the bar on the promotion of the ablest members of the Third Estate as 'a

[1] V. R. Gruder, *The Royal Provincial Intendants: a governing élite in eighteenth-century France* (Ithaca, New York: Cornell University Press, 1968), pp. 223–4.

[2] (Anon.), *Mémoire des avocats du Parlement de Bretagne sur les moyens d'entretenir l'union entre les différens ordres de l'état* (Rennes, 1788), p. 21.

manifest reversal of the social system'.[1] He condemned the nobility for departing from the course which had brought the Third Estate close to it, and of effecting 'the return to barbarism and gothic feudalism'.[2] Count Murat-Montferrand condemned the edict as contrary to the *ancienne constitution*, according to which, anyone could reach the highest point through possessing courage and merit.[3] Even if France of the *ancien régime* lacked a constitution, the historians were doing their best to manufacture one.

The eighteenth-century writings that have been considered in this chapter may well seem to the reader too polemical in character to contribute much to an understanding of the past. Yet, for eighteenth-century authors, who pioneered a new kind of historical writing, prejudice was a less serious defect than for their successors. The desultory pages of Mézeray and Daniel in the seventeenth century are sufficient proof that prejudice could be far less harmful than the lack of general themes that were needed, if unclassified facts were to be shaped into an overall view of the past. The themes that eighteenth-century historians elaborated naturally appear naïve by the standards of our time. However, the present age which itself lacks generally-accepted themes with which to reinterpret the past has little right to condemn those of other periods.

It was the debate over the origins of fiefs which first served to direct French historians to the study of society as a whole. While the majority of these writings were still either narrowly antiquarian or crudely polemical, those by Boulainvilliers and Dubos among others showed keen historical insight. The same is true of works by Letrosne, Bréquigny, the marquis d'Argenson and others in which the genesis and decline of feudalism are discussed. Their ideas, particularly about the role of the communes and trade in undermining the feudal regime, helped to orientate historical study, even if their accounts were far too over-simplified to win acceptance for long. If the imagination of these writers outran the evidence, which was still largely unexplored, the mental attitudes that were essential for the successful reconstruction of the past were already being formed.

[1] (Anon.), *Réformes dans l'ordre social*, p. 7.
[2] *Ibid.*, p. 18.
[3] Murat-Montferrand, p. 27.

It has often been said that the eighteenth century in France was not a period of originality in historical writing. Even if Montesquieu and Voltaire are left out of account, however, many other writers must be given credit for the ways in which they resuscitated history as a serious study, after it had been laid low by Descartes' strictures in the seventeenth century. Doubtless, historiography was far from being rehabilitated in the esteem of many philosophes, even by the end of the century. Yet in terms of development, largely owing to the debate over the origins and nature of feudalism, historiography made more progress in the eighteenth century than almost any other discipline.

III

'Feudalism' in Juristic Thought

The foremost thinkers of eighteenth-century France include scientists, philosophers, economists and even the occasional theologian, who refused to wither away beneath the tirades of the sceptics.[1] Jurists, by contrast, as Professor Church says, 'occupied only a very minor place in the Enlightenment and . . . at no time during the century did they regain the prominence they had enjoyed as political thinkers before the reign of Louis XIV'.[2] This fact is all the more surprising as no less than a quarter of the deputies of the Third Estate in 1789 have been classified as *avocats* or *notaires*.[3] Yet, the practising lawyer and man of affairs was usually ill-equipped in the field of legal theory. No one who reads the fairly representative collection of writings on law reform that were edited by Brissot de Warville in the 1780s is likely to be impressed by their originality.[4] The ten volumes are 'philosophic' only in the title; barrister's rhetoric and the fashionable language of humanitarianism do not obscure the failure to understand French law as a whole and, above all, from within. In *le siècle des lumières*, to find a writer who combined breadth of vision with informed legal argument it was necessary to exhume one from an earlier century. Even so, the ideas of such luminaries were often too radical for

[1] See R. R. Palmer, *Catholics and Unbelievers in Eighteenth-century France* (Princeton University Press, 1939).

[2] Church, *French Historical Studies*, V (1967), p. 24.

[3] A. Cobban, *Aspects of the French Revolution* (London: Jonathan Cape, 1968), p. 101.

[4] J.-P. Brissot de Warville, *Bibliothèque philosophique du législateur, du politique, du jurisconsulte* (Berlin, 1782–5).

eighteenth-century jurists to accept them, while the non-specialist could not understand them.

The scarcity of great legal thinkers partly reflected the development of royal absolutism in France. As long as the Crown had been weak, it had leaned heavily on the support of royal jurists, who supplied the legal principles to give cohesion and direction to the royal administration in its unending struggle against powerful groups and individuals. However, when the Crown became outwardly supreme under Louis XIV, those, like Bishop Bossuet, who sang the praises of the monarch were favoured at the expense of jurists who defended the legal basis of his absolutism. Such complacency provided Louis' two successors in the eighteenth century with a rickety basis for their power. When the nobles re-emerged during the eighteenth century to challenge monarchical absolutism, there was no longer a school of royal lawyers to defend it.

In the reign of Louis XIV when 'might' was so often 'right', the jurist may seem a peripheral figure. If the king had taken pains to provide his oppression with a legal basis, later historians would doubtless have accused him of being over-fastidious. However, Louis' own disregard for law and precedent have often been exaggerated. Even the command in 1673 that edicts should be registered in the parlements before they protested in their *remontrances* was announced as a temporary expedient during the pressing needs of the Dutch War.[1] In local government, it is true, the Crown was more prepared to assert its power. Professor Mousnier has shown, for instance, the dictatorial means by which the royal administration, in its efforts to secure greater uniformity and control, undermined the autonomy of municipal government.[2] Yet, issues of political control apart, the government did little to curb privilege in private hands. Although the abolition of internal tolls was one of Colbert's professed aims, the rights of the owners were treated with so much respect that the situation was not radically altered.[3]

[1] J. H. Shennan, *The Parlement of Paris* (London: Eyre & Spottiswoode, 1968), p. 278.

[2] R. Mousnier, *État et société sous François Ier. et pendant le gouvernement personnel de Louis XIV* (Paris, n.d.), II, pp. 177 ff.

[3] E. F. Heckscher, *Mercantilism*, ed. E. F. Söderlund, 2nd rev. ed. (London: Allen & Unwin, 1955), I, pp. 82 ff.

The forbearance of Louis XIV hardly seems in keeping with his reputation as an absolute monarch. The usual explanation is that Louis XIV tolerated some independence, notably the retention by the nobles of their fiscal and social privileges, on condition that he himself was undisputed political master of France. This view implies that the king, who drove so many hard bargains abroad, was strangely undemanding at home. Moreover, the nobles, who had just demonstrated their political ineptitude during the Frondes, were in no position to impose their terms on the king. Why did Louis XIV not do more to reduce the power of the nobles? Part of the answer lies in his temperament and character. Historians have been too ready to cast him in the role of 'bourgeois king', mainly on the grounds that he drew most of his ministers from men who were originally outside the nobility.[1] A surer guide to his outlook was his pursuit of grandeur abroad through war, which was the traditional, and almost the only, occupation of many nobles. The *hauteur* with which Louis XIV negotiated with the Dutch, especially in 1672 when he ordered them to bear him a gold medal annually as a souvenir of their humiliation, was worthy of one of his own cavalry officers. Anyone who can believe, after walking through the *grands appartements* at Versailles, and, after calling to mind the elaborate ceremonial of the court, that Louis XIV was a bourgeois at heart, can surely believe anything. However, it may seem misleading to stress the importance of Louis XIV's personal outlook, when he would not abandon affairs of state even at the drop of a petticoat. It is more likely that Louis XIV failed to complete Richelieu's reduction of the powers of the nobility because he was preoccupied with foreign affairs at the expense of domestic. While this last point is a truism, Louis XIV can hardly have failed to see that his ventures abroad were jeopardized continually by lack of money, for which the only long-term solution was to subject the privileged to greater taxation. Yet, the *capitation* of 1697 and the *dixième* of 1710 which fell on all classes, although the nobles naturally did not pay their full share, were announced as transient measures. As Dr Shennan comments, 'Even Louis XIV

---

[1] See R. Mousnier, *Les XVI. et XVIIe. siècles: les progrès de la civilisation européenne et le déclin de l'Orient* (1492–1715), (*Historie générale des civilisations*, ed. M. Crouzet, IV, Paris: PUF, 1954), p. 235.

could only invoke the doctrine of *raison d'état* as a temporary and abnormal expedient.'[1] When Louis XIV was so short of money and also had an army of nearly half a million men with which to bring the matter home to his subjects, it is surely remarkable that he should have treated the privileges of the nobility with such respect. Louis XIV's personal outlook and policies obviously cannot provide the whole answer. The king was also held back by law and custom, of which he was rather more aware than most modern historians of his reign. French society of the *ancien régime* was defined mainly in juridic terms. The individual counted for little in himself, except in so far as he belonged to a social group. Besides the 'estates' of the clergy and nobility, there were guilds, municipalities, professional bodies, such as the *Six Grands Corps de Marchands* of Paris, not to mention the particularist privileges of provinces that were recorded in their *coutumes*. 'Each of these,' as Professor Méthivier explains, 'has its right and regulations, its "liberties" or "franchises", its *privilèges*, that is to say, its private laws. Corporative organization, armed with the particular privileges of each body is, therefore, the foundation of the society of the *ancien régime*.'[2] This society possessed a kind of grass-roots resistance to the extension of monarchical absolutism. Those who criticize Louis XIV and his successors mainly for failing to take strong measures against the privileged are transposing a juridical problem into political terms. While few would deny that a readiness to use force was a necessary condition for the extension of royal power, force alone was insufficient. The first requirement was to undermine the legal basis of privilege: to erode the claim of groups and individuals to hold rights against king and State.

As these rights were upheld in a multiplicity of law codes, a necessary step towards this end was the establishment of a single system of royal justice. The elements already lay to hand: there was a hierarchy of royal courts which was headed by the Council of State, which acted as a final court of appeal. The king had long been recognized as the ultimate source of law in France. His will, therefore, took precedence over customary law. The Crown had made good this claim in 1580 when the royal lawyers had

---

[1] Shennan, p. 297.
[2] H. Méthivier, *L'Ancien Régime* (Paris: PUF, 1961), p. 6.

redrafted the *coutumes* of the various provinces. Once the *coutumes* had been demoted from a menace to a nuisance, however, the government did little to reduce their authority further. The traveller across France, as Voltaire pointed out in the eighteenth century, continued to change law codes more often than he changed horses.[1] The *coutumes* were described accurately by Maupeou in a memorandum to Louis XVI as 'unintelligible to the people, obscure and enigmatic to the scholar', while constituting 'between the different provinces barriers which trade and the spirit of the times strive in vain to overturn'.[2] For the *coutumes* gave legal backing to local particularism, and also reinforced within the area the status of groups, such as the holders of fiefs, which aspired to share sovereignty with the Crown.

The failure of the government in the seventeenth century to reduce significantly the authority of the *coutumes* is all the more remarkable, in view of Colbert's ambition to establish a single law code in France. His talents as an administrator, and even his eagerness to resort to savage punishments in defence of the social order, however, failed to equip him adequately for the task. Only a jurist of outstanding ability could have disentangled the Kafkaesque complexities of the French laws. Whether President Lamoignon or Jean Domat, whom some regard as the greatest jurist of the reign, were equal to this undertaking, was never put to the test. However debatable their abilities, they had no rivals among their eighteenth-century successors, whose few ideas were lost on pages where the so-called 'footnotes' climb with inexorable erudition to the top of the page. The huge number of eighteenth-century commentaries on the *coutumes* did not stem from any strong urge to simplify them. Karyeev, in an important work, justly summarized their achievement when he wrote:[3]

The principal work of the *feudistes* of the eighteenth century was not to demand a general reform of the law, but to reduce all the varieties of *coutumes* to general principles, to define accepted principles more

---

[1] Voltaire, *Oeuvres*, XV, p. 427.

[2] Marion, *Dictionnaire*, p. 159.

[3] N. I. Karyeev, *Les Paysans et la question paysanne en France dans le dernier quart du XVIIIe. siècle*, trans. from the Russian by C. W. Woynarowska (Paris: V. Giard et E. Brière, 1899), pp. 255–6.

precisely, to fill gaps, to eliminate misunderstandings, contradictions, and to make a complete system out of all these legal materials. They sought nothing, or practically nothing, beyond that.

When the Crown ceased in the seventeenth century to patronize a school of jurists, they had turned away from the public domain to immerse themselves in the intricacies of private law.[1] It was hardly surprising that most of these jurists transformed their loyalty from the sovereign to the individual seigneur whose rights were enshrined in the various *coutumes* and feudal commentaries which they edited. The jurists who discerned their interests more quickly than the new set of principles which were required to buttress them reached a shaky compromise in the eighteenth century. They usually began by invoking in general terms the time-honoured rulings of earlier royal jurists, such as Du Moulin and Loyseau. Their honour satisfied in this painless way, they proceeded to record in meticulous detail the sordid inventory of the seigneur's claims against his vassals.

The jurist whom they invoked most often and who had done most to curtail theoretical support for feudal and seigniorial rights was Charles Du Moulin. The man who was undoubtedly the greatest French jurist of the sixteenth century had done more than anyone to cast the Crown as the guardian of the common interest against the selfish claims of groups and individuals. An important corollary of the king's power, Du Moulin argued, was the freedom of his subjects to fulfil their obligations to him without interference from others: in this sense, he set all Frenchmen on an equal footing. He was opposed on principle to all feudal and seigniorial rights in so far as they placed a barrier between king and subjects. 'The major significance of the medieval law of property as a basis of social organization,' as Professor Church has explained, 'was that it not only distributed landed properties, the major form of wealth, among persons in the realm but that it also fixed the positions of the holders of those lands in the hierarchical structure.' In this situation not only were tenure and status largely synonymous, but 'often the jurists went to the lengths of giving greater weight to the personal element than to the

---

[1] Church, *French Historical Studies*, (1967), pp. 5 ff.

proprietary'.[1] Du Moulin's influence was vital in reversing this trend, and in restricting the definition of a fief to the proprietary elements alone. Du Moulin insisted that the seigneur's rights were over the fief which was held from him, and not over the person of his vassal.[2] Feudal dues and services, he stated, were little more than 'base servitudes'.[3] He wanted ultimately no less than the abolition of servitudes of every kind, and the reduction of all reliefs to a single lump sum.[4]

Du Moulin's onslaught against feudal and seigniorial rights was closely allied to his attempts to reform the *coutumes*. For it was the *coutumes* which embodied the customary law of the different provinces concerning feudal and seigniorial rights. In the first place he refused to concede full legitimacy to any seigniorial claims that went unsupported in the appropriate *coutume*.[5] Second, the *coutumes* themselves were judged in the light of general principles which he drew from Roman law and other sources. The general effect of his writings was to establish the monarch, enlightened by his jurists, as sole arbiter.[6] His far-ranging ideas, backed as they were by the Crown, had immense practical effect. When the royal lawyers undertook their most ambitious task in the century, the redrafting of the *coutumes* in 1580, they were guided by the principles which he had laid down.[7]

Du Moulin was held in the highest respect during the eighteenth century. The re-editing of his *Traité des fiefs* in 1773 was enough to turn Henrion de Pansey, who had been vegetating 'in the profoundest obscurity' for ten years, into a celebrity overnight.[8] In his edition of the *Traité* he called it 'the torch which has illuminated all the reformers who have presided over the drafting of the *coutumes*, all the judges who have given judgement, all the authors who have written about fiefs during two centuries'.[9] This was faint praise, however, in comparison

[1] W. F. Church, *Constitutional Thought in Sixteenth-century France* (Cambridge, Mass.: Harvard University Press, 1941), p. 184.

[2] *Ibid.*, p. 185.   [5] *Ibid.*, p. 108.
[3] *Ibid.*, p. 107.   [6] *Ibid.*, p. 106.
[4] *Ibid.*, p. 187.   [7] *Ibid.*, p. 109.

[8] A. V. Arnault, A. Jay, and others, *Biographie nouvelle des contemporains* (Paris: Libraire historique, 1820–5), IX, pp. 133–4.

[9] P. P. N. Henrion de Pansey (ed.), *Traité des fiefs de Dumoulin analysé et conféré avec les autres feudistes* (Paris: Valade, 1773), p. i.

with what he wrote in the *Éloge* which appeared in the same volume. 'Du Moulin,' according to Henrion de Pansey, 'substituted reason for a multitude of puerile subtleties . . . he re-created the art of reasoning . . . Descartes only said what Du Moulin had put into practice.'[1] Guyot, who was well enough known to be nicknamed 'Guyot of the fiefs', described Du Moulin as 'this illuminator of fiefs'.[2] Even Hervé, who was probably the most radical commentator on feudal law that the eighteenth century produced,[3] wrote on the eve of the Revolution that Du Moulin undoubtedly held the first place among those who had written about fiefs.[4] The fact that in the *Journal Encyclopédique*, the official organ of the Encyclopaedists, detailed reference was made to the writings of Du Moulin, in order to refute a defender of serfdom, shows that his influence was felt far outside legal circles.[5] Other jurists from the past, notably Charles Loyseau, enjoyed a great, if lesser, reputation in the eighteenth century. Even the authors of short pamphlets about seigniorial justice drew heavily on the great seventeenth-century jurist's *Des Abus des justices de village*.[6]

Yet the eighteenth-century jurists who made a show of venerating their predecessors seldom seem to have been influenced by their ideas. The very fact that Loyseau's *Des Abus des justices de village* was quoted verbatim and at length on the eve of the Revolution, as if it gave the most up-to-date description of the workings of seigniorial justice, itself shows a lack of

---

[1] *Ibid.*, p. 4.

[2] G.-A. Guyot, *Traité des fiefs tant pour le pays coutumier que pour les pays de droit écrit* (Paris: Saugrain, 1746–58), I, iv.

[3] See his remarks on serfdom that are discussed below in chapter V, p. 129.

[4] F. Hervé, *Théorie des matières féodales et censuelles* (Paris: Knapen, 1785–8), I, p. ii.

[5] *Journal Encyclopédique*, vol. 4 pt 3 for 1779, p. 448.

[6] E.g.: Mézard (chevalier et Président de la cour royale d'Ajaccio), *Essai sur les réformes à faire dans l'administration de la justice en France. Dédié aux États-Généraux* (n.p., 1788), pp. 62–4; A. J.-B. Boucher d'Argis, *Cahier d'un magistrat du Châtelet de Paris, sur les justices seigneuriales et l'administration de la justice dans les campagnes* (Paris: Clousier, 1789), pp. 12–14; J. Pétion de Villeneuve, *Les Loix civiles et l'administration de la justice, ramenées à un ordre simple et uniforme: ou réflexions morales, politiques . . . sur la manière de rendre la justice en France, avec le plus de célérité et le moins de frais possible* (London, 1782), pp. 10–11; Fouqueau de Pussy (avocat), *Idées sur l'administration de la justice dans les petites villes et bourgs de France, pour déterminer la suppression des jurisdictions seigneuriales* (Paris: Godefroy, 1789), pp. 54 ff.

interest in the contemporary relevance of his ideas. Even if conditions in the seigniorial courts had changed little over nearly two hundred years, these writers would have carried more conviction if they had corroborated Loyseau's evidence. Again, if Du Moulin's ideas were put into effect at the redrafting of the *coutumes* in 1580, those who professed to admire him did little to continue his work. An occasional jurist advocated the unification of the *coutumes* along the lines that he suggested, but clearly lacked the intellectual capacity for the task.[1]

Whatever the principles they professed, eighteenth-century commentators on feudal law upheld the interests of the seigneur against his peasants. However, like most lawyers, to compensate for their disregard for the spirit of the laws, they were sticklers for the letter. Their scruples could even lead them on occasion to side with the peasant. Thus, La Poix de Fréminville, whose writings will be considered shortly, wrote that rabbit warrens should be destroyed when the seigneur broke the provisions in his title-deeds.[2] Another jurist, Renauldon, likewise reminded the seigneur of his legal obligation to feed his peasants while they were performing the *corvée*, although he admitted that valid deeds could dispense the seigneur from even this duty. In the latter case, he contented himself with exhorting the seigneur to feed the indigent and those who were too far from their homes to return there for a meal.[3] The same conclusions were reached after much legal agonizing by Jean Bouhier, *le grand Président* of the Parlement of Burgundy.[4] No contemporary could lightly set aside the view of this man, whose erudition was a legend in his own lifetime. Even at the age of fifteen his defence of a thesis 'on all aspects of philosophy and the most essential in mathematics' had ranked as 'an occasion'. His life's work, the massive *Observations sur les coutumes du duché de Bourgogne*, which he finished in 1746, the

[1] E.g. P. Challine, *Méthode générale pour l'intelligence des coutumes de France* (Paris: M. Bobin et N. Le Gras, 1666), préface, third page (unpaginated).

[2] E. de La Poix de Fréminville, *Dictionnaire ou traité de la police générale des villes, bourgs, paroisses et seigneuries de la campagne* (Paris: Gissey, 1758), p. 265.

[3] J. Renauldon, *Traité*, p. 212.

[4] J. Bouhier, *Observations sur les coutumes du duché de Bourgogne* (Dijon: Arnauld Jean-Baptiste Augé, 1742–6), II, p. 342.

year of his death, established his reputation as one of the most erudite jurists of the eighteenth century.[1] It is surely an indication that juristic thought had become lost in irrelevancies when a writer of Bouhier's eminence not only speculated over whether those who performed labour-services were entitled to cheese with their bread ration, but found this question altogether too difficult to answer.[2]

The validity of the rights themselves, provided they were recorded in the local *coutume*, was hardly ever questioned. On the contrary, it was a point of honour for most writers to see that no right or privilege, however slight, was denied the seigneur. Thus, whole books were devoted to such topics as the right which some seigneurs had to be accorded, along with the Almighty, special marks of deference in church.[3] 'Honorific rights', such as that of the Founder or possessor of High Justice to be censed in church, gave rise to so many lawsuits that the subject was discussed in the most elaborate detail. Guyot, the leading authority on these complex issues, considers the case for the Founder being censed thrice or only once, and whether his children should be censed individually or collectively, and if so how many times.[4] The authors of such books doubtless suffered more than the seigneurs themselves when one of the few rebellious curés, instead of paying the prescribed honours to his social superior, would sometimes hit him smartly with the holy-water-sprinkler.[5] These incidents perhaps did something to solace those who had to bear the boredom of country life in the eighteenth century.

The conservatism of the commentators on feudal law was particularly apparent in their treatment of the banalities. No other seigniorial right was so unpopular with the peasants as these obligations to have their own corn ground in the seigniorial mill, their bread baked in the seigniorial oven and their grapes

---

[1] J. Balteau and others, *Dictionnaire de biographie française* (Paris, 1393 onwards), VI, pp. 1305–6.

[2] Bouhier, II, pp. 342–3.

[3] See, for instance, G.-A. Guyot, *Observations sur le droit des patrons et des seigneurs de paroisse aux honneurs dans l'église*, ed. A.-G. Boucher d'Argis (Paris: B. Brunet, 1751), and M. Maréchal, *Traité des droits honorifiques des patrons et des seigneurs dans les églises*, ed. J. A. Sérieux (Paris: Barrois, 1772).

[4] Guyot, *Observations*, pp. 329–30.

[5] H. Carré, *La Noblesse de France et l'opinion publique au XVIIIe. siècle* (Paris: Edouard Champion, 1920), p. 317.

crushed in the seigniorial wine-press.[1] The *cahiers*, in which they registered their grievances in 1789, are full of complaints about the cost and inconvenience of the banalities. Yet in the eighteenth century no commentator on feudal law appears to have advocated their abolition. The usual practice was to vilify them briefly for form's sake, while endorsing at length the claims of the seigneur. One of the many writers to adopt this course was Joseph Renauldon. He is an interesting example of an eighteenth-century intellectual vagabond, whose earlier career was enough to curl the calf on his own learned works. Born in 1709, he headed a troop of bohemians until he joined successively the Capuchin friars, the canons of St Geneviève, the army and the household of the marchioness of Romagnesi, before finding his true vocation as a lawyer, and more especially as one of France's best-known commentators on feudal law.[2] With blithe inconsistency, Renauldon announced in one part of his *Traité* that 'the feeling has prevailed that the rights of the banalities are odious',[3] while insisting elsewhere in the same book that the seigniorial oven was always to be used by the vassal, however far he had to go,[4] and that bakers themselves were exempt from the same obligation only under certain specified *coutumes*.[5] Similarly, 'Guyot of the fiefs', despite his respect for Du Moulin, and his conviction that the peasant's obligation to have his own corn ground at the seigneur's mill was an infringement of his liberty,[6] was still ready to accept the seigneur's right to search premises where he suspected flour had been ground illegally.[7]

The banalities, which were accepted by many with a show of reluctance, did not lack their open advocates. President Bouhier, for instance, announced firmly his dissent from the view that their origins could be traced 'to the immoderate power of the seigneurs'. He refused to call them 'odious and contrary to natural liberty', when he saw them as the price of emanci-

---

[1] A. Cobban, *Social Interpretation of the French Revolution*, p. 50.
[2] F. Hoefer, *Nouvelle biographie générale* (Paris: Firmin-Didot, 1857–66), XXI, p. 1001.
[3] Renauldon, *Traité*, p. 251.
[4] *Ibid.*, p. 273.
[5] *Ibid.*, p. 275.
[6] Guyot, *Traité des fiefs*, I, p. 351.
[7] *Ibid.*, I, p. 441.

pation from servitude, or as the result of an equitable contract.[1]

While Bouhier argued his case with impressive erudition, the same views were embroidered in a pseudo-historical vein by another jurist, Pocquet de Livonière. He was a man of some position, as he was a councillor at the *présidial* of Angers and Professor of French Law in the same city. His long experience and diligent study of the *coutume* are said to have established him 'as the oracle of his province'.[2] His very outspoken defence of the banalities, therefore, cannot be discounted as the opinion of an individual extremist.

The majority of our authors [he wrote] see the right of banality as a by-product of the violence of the seigneurs and the abuse of their authority. Because this opinion is founded only on conjectures and probabilities, and as in doubtful cases it is juster to assume good than evil, I prefer to believe that the banalities are established by some kind of agreement between seigneurs and subjects. The latter without the means, or unwilling to undertake the expense, of building mills, ovens and presses for their own use, some seigneurs offered to construct communal and public ones for the convenience of the people dependent on them, but also with a privilege for themselves of a prohibitive and exclusive character.

Pocquet de Livonière's ideas were widely disseminated and extended to all seigniorial rights.[3] According to Renauldon, the vassal should even be grateful to his seigneur for not burdening him more than he did.[4]

A still surer test of a jurist's conservatism was his readiness to justify the maintenance of serfdom in France. As the humanitarian campaign for the abolition of serfdom is considered at some length in chapter V,[5] it is enough to point out here that hardly anyone, apart from jurists and lawyers, notably those in the Parlement of Franche-Comté, wished to halt the rapid decline of servile tenure in France. The most outspoken champion of serfdom was Dunod de Charnage, the Professor

---

[1] Bouhier, II, pp. 348–9.

[2] Michaud, XXIV, p. 628.

[3] P. Lucas-Championnière, *De la Propriété des eaux courantes, du droit des riverains, et de la valeur actuelle des concessions féodales* (Paris: C. Hingray, 1846), p. 574.

[4] Renauldon, *Traité*, p. iii.

[5] See p. 106 ff.

of Law at the University of Besançon. As his family had themselves been serfs until 1642, while he had achieved ennoblement
for himself in 1734, he could almost be described as 'a serf
made good'.[1] Dunod complained in his *Treatise* of the tendency
to regard serfdom as odious and for its spread to be discouraged
as far as possible. While there was a general feeling that the
bonds of serfdom should be weakened, he said, the conditions
of the serf had been greatly mitigated by royal *arrêts* and the
redrafting of the *coutumes*. He felt, in any case, that the seigneur
had done a great favour by reducing serfdom to its present
condition. He reinforced his case with the claim that the serfs
who held their property in common were better protected
against the dissipation of their inheritance than free men. The
lot of the serf, in his view, was not as harsh as it was commonly
represented to be. Consequently, all the provisions of the law
in favour of liberty should not be applied indiscriminately.[2]
Dunod's ideas on serfdom were shared by President Bouhier
who disputed the view held by Du Moulin and others that the
right to own serfs was odious because it was a remnant of
barbarous slavery, and that judgement should be given against
the seigneurs in all doubtful cases. Bouhier rebutted these ideas
on the grounds that the owners deserved some recompense for
having renounced their original rights over their slaves. Like
Dunod, he argued that serfdom promoted better husbandry and
also that 'the peasants in places where serfdom exists are
much better off than those who inhabit lands that are freed from
it.'[3]

Commentators on feudal law who safeguarded the rights of
the seigneurs were also, as I will try to show shortly, promoters
of the so-called 'feudal reaction'. This term, which has long
been popular among historians, could hardly be more misleading. It conjures up a vision of aristocratic rustics in retreat from
the modernity of the eighteenth century to the 'good old days'
of the feudal past. Backwoodsmen of this kind undoubtedly
existed, as some of the pamphlets and *cahiers*, that will be
discussed in the next chapter, show.[4] However, 'the feudal

---

[1] Balteau, fasc. LXVIII, p. 278.

[2] F.-I. Dunod de Charnage, *Traités de la mainmorte et des retraits*, new ed.
(Paris: Dupuis, 1760), p. 15.

[3] Bouhier, II, p. 422.

[4] See p. 101 ff.

reaction' makes little sense if it is seen as an attempt by the nobles to meet their financial needs in the present by resorting to the practices of the past. The nobles were faced by exactly the opposite problem: how to maintain an eighteenth-century standard of living from a seigniorial regime that was geared to the productive methods of the Middle Ages. Even if manufactures and trade had made dramatic progress, agricultural yield, which was still the mainstay of their fortunes, had hardly changed over the centuries. The standard of living of the nobility as a whole was threatened in the eighteenth century by the rapid increase in their numbers that resulted from the fall in the mortality rate. It is true that this did not hold true in the eighteenth century for many of the richer nobles who deliberately restricted the size of their families.[1] However, it is clear from the descriptions of contemporaries that more members of the nobility than ever before were underlining their claims to social status with conspicuous consumption that lay beyond their means. There were, therefore, strong reasons why all sectors of the nobility should look for new means of raising money.

An easy way for many nobles to increase their revenues was to turn feudal and seigniorial rights to better financial account. It is quite misleading to call such profiteering a return to some kind of 'feudal' order. The privileges, in so far as they ever had made sense, were intended to give those who fought for society the means to carry out their duties. While this justification for feudal and seigniorial rights was still quite commonly advanced in the eighteenth century, it bore little relation to the social conditions of the time. Few nobles wished to increase the yield from their fiefs in order to enable them to meet the cost of performing military service. The 'feudal reaction' was itself an attack on 'feudalism', as far as it was an attempt to pervert the original purpose of fiefs.

The 'feudal reaction' took many forms. Until recently, it has been represented as comprising little beyond the arbitrary increase in the burden of existing feudal and seigniorial rights, supplemented by new ones, which the *feudistes* had manufactured along with false charters to support them. A 'feudal

---

[1] J. Hecht, 'Un Problème de population active au XVIIIe. siècle, en France: la querelle de la noblesse commerçante', *Population: Revue Trimestrielle de l'Institut National d'Études Démographiques*, XIX, no. 2 (1964), pp. 279–80.

reaction' of this primitive type appears to have been widespread in Brittany during the reign of Louis XIV, when some Breton seigneurs began to introduce new impositions and to increase their existing demands, especially the labour-services, known as *corvées*.[1] A more effective means of increasing the yield from feudal and seigniorial rights, as some seigneurs discovered in the eighteenth century, was through more systematic book-keeping together with more rigorous means of enforcement. The basic tool for the operation was the *terrier*, which was a kind of register of the seigneur's claims. The *terriers*, as Professor Davies has pointed out, had long been 'becoming technically better as a result of the application of scientific methods, and especially the advances in mathematics which had characterized the seventeenth and eighteenth centuries'.[2] The many complaints in the *cahiers* against the commissioners who compiled the *terriers* show that the peasants themselves understood how the 'feudal reaction' had been carried out.[3] It could also involve, as Professor Forster shows, the use of seigniorial obligations as part of 'a comprehensive adaptation of the noble estate to an expanding market for farm-produce'. Thus, the seigneur could round out his domain lands, for example through the foreclosure of mortgages against peasants who had been reduced to penury by the systematic enforcement of feudal and seigniorial rights. Such methods, as he suggests, were not the practices of fossilized rustics, but rather indicated the application of business techniques to the running of a fief.[4]

The extent of the 'feudal reaction' will never be known, as the French peasants, indifferent to the needs of historians, destroyed many of the seigniorial records in the riots of 1789. It is the shortage of archival evidence which lends particular interest to the published manuals of the *feudistes*. For these gave precise and detailed guidance to the seigneur and his business agent for the maximization of profits. Without a thorough

---

[1] Mousnier, *État et societé*, II, pp. 126 ff.

[2] A. Davies, 'The Origins of the French Peasant Revolution of 1789', *History*, XLIX (1964), p. 36.

[3] A. Chérest, *La Chute de l'ancien régime* (Paris: Hachette et H. Joly, 1884–6), I, pp. 52 ff.

[4] R. Forster, 'The provincial noble: a reappraisal', *American Historical Review*, LXVIII (1963), pp. 684–5.

knowledge and complete record of his 'rights', together with a mastery of the complicated requirements of feudal, and the appropriate customary, law, the holder of a fief was likely to lose most of what was owed him. The practical relevance of these treatises is underlined by the contemporary habit of applying the term *feudistes* indiscriminately both to the writers of the treatises and to the agents who levied feudal and seigniorial rights for the seigneur. Both functions appear to have been commonly combined by the same person, as in the case of La Poix de Fréminville.[1] The publication of these treatises, therefore, gives strong corroborative evidence that a 'feudal reaction' took place.

While advice on the drawing-up of *terriers* figured in many general treatises on feudal and seigniorial rights, the first book that was entirely devoted to the subject, apart from a work that was limited to the royal domain and apanages, did not appear until 1746.[2] La Poix de Fréminville's *la Pratique universelle pour la rénovation des terriers et des droits seigneuriaux* was the unwieldly prototype of the handy manuals of seigniorial extortion that were available from the 1760s;[3] five quarto volumes of instalments over a period of eleven years hardly met the needs of the rapacious. The work, as one reviewer pointed out, suffered additionally from the poor arrangement and the author's repetitious and slipshod style.[4] Above all, despite the title, it was not 'practical' enough. The work of an aspiring jurist, rather than of a legal technician, was the verdict implied by a colleague on the eve of the Revolution.[5] None the less, La Poix de Fréminville could justifiably claim in the full title of his work that it was 'useful for all seigneurs'. The novelty and usefulness of his manual received favourable comment in several contemporary periodicals. In the *Bibliothèque Françoise* the reviewer assured his readers that 'men of affairs value this book, especially interesting for them, as it is the only one of

---

[1] See p. 64.

[2] A. Soboul, 'De la Pratique des terriers à la veille de la Révolution', *Annales. Économies. Sociétés. Civilisations*, XIX (1964), p. 1050.

[3] E. de La Poix de Fréminville, *La Pratique universelle pour la rénovation des terriers et des droits seigneuriaux* (Paris: Morel et Gissey, 1746–57).

[4] *Journal des Sçavans, combiné avec les Mémoires de Trévoux* . . . (Amsterdam, 1754–63), XXXVI, no. 7, June 1758, pp. 111–12.

[5] A. Soboul, *Annales. Économies. Sociétés. Civilisations*, XIX (1964), pp. 1050–1.

its kind'. He added that the author was 'in a strong position to acquit himself well in this work, to which he has long given special study, having been charged by several seigneurs with revising their title-deeds and *terriers* in various provinces'.[1] The *Mémoires de Trévoux* also contained a very favourable review of La Poix de Fréminville's book. 'It was difficult,' the reviewer wrote, 'to work on a more interesting subject. The public could not show too much gratitude to these zealous and hard-working men, who instruct them in all that it is necessary to know and do, to keep by prudent attention what they possess, or to recover what they have lost through negligence and sometimes also through the fraud of their neighbours'.[2] This was indeed high praise from the Jesuits who policed the writings on both worlds. In a review that ran to almost nine pages in a pirated edition of the *Journal des Sçavans*, La Poix de Fréminville's work was commended for its 'general usefulness'.[3] Passing reference many years later in the official version of the *Journal des Sçavans* to 'the good work of Monsieur de Fréminville', suggests that by then it had attained the status of a classic.[4]

Many other writers followed with manuals of a more compact and utilitarian kind. Aubry de Saint-Vibert's *Code des terriers* appeared in one handy duodecimo volume in 1761, with a second edition in 1769. He proclaimed it in the title, 'useful to all seigneurs of fiefs, notaries, commissioners of *terriers* and clerks of the domains'.[5] Roussel's *Instructions pour les seigneurs et leurs gens d'affaires*, which appeared in the same format in 1770, was given a lengthy review in the sequel to the irrepressible *Mémoires de Trévoux*. Although the work was described as 'useful',[6] the reviewer seemed to hint that such works could,

---

[1] *Bibliothèque Françoise, ou histoire littéraire de la France* (Amsterdam, 1723–46), XLII, pt 2 (1746), p. 359.

[2] *Mémoires pour l'Histoire des Sciences et des Beaux-Arts* (Trévoux, 1701–67), vol. 2 for 1746, pp. 2194–5. (The journal was usually called for short, *Mémoires de Trévoux*.)

[3] *Journal des Sçavans, augmenté de divers articles qui ne se treuvent point dans l'édition de Paris, 1665–1753* (Amsterdam, 1685–1753), CXXXVIII (April 1746), p. 531.

[4] *Journal des Sçavans*, vol. for 1762, p. 563.

[5] A. Soboul, *Annales. Économies. Sociétés. Civilisations*, XIX (1964), p. 1050n.

[6] *Journal des Sciences et des Beaux-Arts* (Paris, 1768–78), vol. I for 1770, p. 421.

indeed, be too useful. Roussel was taken to task for contrasting in his book a good and a bad seigneur in a way which made the first a paragon of virtue and the second far from an exemplar of contemporary wickedness. He was reminded of 'those swindles, those base acts, those hateful frauds which some seigneurs, unworthy of their rank, pursue to the ruin of their debtors'.[1] Such were the results, the reviewer seemed to say, when the technical expertise of the *feudistes* fell into the wrong hands. Yet the work of the *feudistes* was usually welcomed in a matter-of-fact fashion and without reservations. When the *Méthode des terriers* of the Jollivet brothers appeared in 1776, the authors claimed that the seigneur lost half the potential yield from seigniorial rights.[2] Without hesitation the reviewer in *Suite de la Clef* declared that the usefulness of the work was apparent in its title,[3] while it was commended in the sequel to the *Mémoires de Trévoux* for its clarity and usefulness.[4]

The works of the *feudistes* and their reception in contemporary periodicals may help to illumine the 'feudal reaction'. The enthusiastic reception of the first work that was devoted solely to the drawing-up of the *terriers* seemed to show that the spirit of the 'feudal reaction' already existed in 1746. Yet the technical expertise to carry it through efficiently can hardly have been readily available until much later. La Poix de Fréminville's own work on the renewal of *terriers* was complete only in 1757 and was at best an unwieldy guide for the task. It seems significant that the first practical manual did not appear until 1761, and apparently had no successors until the 1770s. Allowance should also be made for the time-lag between the appearance of these works and the completion of the actual 'renewal of the *terriers*', which could absorb many years of labour by skilled practitioners, whose services were both expensive and in short supply. Letrosne, in *De l'Administration provinciale*, which first appeared in 1779, cited several cases of *terriers* that remained uncompleted for many years. He instanced, among others, a *terrier* that a team of about ten to twelve clerks had been labouring

---

[1] *Ibid.*, pp. 424–5.

[2] Jollivet (frères et commissaires aux droits seigneuriaux), *Méthode des terriers, ou traités des préparatifs et de la confection des terriers* . . . (1776), p. v.

[3] *Suite de la Clef, ou journal historique sur les matières du temps* . . ., 120 vols (1717–76), January 1776, p. 270.

[4] *Journal des Sciences et des Beaux-Arts, par l'Abbé Aubert*, January 1776, p. 176.

to complete for twenty-five years.[1] It may well be, therefore, that the 'feudal reaction' did not really get under way until the 1780s. It is perhaps significant that the letters patent, which put the greatly increased financial burden of revising the *terriers* on the peasants, did not appear until 1786. Yet, whatever the exact timing of the 'feudal reaction', it clearly received much moral support from society at large, as is indicated by the reviews in the periodicals. Conversely, it was in revolt against this society that at least one *feudiste* claimed to have become a revolutionary: 'It was in the dust of the seigniorial archives,' wrote Babeuf, 'that I discovered the mysteries of the usurpation of the noble caste'[2] — not, it would seem, before he himself as a middleman had taken his cut.

Feudal and seigniorial rights, whether extended by a 'feudal reaction' or not, depended for their enforcement on the functioning of the seigniorial courts.[3] As this is the area in which the whole feudal and seigniorial regime was most vulnerable to attack from the Crown, the activities of the seigniorial courts should be of particular interest to the historian. Unfortunately, historians, who are sometimes only human, have seldom dared to broach the subject, for which the documentation is at once so overwhelming and so incomplete. Some idea of the number of seigniorial courts can be gauged from the fact that in Brittany alone in 1769 there were about 3,700, which gives an average of nearly three to each parish.[4] Yet hardly anything is known about the actual doings of these ubiquitous courts.

The natural starting-point for an inquiry is to examine the formal status of the courts. In the hope that one bizarre French institution will illuminate another, it is worth looking for guidance to the *Académie Française*. The 1762 edition of their famous *Dictionnaire* gives a straightforward description of the

---

[1] Letrosne, *De l'Administration provinciale* (1788), II, p. 440. (The 1788 edition, which is practically identical with that of 1779, has been used for the sake of convenience, as the royal censors who seized most of the first edition have made it relatively inaccessible to the scholar.)

[2] Soboul, *Revue Historique*, CCXL (July–September 1968), p. 39.

[3] For a fuller account see the author's 'Criticism of seigniorial justice in eighteenth-century France' in *French Government and Society*, a volume in memory of Professor Cobban, and edited by J. F. Bosher (London: Athlone Press, forthcoming, 1973).

[4] A. Giffard, *Les Justices seigneuriales en Bretagne aux XVIIe. et XVIIIe. siècles (1661–1791)* (Paris: A. Rousseau, 1903), pp. 39 and 307.

three-fold division, as in the Middle Ages, into High, Middle and Low Justice. The jurisdiction of the first was described as limited to civil and criminal matters that fell outside the province of the royal courts; Middle Justice was confined to civil suits in which a maximum fine of seventy-five Parisian sous could be levied; Low Justice was restricted to the enforcement of the rights that were owned by the seigneur, to a maximum fine in civil suits of sixty sous and also to a maximum fine for misdemeanours — doubtless of a trivial bucolic nature — of only ten sous.[1]

A description of the powers of the seigniorial courts is very misleading, however, if it fails to take account of their relationships with other law courts in eighteenth-century France. Royal, seigniorial, municipal, ecclesiastical and extraordinary courts, not to mention a host of administrative authorities with judicial powers, were in frequent conflict with each other. So great was the confusion that, according to the Procurator-General himself in 1763, a plaintiff was often obliged to plead his case for two or three years before different courts in order to ascertain before which judge he should have the misfortune to appear.[2] It is very difficult to discover how the seigniorial courts fared in their unremitting struggle with other judiciaries, notably the royal courts. The few studies that are available are strictly regional in character and hardly justify the drawing of general conclusions for France as a whole. For the area around Paris, Lemercier found that while the powers of the seigniorial judges had declined since the middle of the seventeenth century in criminal matters, their authority in civil suits seemed to have remained intact during the eighteenth century.[3] In Auvergne, on the other hand, the fact that several ecclesiastical seigneurs surrendered their jurisdictional rights because of the heavy cost of upkeep suggests that the seigniorial courts were in decline there.[4] However, in Brittany, where admittedly traditions died harder than elsewhere, the royal and seigniorial courts have been

---

[1] Académie Française, *Dictionnaire* (1762), I, p. 980.

[2] Marion, *Dictionnaire*, p. 314.

[3] P. Lemercier, *Les Justices seigneuriales de la région parisienne de 1580 à 1789* (Paris: Domat-Montchrestien, 1933), p. 278.

[4] A. Poitrineau, 'Aspects de la crise des justices seigneuriales dans l'Auvergne du dix-huitième siècle', *Revue Historique de Droit Français et Étranger*, 4th ser., XXXIX (1961), p. 564.

described as locked in a war of attrition in which there was no clear victor.[1] Yet, in his *Paysans de l'ouest*, which deals with the nearby area around Le Mans, Monsieur Bois found that the financial yield from seigniorial justice was insignificant. He added that it was not surprising that the right was not exercised in many fiefs.[2] On balance, therefore, it seems likely that, with notable exceptions, particularly in the outlying provinces, the seigniorial courts were in a state of gradual decline.

Criminal justice appears to have been the area in which the seigniorial courts failed most seriously to meet their responsibilities. Seigneurs had long since abandoned the practice, which La Bruyère ridiculed, of hanging a minor villain from time to time by way of advertising their jurisdictional rights.[3] In the eighteenth century the holders of High Justice, which (unlike Middle and Low Justice) conferred the right to try criminals, usually preferred to spare themselves the expense of doing so. The result, as many of these writers who attacked seigniorial justice on utilitarian grounds pointed out, was to turn areas of seigniorial jurisdiction into havens for malefactors.[4] To remedy the situation the royal administration in 1771 produced an edict which contained a skilful formula for divesting the seigniorial courts of their criminal jursidiction when they refused to exercise it. The seigneur who had reported the case beforehand to the royal judge would be reimbursed the legal costs. On the other hand, if the seigniorial judge had to be prodded into action the seigneur was held liable for the legal expenses.[5] Even if the edict was seldom enforced, as seems to have been generally the case,[6] it bore official witness to the reluctance of many seigniorial justices to avail themselves of their criminal jurisdiction.

[1] Giffard, p. 207.

[2] P. Bois, *Paysans de l'ouest. Des Structures économiques et sociales aux options politiques depuis l'époque révolutionnaire dans la Sarthe* (Le Mans: M. Vilaire, 1960), pp. 402–3.

[3] E. A. Combier, *Les Justices seigneuriales du bailliage de Vermandois sous l'ancien régime* (Paris: A. Fontemoing, 1898), pp. 5–6.

[4] See p. 154.

[5] Marion, *Dictionnaire*, p. 320.

[6] This is the view of Marion, *Dictionnaire*, p. 320. See also the contemporary writer G.-F. Letrosne, *Vues sur la justice criminelle. Discours prononcé au bailliage d'Orléans* (Paris: Debare, 1777), p. 113n. For an argument that the edict was applied effectively in Auvergne, however, see Poitrineau, p. 563.

A sign of the decline in the practical importance of seigniorial justice is the tendency of the eighteenth-century holders to prize it mainly as a badge of social status. Those who claimed to be *haut-justiciers* usually took pains to impress their importance on others by erecting a gallows at the gates of their *châteaux*. The owner's rank was further publicized by the number of pillars that were used to support the gallows. Such details were important enough to find a place in the *Encyclopédie* where it is explained that counts could usually erect six pillars, barons four, *châtelains* three, down to two for plain *hauts-justiciers*.[1] Even Voltaire was doubtless proud to have a gibbet, especially as it was upheld by no less than four pillars,[2] although the poet, like others, stubbornly resisted being turned into *le haut-justicier malgré lui* when it put him out of pocket.[3]

When the owners of seigniorial justice were more concerned about the prestige of office than the maintenance of order, the courts themselves were unlikely to be models of legal propriety. Their misdoings were gleefully reported by many eighteenth-century writers. These depicted meetings that took place in taverns, while the judge is often described as an ignorant peasant, whose ignorance, however, did not prevent him from realizing that it was in his interest to pronounce judgement in favour of his master. If he were lucky, the seigneur who could sack him at will might give him the wages of a domestic servant. Otherwise, his only source of livelihood were the sums which he extorted from the unfortunate litigants.[4] It is hardly surprising that the *cahiers* contained many requests for the abolition of the seigniorial courts.

There were many reasons for the Crown to take action against the seigniorial courts. They hampered the royal judges in the work of maintaining order in the countryside. The very existence of private law courts was a challenge to royal sovereignty. The seigniorial courts, capped by the parlements which were the appeal courts for the provinces, guaranteed the maintenance of feudal and seigniorial privilege. While historians are disagreed on the weight of the burden which these

---

[1] D. Diderot (ed.), *Encyclopédie* (Paris, 1751–65), VII, p. 224.
[2] F. Caussy, *Voltaire, seigneur de village* (Paris: Hachette, 1912), p. 3 n. 2.
[3] *Ibid.*, p. 58.
[4] For contemporary descriptions of the seigniorial courts see pp. 152 ff.

privileges placed on the peasantry, there can be no doubt that they played an important part in raising the nobility above the status of ordinary subjects. When the courts themselves had apparently declined, sometimes to the level of opera-bouffe, it seems unlikely that the Crown would have met much opposition in taking measures against them. Many seigneurs were more concerned to preserve the honorific character of seigniorial jurisdiction than their hold over the administration of justice itself. Nor did the king lack the judicial means for intervention. He was recognized universally as the head of the judiciary, and the Council of State was the final court of appeal. At a local level, there were royal courts which ranked above the seigniorial courts, while the intendant also had powers to supervise the course of justice.

For most of the century the Crown hardly attempted to curb the powers of the seigniorial courts. While the edict of 1771 was a step in this direction, it does not appear to have been implemented.[1] In this context, therefore, the edicts of April 1788 are all the more remarkable. They were designed to bring about such fundamental changes in the administration of justice that they have been called 'the most important revolution which France saw before the final fall of the *ancien régime*'.[2] The seigniorial courts themselves in the provisions of the edict were practically wiped out of existence. In civil cases, as each party was authorized to summon the other before the royal judges, attendance at the seigniorial courts became purely voluntary. Criminal jurisdiction was conditional on possession of a court, a sanitary and secure prison, a graduate judge, a procurator fiscal, a scribe and a gaoler in residence. Such counsels of perfection could be prescribed in the confidence that hardly any seigniorial court would reach them.[3]

It is worth considering why these reforms were not attempted earlier when they would have had a better chance of success. The main reason seems to be that the edicts of 1788 were primarily designed as punitive measures against the parlements which had been making political capital out of their judicial

---

[1] See p. 68.

[2] M. Marion, *La Garde des Sceaux, Lamoignon et la réforme judiciaire de* 1788 (Paris: Hachette, 1905), p. 1.

[3] *Ibid.*, pp. 67–8.

role. All the factiousness of the *parlementaires* was needed to prompt judicial reform, and then for the wrong reasons. Yet important reforms, notably the edict of 1771 concerning seigniorial justice, the abolition of serfdom on Crown lands in 1779 and of the *Question Préparatoire* in 1780, had been undertaken in the immediate past. There can be little doubt that the government was well-intentioned and prepared to undertake legal reforms that it deemed necessary. What was lacking was a comprehensive plan and a sense of purpose in carrying it out.

The administration's failure to appreciate the urgent need for the reform of seigniorial justice owed something to the lack of good critical writings on the subject.[1] Published criticism of seigniorial justice came mainly from royal officials who were usually preoccupied with practical matters. Jurists whose specialized knowledge put them in a better position to question the legal basis of seigniorial justice were seldom inclined to do so. Bouhier, for example, insisted that whatever the abuses in the administration of seigniorial justice, it would have been very harsh to despoil the present owners without paying them compensation.[2] While Renauldon admitted that the courts had often degenerated into instruments of brigandage, he was prepared to tolerate this development because the seigneur without his jurisdiction would have been indistinguishable from a mere plebeian.[3] Their uncriticial attitude was fully in keeping with their views, that have been discussed already, concerning feudal and seigniorial rights in general.[4]

The works of the few jurists who were strongly hostile to seigniorial justice, therefore, are the exceptions that call for explanation. Bellami's *Traité de la perfection et confection des papiers terriers généraux du Roy* is of particular interest. Like La Poix de Fréminville's *Pratique universelle*, it was designed to do for the royal domain what the latter attempted for seigneuries in private hands. Bellami, who wrote in effect as a *feudiste* in the service of the Crown, was naturally concerned

---

[1] For a fuller treatment of the subject see the author's article in the memorial volume to Professor Cobban, *French Government and Society*, ed. J. F. Bosher.

[2] Bouhier, II, pp. 8–9.

[3] Renauldon, *Traité*, p. 628.

[4] See pp. 56 ff.

mainly to promote the administration of the royal domain.[1] Therefore, it is hardly surprising that his objection to seigniorial justice is not based on principle, but on his own experience of 'the abuses which are committed in the village law courts in connection with the *terriers* of the seigneurs.'[2] Bellami surely had in mind principally occasions when the interests of the king as a feudal seigneur were thwarted by other neighbouring feudal seigneurs. This is a curious example of a clash between the motives of the king as a sovereign and as feudatory. On the eve of the Revolution the royal administration, which had every reason to curb feudal and seigniorial rights, had slipped instead into the forefront of the 'feudal reaction'.[3]

Another legal commentator who was uncompromisingly hostile to the seigniorial courts was the abbé Claude Fleury, whose *Droit public de France* was reissued in 1769. Both the title and his calling as deputy tutor to the Princes of the Blood about a century earlier made clear where his sympathies lay. The abbé considered what he saw as the decline 'from day to day' of the seigniorial courts as 'very useful to the State'. Although he could not agree with Du Moulin and Loyseau that seigniorial jurisdiction had been usurped, he felt that the only remedy was to suppress it.[4]

Even when seigniorial justice was condemned, as in those legal treatises, there was an almost total failure to argue the case on grounds of principle. The Crown had advocates of its rights, just as the private seigneurs had their *feudistes*, but it had in its service few jurists and certainly none of stature. Such were the effects of the legal 'brain-drain' into the private sector under the Bourbons of the *ancien régime*.

Criticism of seigniorial justice fell by default in the eighteenth century to royal officials, practising lawyers and publicists. The earliest of these writers to condemn seigniorial justice appears to have been the marquis d'Argenson who had been one of

[1] Bellami (avocat fiscal au bailliage et marquisat-pairie d'Herbault), *Traité de la perfection et confection des papiers terriers généraux du Roy* . . . (Paris: Paulus-du-Mesnil, 1746), p. ix.

[2] *Ibid*, pp. ix-x.

[3] Chérest, *La Chute de l'ancien régime*, I, pp. 54–5.

[4] C. Fleury, *Droit public de France, ouvrage posthume de M. l'abbé Fleury, composé pour l'éducation des princes, et publié avec des notes par J.-B. Daragon* (Paris: Pierre, 1769), I, pp. 56–8.

France's less successful Ministers for Foreign Affairs. His *Considérations sur le gouvernement ancien et présent de la France*, in which he made brief but severe strictures on seigniorial justice, appeared, after its clandestine circulation in manuscript among an earlier generation, in 1764.[1] The same year saw the publication of a pamphlet by Linguet,[2] whose *Théorie des loix civiles* has already been discussed.[3] Other writings followed, notably a pamphlet by Letrosne in 1777,[4] one by Pétion de Villeneuve in 1782,[5] while most of the remainder did not appear until 1788–9.[6]

The main preoccupation of these writers was to expose the practical shortcomings of the courts: the costs and delays in the administration of justice, the poor quality of the seigniorial judges and other officials, and the lack of suitable court-rooms and prisons. These charges against the seigniorial courts will be considered in chapter VI along with other 'utilitarian' objections to 'feudalism'.[7] It is sufficient to note here that if the criterion of efficiency had been applied to all eighteenth-century courts, few of the royal courts themselves would have passed the test. What is more to the point is the almost complete failure to make out a case in legal terms for the curtailment of seigniorial justice. The furthest that most of these writers would go was to condemn seigniorial justice as an infringement of royal sovereignty. For this reason the anonymous author of one pamphlet considered seigniorial justice vitiated at source.[8] 'A

---

[1] Balteau, III, p. 554.

[2] S. N. H. Linguet, *Nécessité d'une réforme dans l'administration de la justice et dans les loix civiles en France, avec la réfutation de quelques passages de 'L'Esprit des loix'* (Amsterdam, 1764).

[3] See pp. 36–8.

[4] See p. 68.

[5] See p. 152.

[6] Mézard, *Essai sur les réformes à faire dans l'administration de la justice en France*, cited above, p. 55; Boucher d'Argis, *Cahier d'un magistrat du Châtelet de Paris*, cited above, p. 55; Fouqueau de Pussy, *Idées sur l'administration de la justice*, cited above, p. 55; Bucquet, *Discours qui a remporté le prix de l'Académie de Chaalons [sic] en l'année M. DCC. LXXXIII sur cette question proposée par la même Académie: 'Quels seraient les moyens de rendre la justice en France avec le plus de célérité et le moins de frais possibles?'* (Beauvais, 1789); Challan, *Réflexions sur l'administration de la justice, sur la formation de tribunaux ordinaires et municipaux, afin de rendre la justice gratuite, et d'éviter les abus qui règnent spécialement dans les justices seigneuriales* (Beauvais: Desjardins, 1789)

[7] See pp. 152 ff.

[8] (Anon.), *De l'Administration de la justice dans les campagnes* (n.p., n.d.), p. 6.

dismemberment of royal jurisdiction, rather than a separate type of jurisdiction,' was the comment of another pamphleteer.[1] Fouqueau de Pussy cited authorities to show that all justice was derived from the king.[2] Mézard called to witness in support of the same view a list of authorities that included the *Encyclopédie*.[3] None the less, all this censing of idols, old and new, fell short of reasoned argument.

There were only two writers who developed a case against seigniorial jurisdiction as such. The first was Letrosne, whose perceptive sketch of the historical development of feudalism was discussed in the last chapter.[4] While other writers had assimilated the administration of justice to an inalienable royal domain, Letrosne made the far more radical claim that the sovereign had a duty to give justice to his subjects.[5] He therefore considered the dismemberment of sovereignty and the attachment of authority to property in private hands no less than a disorder in the state, an offence against the people, rather than a slight against the sovereign. However, as Letrosne had the bent of an historian rather than of a jurist, he thought of seigniorial justice in terms of feudal society. 'During a long succession of centuries,' he wrote, 'our history is properly speaking that of the formation of the sovereign authority, and of the efforts necessary to detach it from the fetters of feudal rule.'[6]

Linguet was the other writer to raise far-ranging questions about the administration of justice in France. While his objections to seigniorial justice mainly related to practical matters, and will be discussed in chapter VI,[7] he agreed with Letrosne that the dispensation of justice was a duty of French kings.[8] He was at his most radical in his attack on the whole corpus of laws in France. As the reviewer of the tract in *L'Année*

---

[1] (Anon.), *Nouveau plan d'administration de la justice civile dans lequel on propose les moyens d'assurer au mérite seul tous les offices ou places de judicature, d'accélérer le jugement des procès et d'en diminuer les frais* (Paris, 1789), p. 6n.

[2] Fouqueau de Pussy, *Idées sur l'administration de la justice*, p. 33 n.

[3] Mézard, *Essai sur les réformes à faire dans l'administration de la justice en France*, pp. 62–3.

[4] See p. 35 ff.

[5] Letrosne, *De L'Administration provinciale*, II, pp. 361–2.

[6] Letrosne, *Vues sur la justice criminelle*, pp. 108–10.

[7] See p. 154 ff.

[8] Linguet, *Nécessite d'une réforme dans l'administration de la justice*, p. 63.

Littéraire pointed out, Linguet was greatly concerned about the sheer number of laws in France. Barristers, he said, were obliged to know, or rather to appear to know, everything that was contained in a mass of folio volumes which nobody read. Licentiates of law were wittily compared to the scholars of China, who were raised by their profound knowledge to the highest ranks, and who died before learning how to read.[1]

Linguet, like Letrosne, explained the chaotic state of the laws in terms of their historical development. He traced the vagaries in the law principally to the compilation of the *coutumes* under Charles VII in the middle of the fifteenth century. Then, 'in place of using the royal authority to reform them', he wrote, 'it was used to give them legal authenticity'.[2] The royal commissioners were described in vivid and unkind detail as they set about their task of recording the unwritten *coutumes*. Ideas of village elders were inscribed, he said, alongside any other thoughts which passed through the minds of the commissioners. It was hardly surprising, remarked Linguet, that what was recorded in one village differed from the findings of a colleague a quarter of a league away. Such, he concluded, was the respectable origin of the famous *coutumes* which in his own day took the place of laws in three-quarters of France. In this way, he added, Frenchmen were still ruled by 'the gross barbarism of their ancestors'.[3]

If Linguet gives his imagination too free a rein, as the reviewer in *L'Année Littéraire* suggested,[4] his account goes far to explain the undoubted inconsistencies and vagaries of French customary law. To challenge the letter of the *coutumes* was the first step towards the rationalization of the laws which would have entailed, among other changes, the reform of seigniorial justice. The *coutumes* did more than almost anything else to uphold the fabric of the society of the *ancien régime*.

Seigniorial justice was not the only area from which the jurist as a critic absented himself. He was almost invariably the defender of the existing order. The philosophes had good

---

[1] *L'Année Littéraire ou suite des lettres sur quelques écrits de ce temps* (Amsterdam, 1754–90), vol. VIII for 1764, pp. 40–1.

[2] *Ibid.*, p. 43.

[3] *Ibid.*, pp. 43–4. Voltaire makes rather similar, but briefer, criticism. See, for instance, his *Oeuvres*, XXVI, p. 98.

[4] *L'Année Littéraire*, vol. VIII for 1764, p. 46.

reason to suppose that 'most of the jurists were utterly reactionary and must be circumvented if any significant legal reforms were to be achieved'.[1] In eighteenth-century France the jurist is like the character who dominates the action of a play without setting foot upon the stage. Few historical works make more than perfunctory references to lawyers before the Revolution, when they appear unheralded to take possession of the state. Yet lawyers did much to shape the society of the time. Every administrative authority of the Crown was armed with its own judicial powers; the parlements and other sovereign courts in Paris and the provinces were all staffed by lawyers; practically every village had its own *seigneur justicier*, and in some areas, such as Brittany, three or more were commonplace. Litigation was a pastime of all classes of society down to the peasantry who took their seigneurs to law with stubbornness and even some success, thanks to the support of royal officials. These many appeals to laws which were largely unintelligible to those who professed to administer them bear witness to the extreme traditionalism of eighteenth-century French society. This traditionalism was embodied more completely than almost anywhere else in the remnants of the ancient feudal and seigniorial regime. Custom and habit proved impervious to rational criticism. Historians in consequence have shown their impatience with the Crown for failing to eradicate the harmful legacy from the past. Yet reform without revolution implied a willingness on the part of the Crown to work for change within the existing system. In the case of legal reform this involved the reshaping of the *coutumes* and other sources of French law by a school of royal lawyers. Publicists could suggest legal reforms; they could only be carried out successfully by lawyers. The failure of French jurists to adapt the remnants of the feudal and seigniorial regime to the conditions and needs of the eighteenth century was largely the fault of the government: instead of bringing reason and tradition together, royal officials stood hesitant and bewildered between them.

---

[1] Church, *French Historical Studies*, V (1967), p. 28

IV

The Nobility and Business

The attitude of eighteenth-century French writers towards commerce may seem a far cry from ideas of 'feudal' and seigniorial privilege. Few contemporary writers tried to relate their economic theories to the character of their society. They approached their subject usually as experts, either, like Belloni[1] or Véron de Forbonnais,[2] as writers of general surveys for the layman, or while treating a particular aspect of economic theory, such as interest rates, as in the case of Melon[3] and Dutot.[4] Yet, although the existence of 'feudal' and seigniorial privileges was seldom even mentioned, these writings were implicitly hostile to them. Economic theorists, whatever their intentions, defined the State in terms which left no room for the justification of privilege on grounds of military prowess. By launching a frontal attack, the writers on commerce might have reinvigorated the 'feudal' pretensions of many nobles. Instead they undermined this 'feudal' outlook by advancing ideas which failed to take it into account. Deprived of nourishment in the form of controversy and attention, political and social claims which were based on an imaginary feudal past tended to perish from inanition.

[1] G. Belloni, *Dissertation sur le commerce, traduit de l'Italien par M.A.**** (The Hague, 1755).

[2] F. de Véron de Forbonnais, *Élémens du commerce*, new ed. (Leyden, 1754).

[3] J.-F. Melon, *Essai politique sur le commerce* (n.p., 1734).

[4] Dutot, *Réflexions politiques sur les finances et le commerce: où l'on examine quelles ont été sur les revenus, les denrées, le change étranger, et conséquemment sur notre commerce, les influences des augmentations et des diminutions des valeurs numéraires des monnoyes* (The Hague: Vaillant et Prevost, 1738).

The question of whether the nobility should be allowed to engage in trade was of long standing.[1] The vast expansion of trade under Louis XIV gave a new urgency to the removal of the stigma against participating in it. Yet the ineffectualness of edicts sponsored by both Cardinal Richelieu and Colbert served to show that the prejudices of a whole society could not be changed by government fiat.[2] The Crown repeatedly invited the nobles to engage in commercial enterprises; the nobles continued to invest their surplus wealth in buying land and offices. This outlook continued to be so strong, indeed, that even on the eve of the Revolution France lacked a large capitalist class so badly that Marxist historians had to conjure it up from almost nothing.[3]

Until about the fourth decade of the eighteenth century there is little evidence of concern outside the government that a social stigma was attached to trade. The edict of 1701, which permitted the nobility to engage in maritime and wholesale trade without incurring *dérogeance*, was reproduced in one of France's chief periodicals, the *Journal de Verdun*, only in 1713, and then in a supplementary volume, which surely argues a tardy interest in the government's measures.[4] The same journal, however, perhaps hinted that a change of outlook was taking place when it announced in 1724: 'We live today in the springtime of a century when the greatest sovereigns appear to devote themselves to forming institutions in their states to encourage and promote trade.'[5]

The question of whether the nobles should participate in trade was related to a social problem of long standing, the fact that many of the lesser nobles had become too impoverished to maintain a style of life in keeping with their social status. Poor farming methods reduced their income from the comparatively small area of domain land which they cultivated for themselves. The impoverished condition of most of the French peasantry for the same reason also ensured that the feudal and

---

[1] H. Lévy-Bruhl, 'La Noblesse de France et le commerce à la fin de l'ancien régime', *Revue d'Histoire Moderne*, VIII (1933), pp. 212 ff.

[2] *Ibid.*, p. 216.

[3] Taylor, p. 487.

[4] *Supplément de la Clef* . . ., *contenant ce qui s'est passé en Europe d'intéressant pour l'histoire depuis la Paix de Ryswick* (Verdun, 1713), II, pp. 344–8.

[5] *Suite de la Clef*, XXXVIII (January 1724), p. 48.

seigniorial privileges would also generally produce little for the seigneurs. Their only other possible avenue to wealth was through fulfilling their traditional role of military service, which, however, often impoverished rather than enriched them.[1] It is, therefore, not surprising that there had already been several demands in the seventeenth century that the nobility should be allowed a new access to wealth through trade. In 1646 Jean Eon had headed one of the chapters of his *Le Commerce honorable*, 'That it is licit and useful for gentlemen and officers to enter into a business company, without prejudice to their ranks and rights.'[2] Permission for nobles to engage in trade without loss of caste had been sought in 1614 at the meeting of the Estates General where it was declared that nothing could be more honourable and useful for the nobility than to fit out ships for commerce. In 1627 the nobility asked in a *cahier* to be allowed to engage in trade without incurring *dérogeance*, while two years later Louis XIII opened maritime commerce to them. Similarly, Colbert, when he established the companies for trade with the Indies in 1664, invited nobles to engage in maritime and wholesale trade without loss of status.[3] That social prejudice remained impervious to Colbert's legislation, made the problem all the more acute during the Regency. Nothing showed this better than the fact that Boulainvilliers, whose part in championing the claims of the nobles in French society was considered at length in chapter II,[4] should himself ask the Regent in a *mémoire* for the nobility to be allowed free access to wholesale trade without loss of status.[5] It was almost inevitable that another prominent writer of the Regency period, the abbé de Saint-Pierre, whose inventive and optimistic nature even led him to consider means of making peers and dukes useful, should also produce a project in 1733 for perfecting commerce in France. With the characteristic insight which illumines even his most eccentric views, the abbé saw the

---

[1] P. de Vaissière, *Gentilhommes campagnards de l'ancienne France* (Paris: Perrin 1903), pp. 319 ff.

[2] J. Eon, *Le Commerce honorable, ou considérations politiques contenant les motifs de nécessité, d'honneur et de profit, qui se treuvent à former des compagnies de personnes de toutes conditions pour l'entretien du négoce de mer en France* (Nantes: D. Le Monnier, 1646), pt III, chap. 5, p. 261.

[3] Lévy-Bruhl, *Revue d'Histoire Moderne*, VIII (1933), pp. 214–15.

[4] See p. 20 ff.

[5] Boulainvilliers, *État de la France*, III, p. 506.

problem less in terms of persuading nobles to go into trade, than of raising trade in social esteem by conferring honours on businessmen.[1] The following year, Voltaire, in his *Lettres Philosophiques*, mentioned with approval 'Milord Townshend', who, although a British Minister of State, had a brother in the City.[2] Dutot, the economist and one of the tellers of the *Compagnie des Indes* under Law,[3] also deplored the prejudice which made trade suitable only for commoners, which he considered an obstacle to the development of commerce itself.[4] The manuscript, *Réflexions*, of the marquis de Lassay who died in 1738, and which will be considered shortly, opened disapprovingly, 'it is heard incessantly that the nobility should be allowed to traffic in goods as in England.'[5] There is no reason to suppose that any of these proposals were of a radical kind. A new issue appeared when the age-old problem of resuscitating the fortunes of the decayed nobility was seen to raise in turn the relationship of the different classes to one another. The importance of Melon's *Essai politique sur le commerce* lay, therefore, in the fact that it was the first French work to focus attention on the effects of trade on the character of the state. This was a natural preoccupation for Melon who was close to the centre of power, as first clerk successively to Cardinal Dubois and Law and later secretary to the Regent himself.[6] His *Essai* contained damaging criticism of militaristic government, in which he presumably had that of Louis XIV in mind. His basic idea was that militarism had an innate tendency to overreach itself, while commerce offered a state the surest means of protection. He wrote, 'When the conquering nation ceases to be so, it is soon subjugated; but the commercial spirit is always accompanied with the prudence necessary for self-protection. It seeks less to extend frontiers than to build fortresses for its tranquillity.[7] He concluded the chapter by affirming his faith that Europe had been enlightened by the

---

[1] C. I. Castel de Saint-Pierre, *Ouvrajes [sic] de politique* (Rotterdam and Paris: Briasson, 1733–41), V, p. 225.

[2] Lévy-Bruhl, *Revue d'Histoire Moderne*, VIII (1933), p. 223.

[3] Hoefer, XV, p. 502.

[4] Dutot, II, pp. 313–14.

[5] *Mercure de France* (Paris, 1724–91), December 1754, p. 86.

[6] Michaud, XXVII, p. 588.

[7] Melon, p. 97.

spirit of peace, and that a 'just balance' would always prevent one power from terrorizing the others. And even if one power did try to extend its frontiers, he felt confident that 'everyone will unite to stop its dangerous course', because they would realize that 'a nation is no longer able to increase its power, except through the wisdom of its domestic government'.[1]

Reviews in eighteenth-century periodicals suggest that Melon's *Essai* made a strong impression on contemporaries. The *Mémoires de Trévoux*, which relayed Jesuit opinion in one of the most successful of all the eighteenth-century periodicals, devoted twenty-two whole pages to the *Essai*.[2] Those parts of his argument which were most damaging to traditional ideas of a military nobility, who were cast as the guides and protectors of the rest of society, received prominent mention.[3] The Jesuits concluded by recommending to their readers a work which was 'very important in its subject-matter, solid, and full of profound reflections'.[4] Another leading journal, *Observations sur les Écrits Modernes*, pronounced Melon's views on different matters very useful, and gave him what was surely the highest award among the philosophes, a commendation for the 'noble use of his reason'.[5] Others, the reviewer said, had treated the 'mechanics of trade'; Melon had added *l'esprit philosophique* to useful knowledge. The reviewer seemed to hint at political implications. Melon was said to have refrained from 'parading his conclusions', because he was persuaded that they would not escape those who could profit from the book.[6] Finally, in 1736 the *Journal des Sçavans*, the *doyen* of the French press, conferred the blessing of the learned establishment upon Melon and his ideas. In a review article, which filled eleven quarto pages, commerce was described as 'this new force which begins to arise before our eyes'.[7] The reviewer regretted that he did not dare to be still more outspoken. 'While treating delicate matters,' he wrote, 'authors often only hint at their meaning;

---

[1] *Ibid.*, pp. 107–8.

[2] *Mémoires pour l'Histoire des Sciences et des Beaux-Arts*, March 1735, pp. 542–64.

[3] *Ibid.*, pp. 552–3.

[4] *Ibid.*, p. 563.

[5] *Observations sur les Écrits Modernes* (Amsterdam, 1735–43), II (8 July 1735), p. 39.

[6] *Ibid.*, II (8 July 1735), pp. 25–6.

[7] *Journal des Sçavans*, 1736, p. 501.

they are only being prudent, but the journalist is obliged to be more prudent still. It would not do for him to raise the veil which has been purposefully thrown over certain things.'[1]

The originality of Melon's contribution to economic theory was soon recognized by contemporaries. The *Journal des Sçavans* with the hindsight of eighteen years said that Melon, 'who combined a philosophic mind with a great fund of knowledge', appeared to have been the first writer to treat economic matters 'systematically'.[2] Voltaire used the same word when he described Melon as having a 'mind given to systematizing (*esprit systématique*), very enlightened, but chimerical'.[3] It was Diderot's opinion that without Melon the whole school of economists might never have been born.[4] Reissues in 1736, 1743, 1754 and 1761 bear witness to the popularity of the *Essai*. Its basic ideas were so generally accepted that even Dutot, whose *Réflexions politiques sur les finances et le commerce* was intended as a refutation of Melon's ideas on currency, said that it 'contains excellent things', while taking issue with him on only a few specific points.[5]

No political or social discussion, least of all one which concerned the proper pursuits of the French nobility, was likely to be unaffected by Montesquieu's views. The passing of two centuries, even the publication of Monsieur André Masson's magnificent edition of the *Oeuvres*, have hardly made *De l'Esprit des Loix* any easier to understand. It clearly requires to be read at several different levels, unless the reader is content to let it, so to speak, argue against itself. Montesquieu, at a superficial level at least, was bitterly hostile to the participation of the French nobility in commerce, which he pronounced as contrary to the spirit of the monarchy, and which he added would ruin the nobility without any benefit to commerce.[6] He considered 'very wise' existing practice under which businessmen could not be nobles, and, therefore, had all the stronger motive to

---

[1] *Ibid.*, p. 507.

[2] *Journal des Sçavans*, 1754, p. 596.

[3] P. Harsin (ed.), *Dutot: 'Réflexions politiques sur les finances et le commerce'* (Paris and Liège: E. Droz, 1935), I, p. XVII. Voltaire used *systématique* of Boulainvilliers in the same pejorative sense. See above, p. 21.

[4] R. Hubert, *Les Sciences sociales dans l'Encyclopédie* (Paris: F. Alcan, 1923), p. 285.

[5] Dutot, I, pp. 1–2.

[6] Montesquieu, *Oeuvres*, I, *De l'Esprit des Loix*, p. 462.

succeed in their profession, so that they could later buy their way into the ranks of the nobility. Although Montesquieu admitted to some qualms about giving to riches what in happier circumstances should have been the prize for virtue, he concluded that in the case of France the arrangement could be very useful. Perhaps by way of salving his conscience, he ended the chapter by praising 'that entirely martial nobility', whose foibles he chronicled with gentle irony before he solemnly declared that 'all these things have necessarily contributed to the greatness of the kingdom'.[1] These and similar ideas of the philosopher soon became the stock-in-trade of lesser theorists of aristocratic power, such as the chevalier d'Arcq, whose views will be considered shortly. Yet, at a deeper level, *De l'Esprit des Loix* surely undermined the arguments in favour of a single class. Montesquieu's natural prejudice as an aristocrat against trade should be set against his carefully developed views as a political theorist on the importance of trade in shaping the development of the Europe of his time. In the opening chapter of Book XX, which is devoted specifically to the relationship between laws and trade, he wrote:

> Trade cures destructive prejudices: and it is almost a general rule that everywhere where there are civilized customs, trade exists; and that everywhere where trade exists there are civilized customs.
> Let no one be surprised, therefore, if our customs are less savage than in the past. Trade has had the effect that a knowledge of the customs of all nations has penetrated everywhere: customs have been compared, and great advantages have followed.

Although these views are briefly qualified with references to Plato and Caesar to show that the customs which are perfected by trade are later corrupted by further trade, the force of the original remarks remains. In the following chapter, 'Concerning the spirit of commerce', Montesquieu paid tribute to the harmonizing effects of international trade in terms which should surely have earned him a statue at Brussels. 'The natural effect of commerce,' he wrote, 'is to promote peace. Two nations which do business together make themselves dependent on one another.'[2] Such ideas are lent support in the *Pensées* where the

[1] *Ibid.*, pp. 462–4.
[2] *Ibid.*, pp. 445–6.

triumphant 'spirit of commerce' is seen to complete earlier historical development.

Each century has its own presiding genius: a spirit of disorder and independence in Europe came into being with Gothic government; the period of Charlemagne's successors was infected by the monastic spirit; afterwards that of chivalry reigned; that of conquest appeared with professional troops; and today it is the spirit of commerce that is in the ascendant.

This commercial spirit means that everything is calculated. But glory on its own only enters into the calculations of fools.

Although Montesquieu adds at once that he is speaking only of vain glory and not of that inspired by such motives as duty, virtue, zeal in the service of the ruler and love of one's country,[1] his whole conception undermines the traditional idea of the nobility as a militaristic caste. Perhaps Montesquieu did not intend his readers to take too seriously the passage in which he praised:[2]

That entirely martial nobility, which thinks that whatever its wealth it must seek its fortune; but which is ashamed of increasing its possessions if it has not begun by dissipating them; that part of the nation which serves it with its capital possessions; which when it is ruined vacates its place to another who will serve with its capital again; which goes to war so that no one dares to say that it has not been; which when it cannot hope for riches hopes for honours: and when it does not obtain them, consoles itself that it has acquired honour; all these things have made a necessary contribution to the greatness of the kingdom.

Whatever Montesquieu's exact position on the question of whether the nobility should be allowed to engage in trade without loss of caste, he had raised a more fundamental issue concerning the proper place of nobles in French society. His whole idea that each type of government had its own distinctive *esprit*, or character, seemed to rule out compromise. He made it more difficult, in theory at least, for the nobility to retrieve its fortunes by having recourse to a commerce which it despised.

---

[1] *Ibid.*, II, *Pensées*, no. 810, p. 237.
[2] Montesquieu, I, *De l'Esprit des Loix*, pp. 463–4.

In 1756 the question of whether the nobility should participate in trade first received voluminous treatment in its own right.[1] The controversy was provoked by the publication in 1754 of the declamatory *Réflexions* of the marquis de Lassay. This chivalrous soldier, justifiably famous for his amatory conquests in an age that offered fierce competition in this field, was really an outsider in the world of letters. The posthumous appearance of his *Réflexions* in the *Mercure*, the periodical which catered especially for the court, was a kind of challenge delivered by the fashionable to the literary world. While the foibles and scandals of the great could be described as their own concern, the *Réflexions* of the marquis had strong political and social overtones which could hardly be ignored by the publicists. Lassay rationalized in elegant form the prejudices of the old martial nobility. The kernel of his argument was that France was a 'kingdom established by arms', which was dependent on physical force for its survival.[2] The nobility, he said, provided 'the largest force in our armies', and had frequently been the reason for France's superiority over her enemies. If trade were opened to nobles, 'they would readily follow a path [which was] easier and less perilous', and would consequently leave France open to attack.[3]

The first and most effective reply to the *Réflexions* of the marquis de Lassay came from the abbé Coyer. Behind the façade of a writer of belles-lettres he possessed a mind of considerable originality. His *Plan d'éducation publique* which was to appear in 1770 contained some of the most revolutionary proposals of any contemporary work on that subject.[4] In refuting Lassay's ideas he returned to Melon's conviction that the power of the state was more a matter of economics than of armies. 'The balance of trade and the balance of power,' he wrote, 'are now one and the same.' He added that it was easy to see that trade lay at the heart of political interests and of the balance

---

[1] For a description of this controversy from a rather different angle see Jacqueline Hecht, 'Un Problème de population active au XVIIIe. siècle, en France: la querelle de la noblesse commerçante', *Population: Revue Trimestrielle de l'Institut National d'Études Démographiques*, XIX (1964), pp. 267–89. See also E. Depitre, 'Le Système et la querelle de la *Noblesse Commerçante* (1756–1759), *Revue d'Histoire Économique et Sociale*, VI (1913), pp. 137–76.

[2] *Mercure de France*, vol. II for December 1754, p. 88.

[3] *Ibid.*, pp. 86–7.

[4] Balteau, IX, p. 1142.

between the powers.[1] Coyer devoted much of his pamphlet to meeting the marquis on his own ground. He was insistent in denying the truth of Lassay's belief that the nobility as a whole was synonymous with the *noblesse militaire*. The French nobility, he said, furnished 'a more than adequate supply' of officers to command the army.[2] He also pointed out that many nobles were too poor to undertake military service, and that, therefore, if they engaged in trade, they would not be depriving the army of recruits.[3] He affirmed his belief, which Saint-Pierre had already voiced,[4] that few nobles would in fact abandon a military career for business. The real cause for concern, he said, was that, held fast by its prejudices, the nobility would not engage in trade at all.[5] Thus, his stated purpose was to assist the impoverished nobles, while disclaiming all intention of interfering with the style of life of the remainder.

If the abbé Coyer's protestations of deference towards the nobility had been genuine, his pamphlet would not have caused such a stir. First, he upset the susceptibilities of nobles by rejecting the usual distinction between retail trade, fit only for plebeians, and wholesale trade, which already carried enough social standing to accommodate much aristocratic prejudice. Coyer argued that retail and wholesale trade were 'divided only by a line', and that it was often necessary to pass from the first to the second.[6] As if this veiled invitation to French nobles to roll up their shirt-sleeves was not enough, Coyer poured scorn on the traditional ethos of the nobility in an imaginary dialogue between the nobles and himself; in which the former asked:[7]

What would become of our privileges if we traded? . . . to which the abbé replied, 'Why would you not keep them? You could, as in the past, sport your coats of arms and murmur against the middle classes who assume them; speak about your ancestors to those who do not question you . . . challenge to, or accept, a duel; keep your

[1] Coyer, *La Noblesse commerçante*, pp. 147–8.
[2] *Ibid.*, p. 12.
[3] *Ibid.*, p. 21.
[4] Hecht, p. 275n.
[5] Coyer, *La Noblesse commerçante*, p. 22.
[6] *Ibid.*, p. 166.
[7] *Ibid.*, pp. 152–3. Degrees in eighteenth-century France were normally bought, though in a more irregular fashion than the Oxford M.A. at the present time.

exemption from the *taille*, on condition that you pay under another name . . . pay your salutations to people of birth; hunt inconsiderately over the farmer's crops; beat and belabour those good people; and in case of need be decapitated, instead of perishing bourgeois-fashion by the rope. It would even be possible to revive certain privileges which you have allowed to lapse, such as that of acquiring more knowledge in less time at the universities . . .'

Coyer's challenge was taken up in the same year by the chevalier d'Arcq. Besides being a talented writer, he had the rarer distinction, as a bastard of Louis XIV's own bastard, the comte de Toulouse, of being able to boast that being born the wrong side of a royal blanket was a family tradition. Such a prestigious genealogy alone was bound to secure the chevalier's views favourable consideration in eighteenth-century France. In his brochure, *La Noblesse militaire et le patriote françois*, he advanced Lassay's arguments again in more moderate terms. It was necessary, he said, that monarchs 'should keep alive in the heart of their subjects dispositions appropriate for conquests', even if they avoided wars whenever possible. 'That,' he said, 'is the only means that the monarch has of making himself feared and respected by his neighbours, consequently of letting his people enjoy the benefits of peace.'[1] Doubtless echoing Montesquieu, he said that if the nobility entered trade it would vitiate the character of the state.[2] However, his only proposal for alleviating the plight of the poorer nobility was to increase the proportion of officers to men, which would have had the effect of making the army still more unmanageable. He also set great store by the formation of new corps of volunteers, which were to be entirely composed of gentlemen, and which even he realized would need to be subjected to the most stringent discipline if they were to be kept in order.[3]

The pamphlets by Coyer[4] and d'Arcq polarized opinion on

[1] P. A. de Saint-Foix, chevalier d'Arcq, *La Noblesse militaire, ou le patriote françois* (n.p., 1756), p. 12.

[2] *Ibid.*, pp. 26–7.

[3] *Ibid.*, pp. 97 ff.

[4] Although *La Noblesse militaire* was convicted by the weakness of its arguments, Coyer unwisely wrote in reply *La Noblesse militaire et commerçante; en réponse aux objections faites par l'auteur de La Noblesse Militaire* (Amsterdam, 1756) and even a *Développement et défense du système de la Noblesse Commerçante* (Amsterdam and Paris: Duchesne, 1757). These two works reproduced the arguments of the first in diluted form.

the question of whether the nobility should engage in trade. While 'the satellites of these two works', as one pamphleteer calls them,[1] have little intrinsic merit, they almost certainly reflect contemporary opinion more closely than the works of more discerning writers, such as Montesquieu, Voltaire and Diderot.

The majority of these pamphleteers supported the chevalier d'Arcq. One of those to share his views most fervently was Dame Belot, a lady who possessed the same romantic temperament as the chevalier. Although she was the widow of an impoverished *avocat*, she never lacked innumerable male protectors. Her second husband, the powerful Président Durey de Meynières, was won by the original resource of beguiling him with her charms in his own library, to which pursuits of a more scholarly kind had supposedly brought her.[2] Dame Belot's pamphlet, however, fails to do justice to her alluring personality. She practically contents herself with reminding her readers that 'France is a monarchy' and that 'the dominating spirit in it should be military'.[3] She had earlier cited the chevalier to show that a warlike disposition safeguarded the foundations of the state, while an over-extended commerce was fatal to it.[4] She condemned the whole controversy for arousing the *amour-propre* of *roturiers*. What good, she asked, had been done by drawing the attention of *roturiers* to their supposed inferiority, and of the poor nobility to their supposed destitution?[5]

If La Hausse, another pamphleteer, had used fewer pages, he might have been credited with summarizing d'Arcq's views; as it is, he repeats him at tedious length, while pinning almost all his feeble theorizing to his main theme, that 'each state has its spirit; the nobility has its own, while that of the nobility is quite distinct from that of commerce, which is only a spirit of calculation and interest'.[6] Similar views were expressed by Garnier, who aptly stigmatized himself on the frontispiece of

---

[1] O. G. Du Rey de Meynières (Dame Belot), *Observations sur la noblesse et le tiers-état* (Amsterdam: Arkstée et Merkus, 1758), p. 20.

[2] Michaud, III, p. 603.

[3] Du Rey de Meynières, pp. 109–10.

[4] *Ibid.*, p. 93.

[5] *Ibid.*, pp. 20–22.

[6] De La Hausse, *La Noblesse telle qu'elle doit être, ou moyen de l'employer utilement pour elle-même et pour la patrie* (Amsterdam and Paris: A. M. Lottin, 1758), p. 7.

his pamphlet, *pédant de collège*, although he was soon to establish himself as an authority on the early history of the Franks. He indicated neatly in the title, *Le Commerce remis à sa place*, where his sympathies lay. The nobility were defined as 'a class of men, whose functions consist in the defence or policing of the state'.[1] He affirmed Montesquieu's view that honour was the guiding principle of the monarchy, and equated trade with the spirit of calculation and self-interest. He foresaw with *Schadenfreude* the time when merchants, 'those traitors to honour, proud of their opulence and of their treasures', would reach the point where they dared to look with 'a disdainful smile at the children of glory', before trampling their titles and escutcheons underfoot.[2] The abbé Barthoul, also, made his position clear. He warned Coyer that even if his work were applauded in London, which he seems to equate with the kiss of death for anyone in search of a literary reputation, every Frenchman would dismiss it as the product of a 'master in the sphere of wit'.[3] Barthoul considered 'the project for a trading nobility' as 'impracticable, dangerous to the state if it were possible, finally useless if it were not dangerous'.[4] The same views were echoed by Billardon de Sauvigny, whose lack of literary talents must surely have done much to earn him the post of royal censor in 1777.[5] The nation, he considered, should never lose sight of the fact that it owed its origin not to its merchants, but to its soldiers.[6] Although he leaned towards Coyer's side in describing contempt for trade as 'a Gothic prejudice',[7] he seemed to be more concerned in case the nobility should lose its taste for war.[8] He would doubtless have been relieved to learn that a lust for war, far from becoming exhausted, was to be more democratically diffused throughout society in the future. The vicomte Alès de Corbet, a professional soldier, quoted

---

[1] J.-J. Garnier, *Le Commerce remis à sa place: réponse d'un pédant de collège aux novateurs politiques, addressée à l'auteur de la lettre à M.F.* (n.p., 1756), p. 14.

[2] *Ibid.*, pp. 21–3.

[3] Barthoul, *Lettre à l'auteur de 'La Noblesse commerçante'* (Bordeaux, 1756), p. 7.

[4] *Ibid.*, p. 20.

[5] Balteau, VI, p. 462.

[6] E.-L. Billardon de Sauvigny, *L'Une ou l'Autre, ou la noblesse commerçante et militaire, avec des réflexions sur le commerce et les moyens de l'encourager* (Mahon, 1756), p. 14.

[7] *Ibid.*, p. 93.

[8] *Ibid.*, p. 54.

Montesquieu's dictum that honour was the principle of the monarchy,[1] and the marquis de Vente de Pennes considered d'Arcq's ideas more in conformity with the principles, customs and constitution of France.[2] Finally, the marquis de Mirabeau, in *L'Ami des hommes*, which, unlike the works mentioned above, was far more than a satellite of d'Arcq's pamphlet, dismissed *La Noblesse commerçante* as 'a pretty preliminary discourse for some light treatises on commerce'.[3] He compared the state to a tree of which agriculture represented the roots, industry the branches, and commerce and the arts, the leaves.[4] He hardly needed to stress that the principle from which he invariably started was the need to cultivate the roots.[5] Mirabeau did not so much participate in the controversy as air his views that commerce was unimportant in comparison with agriculture. In doing so, he spoke for most of the large physiocratic school, whose intellectual interests seldom reached beyond the cultivation of the soil and division of its produce.

Coyer was supported in the controversy by far fewer pamphleteers, and, even so, several of them did not follow him the whole way. Although the anonymous author of *Le Citoyen philosophe* dedicated his work to Coyer,[6] and although he professed to demonstrate the 'instability of the principles in *La Noblesse militaire*',[7] he took him sharply to task for his scathing description of the prejudices of the impecunious nobility. 'What indigent gentleman,' he asked, 'would not be smitten, filled with anger and grief to see the biting and ironic description which you draw of his deep poverty?'[8] He stressed that it was only the nobles who were not required to defend the state who should be permitted to engage in trade, and expressly reassured his readers that the harmonious character

[1] P.-A. d'Alès de Corbet, *Nouvelles observations sur les deux systèmes de la noblesse commerçante ou militaire* (Amsterdam, 1758), p. 144.

[2] De Vente de Pennes, *La Noblesse ramenée à ses vrais principes, ou examen du dévelopement de 'La Noblesse Commerçante'* (Amsterdam, 1759), p. 6.

[3] V. R. de Mirabeau, *L'Ami des hommes, ou traité de la population* (The Hague: Gilbert, 1758), II, p. 4.

[4] *Ibid.*, p. 10.

[5] *Ibid.*, p. 16.

[6] (Anon.), *Le Citoyen philosophe, ou examen critique de 'La Noblesse Militaire'* (n.p., 1756), frontispiece.

[7] *Ibid.*, p. 11.

[8] *Ibid.*, p. 4.

of the monarchy would not be infringed.[1] The abbé de Pézeroles, who wrote *Le Conciliateur*, was another of Coyer's luke-warm allies. He did not really try to refute d'Arcq's view that monarchies were by nature imbued with the spirit of conquest, and contented himself with saying that it was unnecessary to push matters to extremes.[2] He was quite horrified by the proposal that merchants should be ennobled, as he feared that this would have removed the indigent nobility's 'greatest resource', that of marrying the daughters of rich *roturiers*.[3] A prominent economist, Véron de Forbonnais, also agreed with Coyer on most points, but was insistent that retail trade was unsuitable for the nobility.[4]

There were only two or three pamphlets which were at all comparable to *La Noblesse commerçante* in their scorn for the traditional mores of the French nobility. In *Le Commerce ennobli* by Séras, the controversy was given a more radical turn when he placed the needs of trade itself above those of the impoverished nobles. He felt that trade would benefit more from the ennobling of merchants than from persuading nobles to enter it.[5] Those nobles who might consider a career in commerce were severely warned in their own interests to avoid arousing antagonism by standing on their privileges. Nobles were informed that they should inscribe their names like others on the *Tableau des Commerçans*, and forget the prejudice which placed them socially above their colleagues.[6]

The other pamphleteer to lard the nobles with sarcasm was Marchand, who was a society jester and thus well-qualified to become one of the royal censors.[7] In *La Noblesse commerçable ou ubiquiste* he outlined a plan by which impecunious nobles could raise money by selling nobility by the year to *roturiers*,[8]

---

[1] *Ibid.*, pp. 25–6.

[2] Abbé de Pézeroles, *Le Conciliateur ou la noblesse militaire et commerçante; en réponse aux objections faites par l'auteur de 'La Noblesse Militaire'* (Amsterdam and Paris: Duchesne, 1756), p. 34.

[3] *Ibid.*, pp. 136–9.

[4] F. Véron de Forbonnais, *Lettre à M.F., ou examen politique des prétendus inconvéniens de la faculté de commercer en gros, sans déroger à sa noblesse* (Paris: Laurens, 1756), p. 81.

[5] Séras, *Le Commerce Ennobli* (Brussels, 1756), p. 28.

[6] *Ibid.*, pp. 26–7.

[7] Michaud, XXVI, p. 474.

[8] J.-H. Marchand, *La Noblesse commerçable ou ubiquiste* (Amsterdam, 1756), pp. 65–6.

which would have had the advantage, he added, of enabling nobles to pay their debts in their own lifetimes.[1] The sale of aristocratic stock was hedged with ingenious safeguards. For instance, the author announced that, 'It will be forbidden to give or sell portions of nobility to any actress or other girl who might procure it by way of seduction, by abusing her charms and the weakness of her admirers.'[2] Although Marchand's pamphlet was in a sense little more than fair comment on the flourishing aristocratic marriage-market of eighteenth-century France, it did reflect the extent to which the whole idea of nobility was being called in question. The same was true of another pamphlet, *La Noblesse oisive* by Rochon de Chabannes, in which he gracefully implied that the nobility was too idle either to fight or to trade.[3] The only commerce for which he deemed them suitable appeared to be 'le commerce des femmes'.[4]

The best available guide to the reactions of the reading public to these pamphlets are the reviews in contemporary journals. Eighteenth-century periodicals offer an important and largely unexplored field for the survey of ideas.[5] The periodicals appear to have had many readers. An analysis of the contents of some libraries auctioned between 1750 and 1780 showed them to be so strongly represented that there was actually an average of more than one hundred volumes in each library.[6] Formey, in his *Conseils pour former une bibliothèque peu nombreuse mais choisie* of five or six hundred volumes which were to suffice for a lifetime's reading, budgeted for no less than

[1] *Ibid.*, p. 72.

[2] *Ibid.*, p. 79.

[3] M.-A.-J. Rochon de Chabannes, *La Noblesse oisive* (n.p., 1756), p. 4.

[4] *Ibid.*, p. 14.

[5] The most comprehensive survey of French eighteenth-century periodicals is still Eugène Hatin's *Bibliographie historique et critique de la presse périodique française* (Paris: Firmin-Didot, 1866). There are a few useful studies which are confined to individual journals, notably, J. de La Harpe, *Le Journal des Savants et l'Angleterre*, 1702–89 (Berkeley: University of California Press, 1941); J. N. Pappas, 'Berthier's *Journal de Trévoux* and the philosophes', in *Studies on Voltaire and the Eighteenth Century*, ed. T. Besterman (Geneva: Institut et Musée Voltaire, 1957), vol. 3; P. van Tieghem, *L'Année Littéraire*, 1754–1790, *comme intermédiaire en France des littératures étrangères* (Paris: F. Rieder, 1917); R. F. Birn, 'Pierre Rousseau and the Philosophes of Bouillon', in *Studies on Voltaire and the Eighteenth Century* ed. T. Besterman (Geneva: Institut et Musée Voltaire, 1964), vol. 29, which deals with the *Journal Encyclopédique*.

[6] Mornet, *Revue d'Histoire Littéraire de la France*, XVII (1910), p. 478.

thirty volumes of literary periodicals.[1] While it is impossible to estimate at all confidently the number of subscribers to any particular periodical, the *Mercure de France*, which probably had the largest if one of the most feather-brained readerships, claimed in 1763 to have as many as 1,600 subscribers, of whom 40 were said to live abroad, 660 in Paris and 900 in the provinces.[2] These figures are all the more impressive in view of the scores of other periodicals which were in existence at any one time. Even if the vast majority failed to establish themselves, there were several journals of high quality which lasted for much of the century. The cumulative influence of many of the more long-lived periodicals, such as *L'Année Littéraire* and the *Journal Encyclopédique*, both of which provided their readers with well over a hundred octavo pages every fortnight, was probably considerable.

The whole controversy about whether the nobility should participate in trade received a tremendous press. All the principal periodicals carried reviews of at least some of the writings which were mentioned above. *L'Année Littéraire*, which was one of the most successful of all the French periodicals, prefaced a review of *Le Commerce ennobli* in July 1756 with a remark that the reviewer had undertaken to give an account of all writings which bore on the subject of *La Noblesse commerçante et militaire*.[3] In December of the same year the editor, Fréron, again announced that he was reviewing *L'Une ou l'Autre*, not for its intrinsic merit, but so that his readers would not miss any of the writings on that topic.[4] Similarly, the editor of the *Journal Encyclopédique*, which was the official organ of the *Encyclopédistes*, wrote that his subscribers had asked for an account of all pamphlets on the subject.[5] The whole controversy received such an airing, in fact, that Grimm, whose *Correspondance Littéraire* aspired to keep the crowned heads of Europe informed about literary matters, was vainly hoping

---

[1] H. J. Reesink, *L'Angleterre et la littérature anglaise dans les trois plus anciens périodiques français de Hollande de 1684 à 1709* (Zutphen: W. J. Thieme, 1931), p. 84.

[2] G. Weil, *Le Journal: origines, évolution et rôle de la presse périodique* (Paris: La Renaissance du livre, 1934), p. 90.

[3] *L'Année Littéraire*, vol. IV for 1756, pp. 206–7.

[4] *Ibid.*, vol. VIII for 1756, p. 241.

[5] *Journal Encyclopédique*, vol. V pt iii, for 1756, p. 72.

as early as August 1756 that the controversy would die out.[1]

In trying to assess the attitude of the different periodicals to the debate between d'Arcq and Coyer, it is necessary to make some allowance for editorial subterfuge. A periodical, appearing as it did at fairly regular intervals, was inevitably more vulnerable to censorship or confiscation by the police than an isolated work. Although censorship in eighteenth-century France can hardly be accused of being either particularly efficient or repressive, it was capricious enough to urge caution, particularly on the editor of a periodical. The fact that it had been royal policy since before the time of Colbert to encourage the nobility to enter trade was hardly a guarantee of royal protection for those who supported Coyer. In 1779 it was the royal censors themselves who seized the copies of Letrosne's *De l'Administration provinciale*, as if to demonstrate that the Crown attacked its friends more fiercely than its foes.[2] In any case, even if the lethargy of the royal censors could usually be relied upon, there was also the threat of censorship by the Sorbonne and the Parlement of Paris. As censors were impelled to act often to protect influential individuals, editors were well advised to treat the views of the chevalier d'Arcq with respect: a royal bastard in eighteenth-century France was near the top of the social scale.

The usual way in which editors avoided committing themselves to an open expression of opinion was simply by summarizing works without making any comment. The *Journal Encyclopédique* provides a good example of how this means was used to camouflage editorial opinion, in its issue of December 1765. In the middle of a long rebuttal of a reader's criticisms of d'Argenson's *Considérations sur le gouvernement ancien et présent de la France*, the editor suddenly remembers to defend himself by announcing, 'Our extract from the work of the marquis d'Argenson was no more than an extract'.[3] Of course, the journal in such a case had already laid down its editorial line by its choice of works for review, and also by the extracts from these which it had chosen to print.

---

[1] *Correspondance Littéraire, Philosophique et Critique par Grimm, Diderot, Raynal, Meister* . . . ed. M. Tourneux (Paris, 1877–82), III, p. 269.

[2] See p. 66.

[3] *Journal Encyclopédique*, vol. VIII pt ii for 1765, p. 61.

There is little doubt that the majority of eighteenth-century periodicals, by what they said, and even more by their choice of extracts for review, showed that they favoured the views of Coyer, as opposed to those of d'Arcq. The chevalier's *La Noblesse militaire* received its most favourable review from *L'Année Littéraire*, where it was said that he 'overthrows the principles of his adversary, brings everything back to its true viewpoint, and saves the French nobility from the kind of degradation to which it was desired to reduce it . . . He shows that it is not advantageous for a monarchy to extend its trade too far.'[1] In the next issue the journal quoted a declaration, ascribed to the Parlement of Grenoble, in which scorn was poured on the 'filthy merchandise and dusty bales'.[2] The *parlementaires* were reported to believe like d'Arcq in the urgent need to close trade to the nobles, so that they would be forced to pursue 'the arduous paths of honour', which in their view naturally included serving in the parlements.[3] Grimm's *Correspondance Littéraire* gave a characteristically graceless support to d'Arcq's views. D'Arcq was described as having written a worse reply to Coyer's bad book. Fortunately, he added, Coyer needed no refutation, as Montesquieu (whose openly expressed views d'Arcq elegantly relayed) had said enough for those in a position to judge.[4] It is well known that Grimm was more deadly as a friend than as an enemy. Fréron, the talented editor of *L'Année Littéraire*, alone gave d'Arcq full support. He was closely identified with the cause of reaction. According to one biographer, he was obsessed with the notion of resistance to change and instinctively detested the philosophes.[5] Voltaire in a single work managed to call this conservative and Catholic journalist, 'a scribbler, scoundrel, toad, lizard, snake, spider, viper's tongue, crooked mind, heart of filth, doer of evil, rascal, impudent person, cowardly knave, spy and hound'.[6] The same detestation for Fréron was given, so to speak, more bite and fewer teeth, in an epigram which is sometimes attributed to Voltaire in which a snake bit Fréron

---

[1] *L'Année Littéraire*, vol. II for 1756, p. 32.
[2] *Ibid.*, pp. 55–6.
[3] *Ibid.*, p. 58.
[4] *Correspondance Littéraire*, III, p. 207.
[5] Cited by Birn, p. 32.
[6] R. R. Palmer, p. 7.

and the snake died.[1] D'Arcq's support, therefore, such as it was, came from the dwindling minority of conservative opinion, which was stolidly opposed to the philosophes. D'Arcq's views were usually countered in other journals, politely but firmly. The doyen of the French press, the *Journal des Sçavans*, which, despite its semi-official standing, was a surprisingly responsible and comprehensive journal, questioned the very assumption that a noble was degraded by engaging in commerce, and considered the fear that the nobility, if given a chance, would rush precipitately into business, as quite unfounded.[2] The journal dismissed d'Arcq's treatise elsewhere as 'a kind of manifesto'.[3] The *Bibliothèque des Sciences et des Beaux-Arts* wrote that d'Arcq, far from disproving Coyer's arguments, had in many respects unwittingly strengthened them.[4] The *Mémoires de Trévoux*, through which the Jesuits infiltrated into journalism, commented bitingly on d'Arcq's *La Noblesse militaire*: 'from his exordium his indignation is exhaled in pathetic outbursts'.[5]

Coyer and his side received on balance very favourable reviews in eighteenth-century periodicals. The *Correspondance Littéraire* was almost alone in being completely out of sympathy with those who advocated the participation of the nobility in trade. Grimm's periodical characteristically announced that *Le Citoyen philosophe*, which, as we have seen, gave moderate support to Coyer's views, was a 'bad brochure on the insipid quarrel of the trading nobility'.[6] Coyer's own work was dismissed as 'a political masterpiece for the bourgeois of the rue Saint-Denis'.[7] *L'Année Littéraire*, however, despite the fact that it later emerged as d'Arcq's chief supporter, while criticizing some aspects of Coyer's treatise,[8] greeted it as a 'remarkable work', and applauded its 'salutary causticity'.[9] The general tone of the long review in the *Journal des Sçavans* was un-

---

[1] Voltaire, *Correspondance* ed. T. Besterman (Geneva: Institut et Musée Voltaire, 1953–65), XLV, p. 235 n.

[2] *Journal des Sçavans*, August 1756, p. 545.

[3] *Ibid.*, July 1756, p. 459.

[4] *Bibliothèque des Sciences et des Beaux-Arts*, 50 vols (The Hague, 1754–80), vol. 5, pt 2 (1756), p. 497.

[5] *Mémoires pour l'Histoire des Sciences et des Beaux-Arts . . .*, June 1756, p. 1462.

[6] *Correspondance Littéraire*, III (May 1756), p. 225.

[7] *Ibid.*, p. 171.

[8] *L'Année Littéraire*, vol. 1 for 1756, p. 46.

[9] *Ibid.*, p. 55.

doubtedly favourable.[1] The *Bibliothèque des Sciences et des Beaux-Arts*, as was easier for an unofficial paper, gave the abbé unqualified support. Lassay's objections to the nobility's entry into trade were declared 'refuted here in a victorious manner'.[2] Coyer's long sarcastic account of the prejudices of the nobility, which was quoted earlier,[3] appeared almost in its entirety in both the *Bibliothèque des Sciences et des Beaux-Arts*[4] and the *Mémoires de Trévoux*.[5] The *Journal Encyclopédique*, in its review of *La Noblesse commerçante*, not only accepted Coyer's arguments, but was bold enough to ask the government to implement his proposals. 'The greatest wrong which this work has to fear', the reviewer wrote, 'is to be read and admired only by literary people, instead of penetrating to the provinces, and being distributed by the intendants to all the nobility'.[6] After more than a year the *Journal Encyclopédique* repeated that Coyer had many supporters, and that it was now time for 'those who hold the happiness of the nation in their hands' to give Coyer's ideas serious attention.[7] The *Journal Encyclopédique*, which had a powerful protector in Malesherbes, the Director-General of the book trade, could perhaps afford to be more outspoken than the other periodicals. Yet, many of these showed their sympathies by printing long extracts from Coyer and other critics of traditional notions of *dérogeance*. To cite one example, *La Noblesse commerçable ou ubiquiste*, which outlined a plan for the sale of nobility at so much the year, was given four pages in the *Journal Encylopédique*,[8] ten in *L'Année Littéraire*[9] and over sixteen in the *Mémoires de Trévoux*.[10] The fact that so many journals could side more or less openly with Coyer shows how far traditional ideas about the role of the nobility were coming under fire. Of course, the periodicals may not have reflected the views of their readership. However, the high

---

[1] *Journal des Sçavans*, July 1756, pp. 451–9.
[2] *Bibliothèque des Sciences et des Beaux-Arts*, V, pt 2 (1756), p. 296.
[3] See pp. 86–7.
[4] *Bibliothèque des Sciences et des Beaux-Arts*, V, pt 2 (1756), pp. 304–5.
[5] *Mémoires pour l'Histoire des Sciences et des Beaux-Arts*, April 1756, pp. 895–6.
[6] *Journal Encyclopédique*, vol. II pt 2 for 1756, pp. 42–3.
[7] *Ibid.*, vol. III pt 3 for 1757, p. 65.
[8] *Journal Encyclopédique*, vol. V pt 3 for 1756, pp. 79–83.
[9] *L'Année Littéraire*, vol. 3 for 1756, pp. 275–85.
[10] *Mémoires pour l'Histoire des Sciences et des Beaux-Arts*, August 1756, pp. 1925–41.

failure-rate among French periodicals and their complete financial dependence on the subscriptions from their readers make it improbable that so many editors would have simultaneously been high-minded enough to follow an unpopular line. Without knowing more about the actual readers concerned, it is hazardous to generalize. However, perhaps this survey of opinion on the controversy about the nobility's participation in trade at least raises the question of how far French society itself was in fact resistant to change. It goes without saying that in the political circumstances of eighteenth-century France the leadership had to come from the Crown. The most that was attempted was an edict of 1767 which was designed to turn wholesale traders into a special class, from which two members would be ennobled each year. It is highly likely, however, that this *arrêt*, like so many others, was a dead-letter. In any case, the government's good intentions do not seem to have lasted very long. Turgot did not even try in 1776 to tack on to his edict for abolishing the guilds a provision against *dérogeance*.[1]

By the late 1750s the controversy over the nobility's participation in trade seemed to have burnt itself out, doubtless to the relief of others besides Grimm. In the end there seemed to be fairly general agreement that nobles should be permitted at least to engage in wholesale trade without loss of caste. When the government sounded the parlements and intendants in 1757 — itself a striking sign of the government's concern to seek advice — thirty-eight out of the forty-seven parlements and intendants that replied favoured the entry of the nobility into trade.[2] On the other hand, there was little sign that the problem was properly understood. Little would be gained by anyone from allowing an impoverished nobility to engage in wholesale trade when it lacked the necessary capital. Those without funds could clearly not make a living unless they were invited to start in retail trade. Yet only a handful of the intendants, who were much more favourable to the project than the parlements, were prepared to go that far.[3] The whole controversy seems to have had very few practical results. The vast majority of

[1] Lévy-Bruhl, pp. 232–3.
[2] *Ibid.*, p. 226.
[3] *Ibid.*, p. 228.

the nobles had neither the means nor the desire to engage in trade.

The pamphleteers and journalists also failed to influence a small group of nobles whose importance has often been overlooked. It has been shown that many of France's leading industrialists at a time when rapid progress was being made, especially in mining and metallurgy, were nobles rather than commoners.[1] The sharp increase in their activities in the late eighteenth century might seem to indicate a considerable weakening of the social prejudice against trade. There is, none the less, strong evidence against this view. Few nobles engaged in trade openly despite the promptings of the pamphleteers. Many of them took care instead, to avoid the stigma of *dérogeance* by carrying on their business enterprises through *roturier* intermediaries, even if they were only their own household servants.[2] Many nobles also preserved the social decencies by concentrating their attention on mining and metallurgy, which had long been considered acceptable pursuits for the holders of fiefs, as well as being further redeemed from social disfavour by their association with war.[3] It is unlikely that the attitude of the nobility as a whole was greatly influenced by the activities of the *noblesse d'affaires*, as these were drawn almost exclusively from diverse, but clearly defined, sectors of the nobility: from *grands seigneurs* at the Court, the *parlementaires* and the recently ennobled.[4] It is true that in Brittany many nobles entered retail trade, even if they usually took the precaution of protecting their personal honour by setting up in business under the names of their wives.[5] Conditions there were exceptional, however, particularly because the *coutume*, with its special provision for *noblesse dormante*, permitted nobles to resume the privileges of their order once they had abandoned business.[6] In any case, commercial activities of all kinds were the exception in a society that was dominated by agriculture. Not just the nobles, but the vast majority of the bourgeoisie

[1] Richard, esp. pp. 512–13.

[2] *Ibid.*, p. 485.

[3] Soreau, pp. 25–6.

[4] Richard, p. 489.

[5] *Ibid.*, pp. 485–6.

[6] G. Lemarchand, 'sur la société française en 1789', *Revue d'Histoire Moderne et contemporaine* XIX (1972), p. 80.

as well, preferred to gain wealth by almost any means other than through manufactures and trade.[1] It was the absence of a strong incentive to combat the prejudice against commerce that ensured its continuation. Even *roturiers* themselves were often opposed to the abolition of *dérogeance*, as they feared that nobles would use their social status to gain an unfair advantage over their bourgeois rivals. The majority of nobles lacked the capital to pursue commercial interests, even if they had wanted to. And the few nobles who did possess sufficient capital had little motive to resent a prejudice, which could be circumvented so easily by the very rich.

The controversy over whether nobles should engage in trade was resuscitated after thirty years of quiet by the *cahiers* of 1789. These form a treacherous source for the study of opinion, especially if the researcher has failed to arm himself with Professor Hyslop's *Guide*.[2] Almost any thesis can be proved and later disproved by the use of selective citation. Many of the requests in the *cahiers* seem to be too parochial or eccentric to fit any of the usual categories. When the reader finds one parish community blaming church bells for causing thunder and hail, while another community asks for the use of bells to ward off storms,[3] he may feel that the *cahiers* prove nothing so well as what Karl Marx called 'the idiocy of rural life'. The *cahiers*, in order to yield reliable results, require to be studied by a statistician who can establish a percentile incidence for a particular demand by one or more of the orders. Alternatively, they can be studied in relation to a specific locality, as Monsieur Bois did recently for the *sénéchaussée* of *Château-du-Loir*.[4] All I shall attempt to do here is to illustrate from the six volumes of published *cahiers* in the *Archives Parlementaires* some of the views which were precipitated by the controversy over the desirability or otherwise of having nobles who engaged in trade.

In many *cahiers* of the Third Estate, and especially in those

---

[1] Taylor, pp. 485 ff.

[2] B. Hyslop, *A Guide to the general cahiers of* 1789 (New York: Columbia University Press, 1936).

[3] J. M. Mavidal and E. Laurent (eds), *Archives parlementaires de* 1787 *à* 1860 (1st ser. 1789–99, 2nd ed., 1879), IV, p. 612 and p. 605, respectively.

[4] P. Bois, *Cahiers de doléances du tiers-état de la sénéchaussée de Château-du-Loir* (Gap, 1960).

of the nobility, permission was sought for nobles to engage in trade without loss of status.[1] In most cases the request is framed in general terms, which seem designed to include retail as well as wholesale trade. It is common, for instance, to ask that virtually no profession should carry with it social stigma.[2] If there are few *cahiers* which ask for nobles to be admitted expressly to retail trade,[3] there appear to be almost as few *cahiers* of the nobility which limit their request specifically to wholesale trade.[4] The reader might, therefore, gain the impression that many nobles were anxious to engage in trade alongside *roturiers*. The demands of the nobility for free access to trade should be balanced, however, by the requests in nearly half the *cahiers* of the nobility that the privileges of their order should be preserved intact. It was quite common for a community of nobles to covet both permission to trade without incurring *dérogeance* and the maintenance of their privileges in general, or of their exclusive right to bear arms. The nobles of Quercy were an extreme case as they combined a request to ply retail trade with another that the exclusive right of the nobility to fill appointments in the army should be maintained.[5] Such *cahiers* suggest that nobles were prepared to preserve their position in French society by any means that came to hand. If some nobles were prepared to trade on grounds of expediency, few would seem to have been willing to accommodate the demands of commercial life within their mental outlook. The strength of the latter is apparent in a few of the *cahiers* where nobles turned their backs completely on the modern world of the eighteenth century. The nobles of Alençon and Touraine, for instance, asked for a new insignia which would mark them and their families out from the rest of the

[1] Mavidal and Laurent, e.g. the nobles of Agenois, I, p. 683; the three orders of Bayonne, III, p. 104; the nobles of Aval, II, p. 142; the nobles of Dourdan, III, p. 250; the Third Estate of Fontenay-sur-le-Bois-de-Vincennes, IV, p. 554; the Third Estate of Neuilly-sur-Marne, IV, p. 759; the Third Estate of Dombes, VI, p. 69.

[2] *Ibid.*, e.g. the Third Estate of Brest, II, p. 470; the Third Estate of Chartres, II, p. 633; the Third Estate of Rouen, V, p. 605; the clergy of Perche, V, p. 321; the Third Estate of Poitou, V, p. 410.

[3] *Ibid.*, the nobles of Quercy, V, p. 490.

[4] *Ibid.*, the nobles of Condom, III, p. 37; the nobles of Sisteron, III, p. 364; the nobles of Rouen, V, p. 596.

[5] *Ibid.*, V, p. 490.

population.[1] In a few *cahiers* nobles showed that they openly hankered after a feudal past, as when the nobles of Nemours and Anjou each declared their wish 'to preserve the right which belongs to our order of marching to the defence of the State, should the *ban* and *arrière-ban* be called'.[2]

If nobles often hesitated to embrace a business career, the Third Estate were sometimes less than overjoyed at the prospect of competing with nobles, who might turn their social position to financial account. The *tiers* of Charly-sur-Marne even asked that trade should be prohibited to nobles altogether. The *tiers* of Vannes wanted to exclude from trade courtiers and certain officials on the royal farm.[3] Interestingly enough, the Third Estate of Paris, and also that of Nancy, asked to exclude from trade not the nobles, but the clergy,[4] who with large reservoirs of unpaid labour in their charitable institutions were doubtless often already dangerous business rivals. At least one *cahier* recorded the request that should the nobility and clergy engage in trade, they should be obliged to pay taxes, in the same way as the Third Estate.[5]

Although a fair number of the *cahiers* of the Third Estate, as we have seen, favoured the participation of nobles in trade, they naturally tended to look at the question less from the viewpoint of the nobles themselves than from that of the trading community. It is hardly surprising that a few *cahiers* asked not for the participation of nobles in trade, but for the ennoblement of merchants. However, as they were interested in raising the status of the businessman, they were equally concerned to keep him in his calling. Therefore, it was sometimes suggested that a condition of ennoblement should be that the head of the family remained in business.[6] As if to belie the widespread intellectual torpitude in French higher education, the University of Orléans argued that this 'business drain' would be stopped only through the outright abolition of hereditary nobility.[7]

[1] *Ibid.*, I, p. 715 and VI, p. 43, respectively.
[2] *Ibid.*, IV, p. 111 and II, p. 37, respectively.
[3] *Ibid.*, IV, p. 405 and VI, p. 109, respectively.
[4] *Ibid.*, V, p. 285 and VI, p. 647, respectively.
[5] *Ibid.*, the Third Estate of Viry and Chatillon-sur-Orge, V, p. 225.
[6] *Ibid.*, e.g. the Third Estate of Pont-l'Evêque, V, p. 605; the clergy of Châlons-sur-Marne, II, pp. 584–5.
[7] *Ibid.*, VI, p. 672.

The rapid increase in industrial production in the eighteenth century made ideas of *dérogeance* appear still more anachronistic. According to one estimate industrial production rose by no less than 60 per cent in the century after 1730, while there was an even more remarkable rise of 220 per cent in exports in the years between 1716 and 1787.[1] Yet, the controversy over the *Noblesse commerçante* in the 1750s appears only to have sharpened the lines of disagreement. It was purely at a literary level that the abbé Coyer and his supporters had triumphed; there was little change in the social attitudes of the rest of society. If by 1789 more nobles wanted society to raise its unofficial ban on their participation in trade, few appear to have adjusted their outlook to give commerce full social recognition; they wished at the same time to retain privileges based on birth, and to tap a source of wealth which could be increased only by reducing the very social privileges which they enjoyed. The same attitude tended to permeate even those nobles who became France's leading industrialists. Many of them did not seek wealth for its own sake, as a good capitalist doubtless should, but saw it rather as a means of shoring up their faltering social status.[2] A similar situation occurred sometimes in agriculture. The growth of a more commercial outlook injected a new character into the 'feudal' practices of some seigneurs. The so-called 'feudal reaction', as Professor Forster has shown, involved far more than the revival of feudal dues that had fallen into disuse: it should be seen rather as embracing the application of business techniques to the financial exploitation of a fief.[3] In both commerce and agriculture there seems to have been a fundamental contradiction between the goal of some of the wealthier nobility and the means they used to attain it; a disparity between the values of the entrepreneur and of the old feudal nobility which coexisted in society and often in the same individuals. In this way a kind of 'feudal flaw' was transmitted to the economy of the nineteenth century, which may partly explain its curious combination of strengths and weaknesses.

---

[1] Soboul, *La France à la veille de la Révolution*, I, pp. 39–41.
[2] Richaud, p. 500.
[3] See p. 62.

V

Humanitarian Objections to 'Feudalism'

The remnants of feudalism, especially serfdom which was associated with them, were attacked on humanitarian grounds. *Humanité*, as Linguet noted at the time, was 'peripatetic'.[1] It could be used in almost any context, as when the Prince de Ligne exhorted horticulturists to be lovers of humanity.[2] In this sense *humanité* was equivalent to the English 'mankind'. Yet, any definition is misleading unless it also carries strong emotive connotations. The author, who was probably Diderot himself, of the article in the *Encyclopédie*, caught the spirit of *humanité*, when he described it as, 'this sublime enthusiasm . . . tormented by the sufferings of others and the need to alleviate them', and added that 'it would like to traverse the whole universe to abolish slavery, superstition, vice and misfortune'. In the writer's view, 'this virtue, source of so many others, existed in many heads and in very few hearts'.[3] This strain, which was emotional to the point of sentimentality, was near the surface in many of the writings which attacked serfdom, and other aspects of 'feudalism', as an outrage against humanity.

The development of humanitarian feeling can scarcely be nailed down with dates. It is hardly questionable, however, that words like *humanité* and *bienfaisance*, which was revived by the abbé de Saint-Pierre,[4] were far more current in the second than in the first half of the century. When, for instance, the philo-

---

[1] Brunot, VI, pt 2, fasc. 1, p. 1276.
[2] *Ibid.*, p. 1120.
[3] *Ibid.*, p. 118n.
[4] *Ibid.*, p. 113.

sophes appropriated Fénelon as one of their forerunners, it was his love for the common good and his philanthropy which they chose to stress.[1] The growth of humanitarian feeling is reflected still more clearly in the titles of the prize-essays of the provincial academies.[2] Their collective role in diffusing ideas, to which Daniel Mornet drew attention many years ago,[3] has scarcely been studied. The academies, of which there were more than thirty on the eve of the Revolution, provided a network for disseminating ideas throughout the provinces. Many of the academies were in close contact with one another; by rewarding the authors of essays on literary and scientific topics with prizes which were often eagerly competed for, they did much to diffuse their intellectual interests among a wider public. The fact that Robespierre, Brissot and Marat among others received 'academic crowns' for their *discours*[4] illustrates the obvious point that revolutionaries are not always cured of their opinions by respectability. More importantly, it also shows that their ideas could be ventilated freely in one of the more conservative quarters of the society which they later tried to destroy. The academies, however, were restrained from expressing more heterodox opinions, or from endorsing those of others, by the fact that they had given hostages to respectability by accepting revocable royal charters. It is not surprising, therefore, that for most of the century they concerned themselves with subjects that were far removed from politics, such as rhetoric, belles-lettres, antiquarianism and science. If the crowning of Bellicart's *Discours sur l'humanité* by the Academy of Nancy in 1762 presaged the future literary fashion for *l'humanité*,[5] the real break with the past came in the late 1770s. Then mendicancy, which

---

[1] E. Carcassonne, *Fénelon. L'homme et l'oeuvre* (Paris: Boivin, 1946), p. 158.

[2] See, for instance, J. Cousin, *L'Académie des Sciences, Belles Lettres et Arts de Besançon: deux cent ans de vie comtoise, 1752–1952. Essai de synthèse* (Besançon: Jean Ledoux, 1954); P. Barrière, *L'Académie de Bordeaux: centre de culture internationale au XVIIIe. siècle, 1712–1792* (Bordeaux and Paris: Bière, 1951); D. Roche, 'Milieux académiques provinciaux et société des lumières' in *Livre et sociéte dans la France du XVIIIe. siècle*, ed. F. Furet and others (Paris and The Hague: Mouton, 1965), pp. 93–184.

[3] D. Mornet, *Les Origines intellectuelles de la Révolution française, 1715–1787* (Paris: Armand Colin, 1933), pp. 145 ff.

[4] A.-F. Delandine, *Couronnes académiques, ou recueil des prix proposés par les sociétés savantes* (Paris: Cuchet, 1787), II, no. 696; I, no. 528; II, no. 897, respectively.

[5] *Ibid.*, II, no. 763.

had long been an acute social problem, became the subject for prize-essays, which were set in 1777 by the Academies of Châlons-sur-Marne and Orléans, in 1778 by that of the Immaculate Conception at Rouen, and in 1779 by those of Lyons and Soissons.[1] Concurrently, and in the 1780s, education,[2] penal reform,[3] and the condition of the peasants[4] were other topics of social concern that were set for essay-prizes. Similar signs of the increasing appeal to humanitarian feeling can be found in some of the periodicals, which would sometimes report deeds that were considered particularly praiseworthy under a special rubric. For example, under the heading 'Traits de bienfaisance' the *Nouvelles Éphémérides Économiques* reported the practical guidance which the Archbishop of Toulouse had given to his curés for dealing with an epizootic epidemic. 'It is thus that genius alone,' wrote the editor, 'knows how to make reason, humanity, patriotism and religion speak.'[5] In much the same way the *Journal Encyclopédique* under the heading 'Traits de bienfaisance et de générosité', reported how a Monsieur Léonard Euler had forwarded to Turgot, when he was Controller-General, his book on the construction and handling of ships. The journal went on to relate approvingly that as Turgot had considered his work 'of interest to the human race' he had persuaded the king to give Euler a present of 5,000 livres.[6]

As in the case of the development of humanitarian feeling as a whole, humanitarian criticisms of feudal and seigniorial rights and of serfdom in particular became prominent during the 1760s. A jurist named Renauldon headed a chapter of his *Traité*: 'Seigniorial rights which have produced forms of servitude,' and warned his readers that 'at every step nature and humanity shudder'.[7] Two years later the campaign for the abolition of serfdom appears to be foreshadowed in the pages of the *Journal des Sçavans*, when the reviewer of an historical work commented

---

[1] *Ibid.*, I, no. 523; II, nos 778 and 854; I, no. 662; II, no. 919, respectively.

[2] *Ibid.*, I, no. 380.

[3] *Ibid.*, I, no. 526.

[4] *Ibid.*, I, no. 529.

[5] *Nouvelles Éphémérides Économiques ou bibliothèque raisonnée de l'histoire de la morale et de la politique* (Paris, 1774–6), III, pt 3 (1775), p. 207.

[6] *Journal Encyclopédique*, vol. I, pt i for 1779, pp. 139–40.

[7] J. Renauldon, *Traité*, p. 197.

on the period 1313–1515, 'the seventh epoch bears a title of interest to humanity, the "freeing of the serfs" '.[1]

If the humanitarian attack on serfdom had followed the growth of humanitarian feeling as a whole, it would hardly have got under way before the late 1770s or early 1780s. It was almost entirely due to Voltaire that the movement received such impetus at the very beginning of the decade. He began his campaign with two works on the serfs of Mont Jura, the first of which was written in collaboration with his friend Christin, who had been briefed to represent the serfs in their legal battle against the Chapter of Saint–Claude. A review of both works in the *Journal des Sçavans* of 1773 brought the matter to the attention of the educated public. The *Dissertation* by Voltaire and Christin was described as being 'of interest to jurists and to all humanity' and summarized the work as a whole with evident approval.[2] The king's edict itself, by which serfs were emancipated on Crown lands in 1779, has been described as 'visibly inspired by Voltaire's last *mémoire*, which the *avocat*, Christin, lodged at the Council'.[3] Voltaire's work was further recognized when the French Academy's prize in 1781 for a discourse on the abolition of serfdom on Crown lands was awarded to Florian for his poem, *Voltaire and the serf of Mont Jura*. The government also publicized the poem by adding to the laurels of the Academy the distinction for the author of incarceration in the Bastille.[4] Even without this publicity, Florian was highly regarded by contemporaries as a poet and was to be admitted to the French Academy on the eve of the Revolution, while his family connection and friendship with Voltaire gave his account added authority.[5] Florian, for whom Voltaire and *l'humanité* were inseparable,[6] made him figure in the poem as a kind of

---

[1] *Journal des Sçavans* (1767), p. 51.

[2] *Ibid.*, February 1773, pp. 85–7. The contents of the two works were outlined in their titles: *Dissertation sur l'établissement de l'Abbaye de S. Claude, ses chroniques, ses légendes, ses chartes, ses usurpations et sur les droits des habitans de cette terre* (Neufchâtel, 1772) and *Collection des mémoires présentés au Conseil du Roi par les habitans du Mont Jura et le Chapitre de Saint Claude, avec l'arrêt rendu par ce tribunal* (Neufchâtel, 1772).

[3] C.-L. Chassin, *L'Église et les derniers serfs* (Paris: E. Dentu, 1880), p. 71.

[4] Hoefer, XVII, p. 954.

[5] Michaud, XIV, p. 250.

[6] J.-P. Claris de Florian, *Fables de Florian, précédées d'une notice sur sa vie et ses ouvrages (par L.-F. Jauffret), nouvelle édition augmentée de fables inédites* (Paris: Pouthieu, 1825), p. 286.

national patriarch who comforts the dying serf, after he has been told that he himself, his possessions and his children belong to his inflexible masters, the Chapter of Saint-Claude.[1] Voltaire assures him in the poem that the Chapter is certain to follow the king's example, and free their serfs, because 'no one dares to be wicked when the monarch is just'.[2] While Voltaire himself had known too many ecclesiastics to have shared this piece of wishful thinking, the poem and its reception give convincing evidence of the respect which contemporaries accorded Voltaire for his part in the campaign for the abolition of serfdom. Boncerf, who attacked 'feudalism' so trenchantly on utilitarian grounds, and whose writings will be considered in the next chapter, as late as 1791 testified to the influence of Voltaire on his circle, and of how the cause of the serfs of Mont Jura had enabled them to grasp 'feudal law as a whole'.[3]

The strength of Voltaire's campaign against serfdom came from his single-minded appeal to humanitarian feelings. While he did not neglect to criticize serfdom on historical and legal grounds, he disliked arguments that revolved around technicalities. His appeal to humanitarianism and common sense cuts through the historical argument from tradition. 'For thirty or forty thousand years, more or less,' he wrote in *Supplique des serfs de Saint-Claude à M. le Chancelier* (Supplication of the serfs of Saint-Claude) 'martens have eaten our chickens, but we still have permission to destroy them when we catch them'.[4] In the same way he refused to meet the legal defence of serfdom on its own terms. In his short piece on the *Coutume* of Franche-Comté he mocked Dunod's attempts to justify it according to the principles of Roman law. He wrote that the Roman laws on slaves were as relevant to serfdom in France as those which dealt with the Vestal Virgins.[5] Voltaire made no secret that he put humanitarian considerations first. 'In almost all my writings,' he claimed, 'humanity, which should be the first characteristic of a thinking being, will be found.'[6] And again, he wrote, 'without humanity, the virtue which comprises all the

[1] *Ibid.*, p. 293.
[2] *Ibid.*, p. 296.
[3] P.-F. Boncerf, *Les Inconvéniens des droits féodaux* (n.p., 1791), p. ii.
[4] Voltaire, *Oeuvres*, XVIII, p. 606.
[5] *Ibid.*, XXVIII, p. 373.
[6] *Ibid.*, III, p. 379.

virtues, a man would scarcely deserve to be called a philosopher.'[1]

The philosophes undoubtedly showed great ingenuity in conjuring up the spectre of the oppressed serf with which to haunt their society. Materials at hand were not so much inadequate as non-existent. Serfdom in eighteenth-century France was already so much in decline that there were, perhaps, no more than some 140,000 serfs out of a total population of nearly twenty-six million on the eve of the Revolution,[2] while the edict by which serfs on Crown lands were freed in 1779 had affected only a small proportion of the total. Such facts, however, did not deter a leading critic of serfdom, the abbé Clerget, in the title of his main work, from insisting that there were more than a million and a half serfs in France.[3] Publicists took similar liberties in describing the conditions in which serfs lived. Although the most stringent form of serfdom, personal servitude, was practically extinct in France by the eighteenth century, the reader might well get the impression from the publicists that no other type existed. Almost all serfs in fact owed their status to the property which they held under that tenure. A person could free himself from this type of serfdom, *mainmorte réelle*, as it was called, to distinguish it from *mainmorte personnelle*, at any time by simply abandoning the possessions which he held under that tenure.[4] Publicists also misrepresented the facts when they said that any serf could be forceably reclaimed by his former master. The 'right of pursuit' applied only in the few cases of personal servitude. Even so, this right was rarely invoked by the seigneur, and seldom upheld by the courts, especially after a famous ruling by the Parlement of Paris in 1760. The publicists also misled their readers when they said that servile status could be acquired unawares. In reality it could be contracted only by settling in one of the few, and doubtless also notorious, places where *mainmorte réelle* still existed. Many of the harsher aspects of serfdom, which provided the publicists with picturesque copy, had in fact disappeared several centuries earlier.[5]

The smugness of contemporaries, however, goes far to

[1] *Ibid.*, XXII, p. 422.
[2] Marion, *Dictionnaire*, p. 509.
[3] Clerget, *Le Cri de la raison* . . .
[4] Marion, *Dictionnaire*, p. 507.
[5] *Ibid.*, pp. 507–8.

excuse publicists from overstating their case. They even had to contend with those who refused to credit the very existence of serfdom in France. Thus, Née de La Rochelle, in his *Mémoires pour servir à l'histoire du Nivernois et Donziois* of 1747, despite the fact that he was a sub-delegate in Nivernais,[1] which was one of the places where the remaining serfs were most concentrated in the eighteenth century,[2] wrote about serfs in the past tense, and dated their emancipation from a thirteenth-century charter.[3] Similarly, the jurist Lalaure, in his *Traité des servitudes réelles*, was quoted in the *Journal des Sçavans* as saying, 'Among the Romans personal enslavement still existed. . . . But we have no slaves in France, or at least, if there remain some traces, they are found only in the *corvées*, or in the provisions of some *coutumes*.'[4] Lefèvre de Beauvray, a member of the Academy of Châlons-sur-Marne,[5] which did so much to focus public attention on social issues in the 1770s, was certainly himself a man of progressive ideas. Yet, although his views on commerce and inoculation were those of a typical philosophe, he barely mentioned the traces of serfdom in his own day.[6] In 1789 the marquis de Villette could claim in his *Protestation d'un serf du Mont-Jura* that people tried to make believe in the capital that serfdom no longer existed in the provinces.[7] It was one of Voltaire's main aims in his campaign against serfdom to demonstrate to those who denied the existence of serfs in France that 'there are still serfs who work three days each week for the seigneur'.[8] The revelation, as Cahen wrote, that serfdom still existed at the end of the eighteenth century provoked a general feeling of indignation and horror.[9] To make Frenchmen aware of the presence of serfdom in France was, therefore, the first and not the least important step towards securing its abolition.

In order to arouse the sympathies of their contemporaries,

[1] Michaud, XXX, p. 278.

[2] Marion, *Dictionnaire*, p. 508.

[3] J.-B. Née de La Rochelle, *Mémoires pour servir à l'histoire du Nivernois et Donziois, avec des dissertations* (Paris, 1747), pp. 381–8.

[4] *Journal des Sçavans* (1762), p. 501.

[5] Michaud, XXIII, p. 591.

[6] P. Lefèvre de Beauvray, pp. 54 ff., 235 ff. and 492, respectively.

[7] C. M. Villette, *Protestation d'un serf du Mont-Jura* (n.p., 1789), p. 4.

[8] Voltaire, *Oeuvres*, XVIII, pp. 604–5.

[9] L. Cahen, *Condorcet et la Révolution française* (Paris: F. Alcan, 1904), p. 70.

several writers purposefully gave the misleading impression that it was perilously easy for the ordinary Frenchman to contract servile status unawares. The great *Encyclopédie* of Diderot in the article on *Main-Morte*, listed various fictitious ways in which servile status could be contracted. Besides the only real one, that is by residing in a place of servile tenure for a year and a day, the *Encyclopédie* also gave ownership of any servile property, and finally death while in possession of such property,[1] neither of which in itself carried that penalty for the owner or his heirs. Condorcet in his *Vie de Voltaire*, seriously counselled his readers never to live on the notorious *terre* of Saint–Claude, since it was 'stricken by feudal anathema', and 'he would forfeit his goods to the monks'.[2] Voltaire, as a persistent anti-clerical, loved to make the same charge.[3] Under the heading, 'Goods of the Church,' he wrote in his *Dictionnaire Philosophique* for credulous readers:[4]

It has happened sometimes that a French businessman, the father of a family, drawn by his concerns into those barbarous parts, after renting a house there for a year, has died in his homeland in another province of France. His widow and his children have been completely astonished to see their moveables seized by ushers, with executors to sell them in the name of Saint–Claude, and to chase an entire family from its father's house.

In much the same way the abbé Clerget tried to convince his readers that the danger of becoming a serf oneself was no 'puerile fear'.[5] The generalized character of such references needs little comment. Had Condorcet's 'foreigner' or Voltaire's 'French businessman' existed, their names would doubtless be as well known as those of Calas and La Barre. None the less, the stress on the danger which any Frenchman was supposed to run of contracting servile status had the effect of putting all Frenchmen on an equal footing before a barbarous code that was represented as a relic of the feudal regime. It was an obvious, but important, point of humanitarian writers that serfs and vassals were human beings like other people.

---

[1] Diderot (ed.), *Encyclopédie*, IX, p. 878.
[2] Voltaire, *Oeuvres*, I, p. 267.
[3] *Ibid.*, e.g. XV, p. 427, and XVIII, p. 605.
[4] *Ibid.*, XVII, p. 593.
[5] Clerget, *Le Cri de la raison*, pp. 57–8.

The humanitarians tried to arouse the pity of their readers by bringing home to them in graphic detail what it was like to live and die a serf. The day-to-day life of the serf revolved around the *communion*, that is to say his communal existence in patriarchal groups. To inherit property from the head of the family, according to customary law, it was necessary to live in the *hutte paternelle*, and to give proof of full membership of the household by sharing the communal life of the family, right down to use of the same fire and cooking-pot. Even Dunod, who was the foremost defender of serfdom in his *Traités de la mainmorte et des retraits*, admitted that life in the *communion* was 'a rather hard servitude', owing to the way in which it threw close together many people of different ages and temperaments, with nothing in common besides their rival claims to inheritance.[1] Denunciations of these hardships figured prominently in the campaign against serfdom. The abbé Clerget, whose writings will be considered shortly, insisted in one of his vituperative chapter headings that 'the *communion* of serfs is a real tyranny'.[2] He argued that the gathering of all heirs under one roof was disruptive of family life to the point of promoting the murder of close relatives. The fact that property reverted to the seigneur in default of an heir, he saw as an invitation to immorality. In practice it meant that the family had to be sure that an heir was on the way before marriage, and that when a family was childless the wife was turned over 'to the first comers'.[3] The effect of the *communion*, he says, was to turn each house into a kind of stud-farm where individuals multiplied to the seigneur's profit.[4] The principal point in the humanitarian case against serfdom was precisely that it treated serfs more like chattels than human beings.

It was the laws of *reprêt* and *échute* which put serfs legally at the seigneur's mercy. According to these laws, anyone who had absented himself from the *hutte paternelle* was said to have 'broken the *communion*', and thereby to have forfeited his rights to inheritance, even if he later returned. Publicists liked to write as if such cases occurred every day. Boncerf, in the

---

[1] Dunod de Charnage, *Traités de la mainmorte et des retraits* (1760), pp. 134–5.
[2] Clerget, *Le Cri de la raison*, bk 2, chap. 16, p. 159.
[3] *Ibid.*, pp. 166–9.
[4] *Ibid.*, p. 164.

pamphlet which created a real crisis for Turgot his sponsor in 1776,[1] cited from the writings of Voltaire the case of a woman who, after living with her father for eighteen years, was disinherited because she had passed the first night of her marriage away from the *hutte paternelle*.[2] In the same vein Voltaire spoke of the Chapter of Saint-Claude causing infants at the breast to be abandoned, and girls chased from their father's house into the snow.[3] Another injustice, which on the face of it sounds more likely to have caused greater hardship in everyday life concerned the fate of a serf's widow when there were no children. According to a lawyer named Laurent, when there was no marriage-contract in which property was divided on a half-and-half basis, the seigneur could take everything 'down to the ashes in the grate'. Even when a contract did exist, Laurent claimed that the property was divided equally between the seigneur and the widow, including the last pound of lard or cheese. He added that a similar scene had remained continually in his mind, ever since he had witnessed it at the age of ten.[4] These, however, were the sort of practical matters that tended to be overlooked by the publicists in their attacks on serfdom.

Humanitarian writers paid more attention to the laws which governed marriages in the *communion*. As the serf was his lord's property, it was to the lord's advantage that the offspring of all his serfs should also become his property by being born on his land. Hence a restriction had been placed on marriages between the serfs of different overlords. Under the right of *formariage*, a female serf was obliged to obtain permission, which was usually granted on payment of a fine, to marry a serf outside the seigneurie. Although such a marriage 'broke the *communion*', various *coutumes* arranged that a daughter should retain a right to inherit a share of her father's property, provided she came 'to lie the first night' of her marriage in her father's house. In the province of Burgundy, according to one

---

[1] See p. 164 ff.

[2] P.-F. Boncerf, *Les Inconvéniens des droits féodaux. Nouvelle édition, augmentée de fragmens sur l'origine des droits féodaux, et de l'examen de la règle, nulle terre sans seigneur, par M. Francaleu* (London, 1776), p. 5.

[3] Voltaire, *Oeuvres*, XXVIII, p. 370.

[4] Laurent (avocat en Parlement), *Lettre d'un franc-comtois aux députés de sa province* (n.p., n.d.), p. 5.

contemporary writer, even this requirement had been relaxed, so that the girl had only to present herself for a moment at her father's house after the celebration of the marriage. Yet, what the author called a 'not very painful' gesture of submission to the seigneur became for publicists the ultimate human indignity.[1] Voltaire exploited the point with obvious relish. His indignation and ridicule reached a crescendo in a *Mémoire* in which he advocated the complete abolition of serfdom in France. He described how the Chapter of Saint–Claude solemnly despatched judicial letters of inquiry, called *monitoires*, to discover where a girl had lost her virginity.[2] He implied that a system which based itself upon such matters was beneath contempt. It was typical of the humanitarian case that this should provide a central plank in its platform. Chassin's *L'Église et les derniers serfs* provided a useful corrective to the writings of the philosophes. He focused attention on some of the important practical issues which humanitarian writers in general found so less absorbing than their own poignant anecdotes. The population of Mont Jura protested, for instance, that it was hard for a daughter to make good her claims to the property of her dead father, owing to the difficulty of proving that she had passed the first night of her marriage in her father's house. As many years had often elapsed between the marriage of the daughter and the death of her father, the witnesses might have died or disappeared. Even when there were witnesses, the other side might seek pretexts for calling their testimony in question. They added that while the husband could call in a notary to his father-in-law's house to testify to the presence of his wife, and of her declaration of her intent to spend the night there, this cost money, and might be difficult to arrange at the time.[3] Yet, such practical matters did not carry as much weight with publicists as one night's separation, or forced sojourn in the bride's house, of the newly-wed. The very fact that some writers referred to a separation and others to the marriage being consummated at the bride's home, itself argues that they had not taken the trouble to investigate the matter. Whatever the

---

[1] Cited by G. Demante, *Étude historique sur les gens de condition mainmortable en France, au XVIIIe. siècle* (Paris: A. Picard, 1894), p. 101.

[2] Voltaire, *Oeuvres*, XXIX, p. 404.

[3] Chassin, *L'Église et les derniers serfs*, pp. 112–13.

frustrations in the life of the serf, they can hardly have equalled those of some of the publicists who appear to have lived their entire sex-life in their own polemics.

As the above descriptions show, eighteenth-century publicists, with their talent for romanticizing, delighted in giving concrete form to general grievances. They gave French literature almost a new genre, which should, perhaps, be called 'the tearful anecdote'. Voltaire seems to have been the first writer to popularize it. For instance, instead of inveighing against the iniquity of a law of inheritance that gave the seigneur a direct interest in hastening the death of his vassal, he took an example from life, doubtless the life of his imagination. The surgeon Nicod, he related, was refused payment for his services by an indignant Chapter of Saint-Claude. 'Far from paying you,' he was told by their agent, 'the Chapter should punish you. Last year you cured two serfs, whose death would have brought my masters a thousand *écus*.'[1]

A tale of the same provenance served as the nucleus for *Protestation d'un serf du Mont-Jura* by the marquis de Villette. This man, who pursued a life of flamboyant folly with such evident success, is of interest mainly because of his close association with Voltaire. The marquis even claimed Voltaire as his father, which, if true, reflects scant credit on the poet. His only saving grace appears to have been his good sense in selecting a talented ghost-writer for his numerous literary productions. His writings attracted attention, particularly the *cahier* which he wrote for the *bailliage* of Senlis, on account of the bold presentation of the complaints and desires of the inhabitants.[2] In his *Protestation d'un serf du Mont-Jura* the marquis recounted a story about a brave officer, a holder of the Cross of Saint-Louis, who had acquired the status of nobility after forty years' service in the army while none the less remaining a serf of Saint-Claude. On his deathbed the old soldier bequeathed his sword to the nephew who was to follow in his footsteps. However, as Villette related, the sword was the seigneur's property by the law of *échute*. The nephew was accordingly thrust into prison for accepting the sword, but was released after his military superiors had intervened. Only then

---

[1] Voltaire, *Oeuvres*, XXVIII, p. 370.
[2] Michaud, XLIII, pp. 515–16.

did the seigneur, 'ashamed of his cupidity', withdraw his claim.[1]

It was the abbé Clerget, however, who brought 'the tearful anecdote' as near to perfection as the genre allowed. Clerget is one of many interesting eighteenth-century writers concerning whom the scantiest biographical facts are known. Unlike the typical abbé with literary pretensions, he does not appear to have gone the round of fashionable drawing-rooms, but rather to have lived the life of a simple parish priest at Ornans. He had important links with the philosophes, however, through his friend the abbé Baverel, who himself had ties with both Sébastien Mercier and the abbé Raynal.[2] The abbés Clerget and Baverel had collaborated in publishing in 1785 a brief essay, *Coup d'oeil philosophique et politiques sur la main-morte.* Far more outspoken, however, was *Le Cri de la raison,* which appeared under Clerget's name alone in 1788. The book justifies its title; it is a kind of literary brain-storm in which typical eighteenth-century rationalism is engulfed in a tempestuous eloquence. Despite its melodramatic style, *Le Cri de la raison* can still arouse the reader's feelings. It would be surprising if this were not one of the more influential tracts of the time.

One of the best introductions to *Le Cri de la raison* is to read Clerget's account of his first encounter with the laws of *communion* and *reprêt.* While passing through a village, he related, his curiosity was aroused by the sight of armed henchmen around a house. Assuming that a criminal was being arrested, he approached one of the guards only to be told that on the contrary they were waiting for a serf to die, so as to make good the lord's claim to his possessions. The dying serf was prevented from seeing his son and daughter, for fear that he would give them some money, despite the fact that they had 'broken the *communion*'. When the abbé understood the situation, he said that he was so overcome by emotion that he burst into the room where the old man was dying, and interrogated his victim concerning 'the cruel customs of this unhappy province'. The serf told him that his daughter had 'broken the *communion*', through neglecting to observe the formalities, which were prescribed by the law of *reprêt,* and that his son had been driven from his house by the intrigues of a stepmother. The abbé was

---

[1] Villette, *Protestation d'un serf du Mont-Jura,* pp. 16–17.
[2] Balteau, V, p. 985.

so moved that he persuaded the sergeant of the guards to admit the serf's children to his deathbed, although they continued to be kept under close surveillance. Clerget added that, although he left after he had briefly witnessed the dying serf in the embraces of his children, 'the memory of this touching scene has never left my heart'.[1]

These stories had a sort of cumulative effect, which defies analysis along the lines of the other four chapters which deal with the historical, legal, commercial and utilitarian attacks on 'feudalism'. Such stories do not develop a theme, so much as contribute to a change of heart. In this light they may perhaps be considered a lowly part of the Romantic Movement. The rather quaint blend of passionate entreaty and a sort of *littérateur's* social observation seem to point to the awakening of a social conscience. In their use of exaggerated language these writings are part cause and part effect of an emotional atmosphere in which no charge was too absurd to be levied against the hated 'feudal regime' and the serfdom, which they usually associated with it. The word *mainmorte* itself provided publicists with a useful *point de départ* for erecting a mystique of horror around serfdom. They had to look no further than Dunod's notorious treatise to find the ridiculous legend, though reported there only as hearsay, that *mainmorte* was derived from the practice of cutting off the right hand of the dead vassal for his lord.[2] Séguier, the Advocate-General, who was foolish enough in 1786 to tell his contemporaries that French laws had reached the limits of human perfection,[3] was already foolish enough in 1760 to accept the legend as established fact. The right hand of the serf who had died without leaving any possessions to his master, he said, had been cut off in the past *in signum dominii et servitutis*, just as it was customary to give the seigneur the left foot of game that had been hunted on his land.[4] The celebrated *Dictionnaire de Trévoux*, which was compiled by Jesuits who should have known better, and who probably did, solemnly quoted from Laurière's ancient *Glossarium*: 'It is said that a bishop of Liège . . . abolished an

---

[1] Clergot, *Le Cri de la raison*, pp. 162–4n.

[2] Demante, p. 38.

[3] A. Esmein, *Histoire de la procédure criminelle en France* (Paris: Larose et Forcel, 1882), p. 376.

[4] Demante, p. 38.

ancient custom in the area around Liège, which was to cut off the right hand of each deceased peasant, and present it to the seigneur to whom he was enserfed, to show that he would no longer be subject to servitude.'[1] The same reference is also to be found in Diderot's *Encyclopédie*.[2]

These learned derivations were useful ammunition for the critics of serfdom. Thus, it suited Voltaire's purpose to speak as if it were a matter of course that the right hand of the vassal had been cut off by way of compensating the seigneur for what he could have extorted from the live serf.[3] The *Protestation d'un serf du Mont-Jura* also shows how the bogus etymology of mortmain could be used for propagandist purposes. The marquis de Villette wrote:[4]

To what point has the noble feudatory not carried tyranny? I am seized with horror. Not content with despoiling the serf during his lifetime, he had his hand cut off after his death. This hand which had made his fields fertile, which the callouses from work made so venerable fell under the priestly hatchet. O alas! It was nailed up on the door of his strongholds among the heads of animals. And it is from the custom of cutting off the hands of serfs that the etymology of *main-morte* is derived.

A few writers demurred. Perreciot, the antiquarian and royal official who wrote *De l'État civil*, refused to believe that 'this disgusting and bizarre tribute', if it had indeed existed, was ever common.[5] Several legal commentators, such as Claude-Joseph de Ferrière, pointed to mortmain's second meaning, 'hand dead in the sense of unable to bequeath property', and reminded contemporaries that the term *gens de mainmorte* for that reason was applied to the clergy.[6] Yet, although this common use of the expression spoke for itself, the macabre etymology of *mainmorte* exercised an irresistible fascination over some of the publicists.

The other principal legend about feudal times was that of the notorious *droit de seigneur*, which was supposed to have entitled

---

[1] *Dictionnaire universel françois et latin, vulgairement appelé Dictionnaire de Trévoux* . . ., ed. abbé Brillant (Paris, 1771), V, p. 742.

[2] Diderot (ed.), *Encyclopédie*, IX, p. 878.

[3] Voltaire, *Oeuvres*, XV, p. 427.

[4] Villette, *Protestation d'un serf du Mont-Jura*, p. 26.

[5] Perreciot, I, p. 399.

[6] Demante, p. 11.

him to spend the first night of the marriage with his vassal's bride. Barthélemy, who devoted a small book and much loving care to the subject, found that legal writers of the sixteenth century, although aware of the possible existence of *marquette*, as it was also called, were far from dogmatic. He found that Laurière's *Glossarium* had played the chief role in disseminating the legend from the seventeenth century onwards, just as we have already seen that it also helped to attribute a macabre origin to mortmain. In Barthélemy's own words:[1]

from the middle of the seventeenth century up to 1854, Laurière's assertions had been repeated with such naivety, exaggerated so zealously for polemical motives that the existence of the *droit du seigneur* became an historic truth. Many decent people believe in it more than in the existence of God . . . I have known a person who boasted of having exercised this right, for the sake of appearances, when he had scarcely left the arms of his nurse. In this fashion in 1839 he wanted people to believe that the estate of which he bore the name, as a result of a quite recent ennoblement, had formerly possessed High Justice.

If motives for perpetuating the legend could exist in the early nineteenth century, eighteenth-century publicists had still stronger ones for propagating the legend among their readers. Even the great *Encyclopédie*, under the heading, *Prélibation*, which may be translated 'first offering', described it as,[2]

this right which the seigneurs arrogated to themselves before, and during, the time of the Crusades, of sleeping the first night with the newly-married [brides] of their plebeian vassals . . . Bishops and barons assumed this right for themselves on the strength of being high barons; and some exacted payment in the last century from their subjects, for the renunciation of this strange right, which long held sway in almost all the provinces of France and Scotland.

It is interesting to see how the chevalier de Jaucourt, the author of the article, attempted to associate the right with the recent past. The abbé Clerget paraphrased Velly, the author of a standard national history, to the same effect.[3] Voltaire, of course, could not resist a chance of ridiculing the clergy. He

---

[1] A. de Barthélemy, *Le Droit de seigneur* (Paris: Auguste Aubry, 1886), pp. 4–5.
[2] Diderot (ed.), *Encyclopédie*, XIII, p. 287.
[3] Clerget, *Le Cri de la raison*, pp. 32–3.

announced that prelates had only recently changed the right of *cuissage* into a money payment. He added with ironic condescension that they had as much right to it as to the virginity of girls.[1] For a bookseller called Rozet, Voltaire's interpretation was too kind to the clergy. In a work which purported in its title to show how the clergy, both secular and regular, had enriched themselves in France, he tried to show that ordinary curés, as well as their superiors, had enjoyed what was perhaps the most enjoyable of all the feudal rights. He insisted that if the right of *cuissage* itself had been proscribed, it persisted, commuted into a payment in money, which the clergy still received. Even Renauldon, the author of a well-known legal textbook, could write under *Droit de marquettes*: 'I have seen seigneurs who claimed to have this right, but which has been, like many others of this kind, wisely proscribed by the judgments of the Court.'[2] If the eighteenth-century seigneur did not share the favours of his female vassals with their husbands, it was hardly for want of wishful thinking on the part of these writers.

Those today who share their fantasies will be sad to learn, that there appears to be no reliable evidence that the *droit de seigneur* ever existed. The texts that are cited in support of it, as Marion has shown in a learned entry of his *Dictionnaire*, cannot withstand close examination. If the slightest traces of the *droit de seigneur* has survived in 1789, the *cahiers* in which the peasants recorded their grievances in such circumstantial detail, would certainly have mentioned it. Marion speculates that the legend probably originated in lewd threats which the seigneurs used in backing up their feudal and seigniorial demands. Rustic customs of various kinds, which have their counterparts in Fraser's *Golden Bough*, may also, he believes, have become associated with the *droit de seigneur* itself.[3] There is no reason to suppose, however, that the absence of a specific right to lasciviousness cramped the amatory style of the eighteenth-century seigneur.

The ways in which some writers handled topics such as the origins of serfdom and the *droit de seigneur* had affinities with

---

[1] Voltaire, *Oeuvres*, XVIII, p. 300.

[2] Rozet (Libraire), *Véritables origines des biens ecclésiastiques* (Paris: Desenne, 1790), pp. 115–16 and Renauldon, *Traité*, p. 450, respectively.

[3] Marion, *Dictionnaire*, art. *Marquette ou droit de seigneur*, pp. 366–7.

accounts of the 'feudal anarchy', which were considered in chapter II. While it is true that many of the writings quoted there showed their authors to possess a very rudimentary understanding of historical causation and development, there was at least some attempt to convey the spirit of the times. Those who attacked serfdom on humanitarian grounds, however, nearly always had too emotional a relationship with their past for it to be called 'historical'. In fact, their writings were often 'anti-historical' in the sense that, either purposefully or not, they blurred the line between past and present, as they summoned the scandals of the past to reinforce those of the present. This trait emerges most clearly perhaps in one of the abbé Clerget's set-pieces against feudal oppression. It is clear that the abbé staked no claim to historical detachment, as he boasted to his readers that the memory of the incident had made his blood boil in his veins, and his pen fall from his hands. However, he had succeeded in controlling his feelings sufficiently to relate that a certain seigneur at the Parlement of Franche-Comté had claimed the right to impose a *corvée* and a payment in wheat and oats for sixty years in return for waiving the ancient right over his vassals 'to lead them to the hunt and in winter to make them open their bowels, so as to warm his feet in their steaming entrails'. At these words, the abbé relates, the virtuous magistrate who was acting as recorder 'could not hide the torment in his soul', and broke out: 'I do not know, *Monsieur le comte*, how your ancestors have acquired such a strange right, but I do know that it makes your other seigniorial rights very suspect in my eyes.'[1] As the last sentence illustrates, once humanitarian feelings had been aroused they could be turned against any aspect of 'feudalism'; all the horror which was inspired by some past, and often imaginary, act rubbed off, so to speak, on any contemporary usage with which it could be associated. This sort of approach was fairly common in many of the *cahiers* of 1789. Thus, the *tiers* of Avesne in their *cahier* on the subject of serfdom asked for 'the absolute suppression of an odious right, and of all those shameful acts of past servitude, of which the honour of humanity demands that even the memory should be lost'.[2] The *tiers* of Ploermel asked for the abolition

[1] Clerget, *Le Cri de la raison*, pp. 106–7.
[2] Chassin, *L'Église et les derniers serfs*, p. 171.

without delay of 'all indecent, ridiculous, absurd rights, which only serve to recall the former tyranny of the seigneurs and the servitude of the people.'[1] Pamphlets and *cahiers* on the eve of the Revolution inveighed against such *droits bizarres* and customs reminiscent of serfdom, out of all proportion to their nuisance value. An almost fanatical preoccupation with human dignity was very much a feature of eighteenth-century French humanitarians, especially among the less articulate assailants of 'feudalism'.

A sign of the general acceptance of humanitarian principles was the fact that the defenders of serfdom and of other seigniorial privileges felt equally obliged to make the same appeal. The outstanding example was Dunod, the author of a much-cited treatise on serfdom. Dunod spoke with some authority, as he was a former *avocat* at the Parlement of Franche-Comté, as well as being a Regius professor at the University of Besançon.[2] Even as early as 1733, when the first edition of his *Traité de la mainmorte et des retraits* appeared, Dunod sometimes cloaked what was essentially a legal argument in humanitarian language. Thus, he stressed that the harsher characteristics of serfdom had been considerably eroded by exposure to the general climate of opinion in France and to the interventions of the Crown. The seigneur, in his view, had already done a great service to his serfs by reducing their obligations to their existing proportions. Serfs in Burgundy, he claimed, were actually more prosperous than peasants who had their freedom. He had little difficulty in reaching the conclusion that 'the condition of serfdom is, therefore, not as harsh as it appears, and as it is commonly reputed. That is why, he concluded, 'I do not believe that all that the laws have established in favour of liberty should be applied indiscriminately.'[3] The whole tone of the work was indeed that of a Regius professor.

The pontifications of the professor were consecrated by the Benedictine monk, Dom. Grappin, in an essay that won a prize from the Academy of Besançon in 1778. He wrote that modern philosophers 'see heavy chains where I perceive only simple

---

[1] Mavidal and Laurent, V, p. 379.

[2] F.-I. Dunod de Charnage, *Traités de la mainmorte et des retraits* (1760), frontispiece.

[3] Dunod de Charnage, *Traités de la mainmorte et des retraits* (Dijon: de Fay, 1733), pp. 10–11.

ties undertaken voluntarily, and which can be abandoned in the same way'.[1] Like Dunod, he saw serfdom as 'a source of riches', and insisted that there was nothing odious about a system which was in fact more 'gentle and humane' than ever before.[2] In conclusion he exhorted his readers 'not to depict in the colours of barbarism and slavery what in origin was often a mark of humanity'.[3]

The reader may well feel that Dom. Grappin's remarks are hardly worthy of that urbane religious order that is equally renowned for its liqueurs and its historians. Even if his *Discours* has some social overtones, however, he wrote primarily as an antiquarian, in which capacity he was held in high esteem in the eighteenth century. When he did turn consciously to social problems, it was to accede to the request of the Keeper of the Seals, who had asked him to write pamphlets that would prepare the province to accept certain reforms which the government favoured. The man who was supposedly a diehard reactionary welcomed the Revolution, as a means of abolishing abuses in society.[4]

The Remonstrances of the Parlement of Franche-Comté in answer to the edict of 1779, which freed serfs on Crown lands, and which rather optimistically invited landowners to follow suit, is interesting as it shows how a body that represented the interests of landowners could defend serfdom almost entirely in humanitarian terms. The *parlementaires* justified serfdom in their long Remonstrance of 1780, as follows: 'a seigneur grants to a poor wretch who has nothing, land with the livestock and implements necessary for tilling, at the cost of cultivating it, and for as long as he and his family wish to farm it. That surely does not constitute an idea that revolts humanity?' They went on to boast that the agreement between the seigneur and the serf 'compromises personal freedom so little, that it is the only contract which allows the debtor even the freedom to break it at will'. 'It is true,' they admitted, 'that serfdom in particular instances can present a moving spectacle of children despoiled of their

---

[1] P.-P. Grappin, *Quelle est l'origine des droits de main-morte dans les provinces qui ont composé le premier royaume de Bourgogne* (Besançon: J. M. Cuché, 1779), p. iii.

[2] *Ibid.*, p. iv.

[3] *Ibid.*, p. 71.

[4] Michaud, XVII, pp. 369–70.

father's property, and give rise to scenes which stir humanity. Such cases should be very rare, however, and could always have been averted, by observing the *communion* or renouncing ownership.' They added, rather inconsequentially, that the serfdom, to the supposed advantages of which they had devoted most of the *remontrance*, was already on the wane, and that it was only a matter of time before a general emancipation of the serfs took place.[1]

The humanitarian defence of feudal and seigniorial rights was largely paternalistic in spirit. There was nothing new in the idea of the seigneur watching over the welfare of his vassals. Under Louis XIV, in his *Les Soupirs de la France esclave*, the author, who is thought to have been Michel Le Vassor, a close friend of Bayle, looked back nostalgically to the time of the cardinals when 'the powerful gentleman of standing protected his parish, and particularly his tenants from the *taille*, and when the strong seigneur secured his vassals from oppression'.[2] Yet, with feudal and seigniorial rights coming under at least literary attack, there was naturally a tendency for eulogies of feudalism to wax more eloquent. The paternalist argument is seen at its most fulsome in Renauldon's *Treatise*, which has already been mentioned:[3]

As one travels through the provinces [he wrote] out of a hundred estates where seigneurs live, perhaps one or two can be found where they tyrannize their subjects; all the rest share patiently the poverty of those over whom they exercise justice; they live with them, give their debtors time in which to pay; they cancel debts, procure them every facility to pay. They mitigate, they temper, the prosecutions which are sometimes too rigorous, of farmers, bailiffs and agents.

Roussel, in his *Instructions pour les seigneurs et leurs gens d'affaires*, which was reviewed in the journal which succeeded the *Mémoires de Trévoux* after the expulsion of the Jesuits, wrote a glowing testimonial for the benevolent seigneur: 'If his vassals groan under the weight of public misfortunes, he sacrifices a part of his income to succour them; I see him loved,

[1] F. Prost, *Les Remontrances du Parlement de Franche-Comté au XVIIIe. siècle* (Lyons: Boscfrères, M. &. L. Riou, 1936), pp. 171–3.
[2] M. Le Vassor, *Les Soupirs de la France esclave, qui aspire après la liberté* (Amsterdam, 1689–90), p. 21.
[3] Renauldon, *Traité historique et pratique des droits seigneuriaux*, p. v.

cherished and respected.' In fairness to the Jesuits it should be mentioned, however, that Roussel was taken to task in the review for his indulgent sketch of this class, which, it was pointed out, contained swindlers as well as saints.[1]

How traditional paternalism could be presented in the guise of a fashionable humanitarianism is shown well in a minor and very characteristic work of the times, de Sapt's *Le Bon seigneur, un conte moral*, with which he prefaced his longer work, *L'Ami du prince et de la patrie, ou le bon citoyen*. The tale opens with a description of a meeting between a neighbouring and self-indulgent seigneur and one of the Good Seigneur's vassals, who was engaged in shedding tears of joy — doubtless a frequent occurrence on that idyllic *terre* — because the Good Seigneur had just intervened to save his son from being conscripted into the militia.[2] When the neighbouring seigneur was unwise enough to volunteer the comment, 'I see you like your seigneur', the peasant unleashed a panegyric which started: 'What! Who would not love him! He is so good! so gentle! so beneficent! He looks on us as his children. Oh! truly, he is indeed the best, the most tender, the most attentive of all fathers. His good offices have banished domestic quarrels which brought sorrow to our families . . . he shares our losses.' And when asked how his seigneur managed to meet all the expenses which these kind offices entailed, the peasant replied simply, 'humanity procures him resources'.[3] His listener, naturally, had no alternative but to be converted by this eloquent tiller of the soil.[4]

Meanwhile, news of the Good Seigneur so intrigued a charming seductress at the Court that she decided to pay him a visit. As befitted a *conte moral*, it was the lady who was captivated. Her elevating conversations with the Good Seigneur soon showed her the error of her ways.[5] The kindly hospitality of a peasant who expressed his gratitude to the Good Seigneur was enough to make 'tears of tenderness flow from her eyes'.[6] From that moment onwards it seems that the Good Seigneur was

---

[1] See p. 65

[2] Abbé de Sapt, *L'Ami du prince et de la patrie, ou le bon citoyen* (Paris: J.-P. Costard, 1769), pp. xiii–xiv.

[3] *Ibid.*, pp. xiv–xv.

[4] *Ibid.*, pp. xv ff.

[5] *Ibid.*, pp. xxvii ff.

[6] *Ibid.*, pp. xxxvi–vii.

hardly ever out of her thoughts, or tears out of her eyes. A lesser writer than de Sapt would have married off the two principal characters so that they could live tearfully ever afterwards. The author, however, cleverly rounded off the story with a kind of conversion in reverse. After the death of the Good Seigneur, the lady intervened to bring his erring son back to his father's ways. The reader's credulity might have been strained if the result had been achieved by another series of elevating conversations. Instead, in more convincing fashion, using her own daughter as the bait, 'the affectionate, ever attentive mother seized the opportune moment' to establish, by a double coup, conjugal bliss and philanthropic landowning.[1] In this way de Sapt ensured that the virtue of the Good Seigneur would be rewarded not in the Christian's hereafter, but in the humanitarian's here and now.

It goes without saying that it was argued from the paternalist standpoint that the abolition of feudal dues was against the interests of the vassals themselves. A lawyer called Villemonney, in the year that 'feudalism' was declared abolished by the National Assembly, warned that if the vassals were freed from feudal dues the seigneur would lose all interest in their welfare. 'He will coldly abandon,' Villemonney wrote, 'his former vassals and subjects put at the mercy of the ravages of the weather, of dishonesty and of the myrmidons of the law.'[2] Linguet mischievously gave the argument a further twist. He said that the slave, and so by inference the serf, was better off than the impoverished but technically 'free' labourer; the master of the former at least realized that to endanger his slave's health was to put his own property at risk.[3]

The practical effects of the growth of humanitarian feeling must be largely conjectural. The propaganda which doubtless should have scorched the souls of brutish landlords may well have been read largely by those who either did not own feudal and seigniorial rights, or for whom they represented only a small proportion of their total revenue, as was true in various parts of France.[4] Even if the seigneurs, under the influence of humani-

---

[1] *Ibid.*, p. xlvii.

[2] Villemonney (avocat en Parlement), *Considérations sur la destruction du régime féodal, avec un projet de nouvelle législation censière* (Paris: Laurens, 1789), p. 20.

[3] S. N. H. Linguet, *Théorie des loix civiles*, II, p. 465.

[4] A. Cobban, *Social Interpretation of the French Revolution*, p. 33.

tarian writings, were less exacting in their demands upon their vassals than in the past, there is good documentary evidence to show that, at least in some areas, in the latter half of the century feudal and seigniorial privileges tended to be administered more efficiently, and in that sense more harshly, than in the past.[1] Besides, humanitarian writings were aimed almost exclusively against serfdom. Yet the life of many nominally 'free' peasants can hardly have been much more enviable than that of the small and dwindling number of serfs. It was, perhaps, just because there were so few serfs that the institution was attacked so strongly; the abolition of serfdom throughout France would affect few landowners, and a satisfying proportion of these were ecclesiastics. A reader of Voltaire, for instance, might be excused if he got the impression that the poet wrote as much against the monks of Saint-Claude, as for their serfs in Mont Jura. In many ways an attack on serfdom was an ideal exercise for publicists who were seldom social radicals. They could hope to lead a majority of Frenchmen against a small vested interest, and by concentrating their propaganda against the ecclesiastical owners of serfs they could count on sweeping into their camp all those who hated the clerical establishment.

Any reform which required a change in the legal status of a whole class necessitated the active intervention of the royal government. For this reason it is worth examining the edict by which serfs on Crown land were emancipated in 1779 in the light of humanitarian writings. It is clear that these alone were not responsible for the improvements in the serfs' condition which preceded the edict. There had been some important legal judgments in favour of the serfs long before the publicists took up their cause. Dénisart, whose *Collection de décisions nouvelles* became a recognized work of reference on its appearance in the 1750s,[2] recorded that the Crown intervened at least twice to protect the interests of serfs against the rulings of their masters in the local parlements. In 1720 when Pierre Clement, a former serf, had died in Rome, the Parlement of Besançon had granted his lord the right to succeed to his property, only to have their decision quashed by a royal *arrêt*. In the case of Luiset in 1729 the Council of State had likewise rescinded the permission which

[1] See p. 62.
[2] Balteau, X, p. 1055.

the same parlement gave to a seigneur of Savoy to seize the goods of a serf who had absconded from his seigneurie. The 'right of pursuit', it was declared severely in the *arrêt*, had 'pernicious effects on the tranquillity of the people'.[1] Another decision of 1760, this time by the Parlement of Paris, in which it had dismissed the claim of a seigneur to the possessions of a serf who had died in Paris, 'had delivered a severe blow to "the right of pursuit" '.[2] There seemed to be much support for Dunod's contention, in the 1760 edition of his treatise on serfdom, that there had been a general erosion in practice of the harsher aspects of serfdom: 'We see in short that the prevailing attitude in the nation is to weaken serfdom, even to banish it from the kingdom, and that in the provinces where it has been preserved, it has been mitigated by the statutory decisions of the *arrêts*, and through the reform of the *coutumes*.'[3]

The publicists, however, contributed to the change of outlook that welcomed, even if it did not bring about, the edict which abolished serfdom on the royal domain. Some of these writings express surprise that serfdom continued to exist even in their own day. For instance, in a highly critical review of Dom. Grappin's eulogy of serfdom, the *Journal Encyclopédique* asked: 'How does France, this enlightened nation, for whom humanity has become the prevailing slogan, still see unfeelingly a multitude of degraded men, whose plight should touch sensitive hearts more than the very slavery of the Romans?'[4] As for the influence of the philosophes in securing the promulgation of the edict, it does at least appear to be closely modelled on Voltaire's *Requête au roi.*[5]

If the edict of 1779 came in answer to humanitarian demands, it was an anticlimax. Apart from the general abolition of 'the right of pursuit', which had largely fallen into disuse anyway, the edict applied only to serfs on Crown lands. The royal government advertised its impotence when it proclaimed in the edict that 'We would have wished to abolish these vestiges of a rigorous feudalism, without exception; but our finances not

---

[1] J.-B. Dénisart, *Collection de décisions nouvelles et de notions relatives à la jurisprudence actuelle* 6th ed. (Paris: Desaint, 1768), II, p. 109.

[2] Marion, *Dictionnaire*, pp. 507–8.

[3] Dunod de Charnage, *Traités de la mainmorte et des retraits* (1760), p. 15.

[4] *Journal Encyclopédique*, vol. iv, pt iii for 1779, p. 449.

[5] Chassin, *L'Église et les derniers serfs*, pp. 71–2.

permitting us to repurchase this right from the hands of the seigneurs; and restrained by the respect that we will always have for the laws of property', the king announced that he did no more than hope that others would follow the royal example, while removing legal formalities from their path.[1] It is true that both Clerget in *Le Cri de la raison* and Necker (who, of course, as the author of the edict was an interested party), in his *Compte rendu au Roi* of 1781, publicized the names of seigneurs whom they claimed had followed the king's example by freeing their serfs.[2]

The edict, however, gave much encouragement to the publicists. The complete abolition of serfdom now appeared to them only a matter of time. Boncerf, whose *Les Inconvéniens des droits féodaux* had partly provoked the political crisis of 1776, wrote shortly before the Revolution that although it was sad to be still pleading the cause of more than 300,000 serfs, the day was at hand when France would have only free citizens.[3] Hervé, despite the fact that he was engaged in commentating on the other intricacies of feudal law right into the Revolution, could write in 1785 that 'It is hardly useful to write about serfdom. Soon only the memory of this hateful servitude will remain in France.'[4] For Clicquot de Blervache, the author of a work on the problems of rural poverty, the king's edict itself was immaterial. In his opinion, 'example and custom had happily preceded the edict of Louis XVI. The effect had been carried out; he had only to confirm it.' He complained that without a second edict to abolish *mainmorte réelle* the gains of the first would be illusory.[5] *L'Esprit des Journaux* also damned the edict with faint praise. In a review of Prost de Royer's *Dictionnaire*, the author was quoted as saying that the edict was remarkable less for its effects than for giving expression to the sovereign's wishes. 'When a strong monarch has expressed himself thus,' he was reported as saying, 'if he is not

[1] F. A. Isambert, and others, *Recueil général des anciennes lois françaises* (Paris: Et. Imbert, 1822–8), XXVI, pp. 139–40.

[2] F. V. A. Aulard, *La Révolution française et le régime féodal* (Paris: F. Alcan 1919), pp. 18 ff. See also Hervé, I, p. 162.

[3] P.-F. Boncerf, *La Plus importante et la plus pressante affaire, ou la nécessité et les moyens de restaurer l'agriculture et le commerce* (n.p., n.d.), pp. 32–3.

[4] Hervé, I, p. 162.

[5] Clicquot de Blervache, p. 13.

understood, it is very necessary for him to finish the work.'[1] Later, in the same article, the periodical seemed to imply that the king's edict was only part of a general movement that he himself was powerless to resist. 'The human spirit,' it reported, 'goes straight towards happiness and liberty. This great revolution, which has been slow and hidden for two centuries is today perceptible and completely open. Woe to the great who delay it! Their power will collapse upon themselves. Woe to the sovereign who may be incapable of following the great examples which instruct him!'[2] Thus, while the edict on the one hand could arouse the opposition of conservatives, like the *parlementaires* of Franche-Comté, as an infringement of property rights,[3] on the other hand it was criticized for not going far enough. Necker, who had been the chief minister when the edict was promulgated, was reproved for failing to carry on his work. The marquis de Villette, whose *Protestation d'un serf du Mont-Jura* has already been discussed, published an open letter to Necker soon after the assembly of the Estates General in May 1789. Villette in the pamphlet claimed archly to have been embarrassed when he had been asked as chairman of one of the political clubs: 'Why this great minister, had not deigned to throw a single glance on the poor serfs whose civil status is the disgrace of French legislation.' Necker was reminded that in his *Compte rendu au Roi* of 1781 he himself had drawn attention to the fact that half the provinces protested against the continuation of 'these remnants of barbarism'. Villette claimed that 'in all the *cahiers* of the nobility, who cling so tightly to what it calls its *prérogatives*, there is not a single one which says expressly that it still prizes its serfs'. Accordingly, Necker was exhorted to delay no longer in completing the emancipation of the serfs and thereby add 'this palm', to his 'civic crown'.[4]

The effects of humanitarian writings with their emotional appeal is hard to assess. In some ways it appears to have been a showy failure. It was too much the single-handed creation of

[1] *L'Esprit des Journaux, François et Étrangers* (Paris and Liège, 1772–1818), XII (December 1784), pp. 129–30.

[2] *Ibid.*, p. 135.

[3] Prost, p. 169.

[4] C. M. Villette, *Lettre de M. de Villette à M. Necker* (n.p., 17 May 1789), pp. 1–3.

Voltaire and his immediate circle to be a spontaneous movement. By concentrating on serfdom they achieved some success, but at the cost of limiting humanitarian criticism to a single aspect of 'feudalism'. There is no denying that the life of the serf was a hard one. Yet starving peasants that were freedmen were also far from unknown in eighteenth-century France. The *cahiers* of the peasants show that they had plenty to complain about. On the face of it, it seems likely that the *banalités*, which were so often denounced in the *cahiers* of 1789, caused as much hardship as serfdom itself. The squalor and penury of peasant daily life, however, lacked the romantic appeal of serfs tied to the soil and often at the tender mercy of the clergy. In general, the serf is a stereotype, and there are few instances of informed social observation. This fact is all the more surprising as there is evidence elsewhere of a keen interest in the occupations of the poor, at least in their technical aspects. The most obvious examples are the famous plates in the *Encyclopédie*, and the beautifully produced *Description des arts et métiers* which appeared in innumerable folio volumes under the aegis of the Royal Academy of Sciences.[1] The same preoccupation with manufacturing techniques is also reflected in the contents of some of the eighteenth-century periodicals. For instance, the *Mémoires de Trévoux* of January 1768, out of a total of one hundred and ninety pages, devoted eight to a review of Garsault's *L'Art du perruquier*, and a further fourteen to Malouin's *Description de détails des arts du meunier, du vermicelier et du boulanger; avec une histoire abrégée de la boulangerie et du dictionnaire des arts*, which gives an overall total of more than a tenth of the whole number.[2] Yet an interest in technology does not seem to have been accompanied very often by concern for those who plied the trades in question. As the philosophes were essentially an urban, not to say a Parisian group, they tended to show much less interest in agriculture than in trade. With the exception of some of the physiocrats, whose ideas will be considered in the next chapter, there were hardly any publicists who had a first-hand knowledge of the lives of the peasants.

[1] Académie Royale des Sciences, *Description des arts et métiers, faites ou approuvées par Messieurs de l'Académie Royale des Sciences* (Paris: Desaint et Saillant, 1761–88).

[2] *Journal des Sciences et des Beaux-Arts par l'abbé Aubert*, January 1768, pp. 30–8 and 39–52, respectively.

As long as social criticism in the eighteenth century was, in Lichtemberger's words, 'not in the order of facts, but in that of speculation',[1] much humanitarian writing was inevitably a form of literary escapism. None the less, there are signs in the late eighteenth century of the growth of a social conscience. The rapid growth of humanitarian writings from the late 1760s was itself symptomatic of the deep disturbance and swift realignment of ideas that transformed French thought in the eighteenth century.

---

[1] A. Lichtemberger, *Le Socialisme au XVIIIe. siècle* (Paris: F. Alcan, 1895), p. 25.

VI

The Inutility of 'Feudalism'

Those who questioned the usefulness of 'feudalism' struck a blow where it was least expected. Feudal dues and privileges had long been seen as rights that needed no justification beyond the laws and immemorial usage. When the physiocrats and other economists argued that these 'rights' did not benefit their owners, there seemed a chance that what an appeal to conscience could never achieve would soon be done through the promptings of self-interest. If enough holders of these privileges had been persuaded that they were unprofitable, the Crown might have been able to secure their abolition. The success of the 'utilitarians' might then have depended on their ability to convert both the privileged and the government to their ideas.

It is hard, as in the case of the growth of humanitarian feeling, to trace the shift in outlook which eventually brought forth a school of utilitarian writers. Recognizable forerunners of the French utilitarians date from at least the end of the seventeenth century. So much advice from this quarter had rained down upon the unfortunate government that in 1716 a special committee was established to consider it. The king, it was stated in the royal edict, had been informed 'that several people zealous for the public good daily presented memoranda, propositions and advice' on such matters as 'ways of reducing expenditure and promoting trade'.[1] The very phrase, 'zealous for the public good' was a favourite boast of later utilitarians. The writing of memoranda was equally the dismal hallmark of the utilitarian, before it later became the hobby of the crank.

[1] *Arrest du Conseil d'Estat du Roy*, 25 April 1716, *Archives Nationales*, ref: AD XI 9.

If the committee was established by the government in the hope of killing the early utilitarians with kindness, it did not succeed. By 1757 a writer in the periodical of the *Encyclopédistes* could say: 'There is no writer who does not believe that he has a duty to enlighten the government on some point of administration.'[1] At about the same time the prevalence of words like *utile* and *bonheur* showed how fashionable utilitarianism had become. 'In the first half of the eighteenth century,' writes an intellectual historian of world renown, 'the rhetoric of natural law had still been prevalent: in the second half it was largely supplanted by utilitarianism.'[2] Evidence of the progress of these ideas in intellectual circles with even a pronounced conservative bent can be found in the very essay titles of the provincial academies. From about the late seventies, typically 'utilitarian' preoccupations, such as mendicity, education, penal reform and the improvement of agriculture were represented in the subjects set for their prizes. *Utile* and its derivatives figured frequently in the titles of these academic discourses. For instance, in 1777 the Academy of Châlons-sur-Marne asked: 'What are the means for eliminating mendicity, while making beggars useful to the State, but without causing them unhappiness?'[3] The Royal Academy of Angers in similar vein asked: 'What are the most suitable and least costly means of providing care in the provinces for foundlings, and of giving them the education most useful to the State?'[4] These and other similar titles show the utilitarian preoccupation with a transformation of society that was to be wrought, above all, at the least possible expense. Utility was so widely accepted by the publicists as a criterion for social reform that Boncerf, one of the foremost critics of feudal and seigniorial rights, in 1776 could describe it as 'the only accurate measure of things'.[5] 'Social utility is a higher and binding principle,' wrote Sagnac, 'the legitimacy of which almost all the thinkers of the century recognize.'[6]

[1] *Journal Encyclopédique*, vol. VII pt 1 for 1757, p. 45.

[2] Cited by A. M. Wilson, 'Why did the political theory of the Encyclopedists not prevail?', *French Historical Studies*, I (1960), p. 289.

[3] Delandine, I, no. 523.

[4] *Ibid.*, no. 380.

[5] P.-F. Boncerf, *Les Inconvéniens des droits féodaux* (1776), p. 21.

[6] P. Sagnac, *La Législation civile de la Révolution française, 1789–1804* (Paris: Hachette, 1898), p. 23.

The abbé de Saint-Pierre seems to have been the first French writer to apply ideas of utility to feudalism as a system of government. The abbé, who held out hope for introducing perpetual peace in Europe, and even of making peers and dukes useful, clearly viewed feudalism with a less indulgent eye:[1]

Through experience we have become disgusted with this kind of service [he wrote concerning the holding of land in return for military service], since we have seen that a disciplined militia . . . are worth incomparably more than the troops of the *ban* and *arrière ban*, that is to say of those who owed their services because of their fiefs . . . The King has fewer troops, but they are better and can be used throughout the year. This type of government [he added] is very harmful to the civil government today in peace-time.

Many other writers joined Saint-Pierre in maintaining that feudalism, even in its heyday, had served no useful purpose. D'Argenson admitted in his *Considérations sur le gouvernement ancien et présent de la France* that feudalism had provided an army for nothing, but one that was ill-disciplined, arrived late and left early.[2] Voltaire also wrote in *Essai sur les moeurs*, that if the feudal lords had served the state for twenty-five or forty days, they had torn the country apart for the remainder of the year.[3]

The most contemptuous of all the terms that was applied to feudalism was probably the *inconvenient* of Saint-Pierre. One of the *observations* in his *Ouvrajes de politiques* is headed, *inconvénient de l'institution des fiefs, moyens d'y remedier.*[4] Considering the social prestige which possession of a fief still brought its owner, in using the noun, *inconvénient,* the loquacious abbé seems to have stumbled for once upon the *mot juste* for expressing his contempt. Although Saint-Pierre, as befitted one of the first utilitarians, was more inclined to use *utile* and its derivatives, *inconvénient* became popular with many writers who voiced similar criticisms of feudalism. The marquis d'Argenson, in a famous passage that has been quoted already,[5] denounced the inconveniences of feudal government as endless; Boncerf,

---

[1] Saint-Pierre, *Ouvrajes*, VII, pp. 90–1.
[2] Argenson, pp. 133–4.
[3] Voltaire, *Oeuvres*, XI, p. 348.
[4] Saint-Pierre, *Ouvrajes*, VII, p. 88.
[5] See p. 43.

whose pamphlet in 1776 did much to incite the wrath of the Paris *parlementaires,* called it *Les Inconvéniens des droits féodaux;* the full title of Letrosne's essay on feudalism was, *Dissertation sur la féodalité dans laquelle on discute, son état actuel, ses inconvéniens, et les moyens de la supprimer;*[1] the subtitle of book III of the abbé Clerget's *Le Cri de la raison* read, *Des Inconvéniens de la main-morte,*[2] while Perreciot claimed that the inconveniences of feudalism had been described in detail throughout the first seven books of his work.[3]

Those who criticized feudal and seigniorial rights on grounds of practicality come from two distinct, if inter-related, groups. First, there were the *agronomes* whose interests were confined to farming itself. Second, there were the physiocrats who wished society to be reordered to meet the needs of agricultural production. Although a physiocrat, such as the marquis de Mirabeau, who claimed to see the whole of philosophy in a grain of wheat, could also be concerned to improve the quality of real grains of wheat, the two interests did not necessarily go together.

The *agronomes,* after interest in husbandry had been in relative eclipse for fifty years, only began to emerge in the 1750s, and most of their works appeared in the following two decades. Although farming in France undoubtedly suffered from the existence of feudal and seigniorial rights, explicit references to them are rarely found in the writings of the *agronomes.* Experts on ploughs, clover and grasses seem to have been reluctant to jeopardize their professional reputations by indulging in political and social comment. This tendency towards specialization on their part may have been reinforced by the fact that in the first half of the century agrarian research and experiment in France had been confined to a few royal and private gardens, above all to the *Jardin du Roi,* which appeared as so many islands of experimentation in a sea of indifference.[4] Whatever the precise reason, it is significant that the marquis de Costa, a man of enlightened views,[5] who claimed member-

[1] Letrosne, *De l'Aministration provinciale* (1788), II, p. 438.

[2] Clerget, *Le Cri de la raison,* p. 195.

[3] Perreciot, II, p. 197.

[4] A. J. Bourde, *The Influence of England on the French agronomes, 1750–1789* (Cambridge University Press, 1953), pp. 9–10.

[5] M. Bruchet, *L'Abolition des droits seigneuriaux en Savoie, 1761–1793* (Annecy: Hérisson, 1908), p. xl.

ship of the famous Economic Society of Berne,[1] appears to make no mention in his *Essay on the improvement of agriculture* of feudal and seigniorial rights. Jean Bertrand, it is true, in a similar work, which was crowned by the same Economic Society,[2] referred to 'feudal obstacles' to farming, although without attempting to define them.[3] Perhaps the attitude of the *agronomes* to feudal and seigniorial rights was expressed best by Fresnais de Beaumont. This writer is notable for his proposal to raise farmers to the nobility as a way of improving the social prestige of their calling.[4] He occupied among the *agronomes* a position that, although far less prominent, was similar to that of the abbé Coyer among writers on trade.[5] Yet his criticism of feudal and seigniorial rights was very oblique. He said little, except that they ought not to be included in the value of the land, 'because this part of the revenue does not seem susceptible of improvement, at least in a way that is exactly useful to the public'.[6] However, even those *agronomes* who claimed to treat the political dimensions of their subject were not much more explicit about the harm done to agriculture by feudal and seigniorial rights. For instance, Girard's *Traité des usemens ruraux de Basse-Bretagne, où l'on parle de tout ce qui peut favoriser les progrès de l'agriculture,* is far less comprehensive than its title suggests. Another broken promise appeared in the preface where he claimed: 'This work is less a juridical treatise than a political essay on ways to increase the produce from the land.'[7] In fact, the self-styled 'volunteer deputy for the small-holder',[8] limited himself almost exclusively to the discussion of a different topic, the landlord's power to dispossess his tenants, which was, admittedly, a serious

---

[1] J.-H. Costa de Beauregard, *Essai sur l'amélioration de l'agriculture dans le pays monteux, et en particulieur dans la Savoye* (Chambéry: F. Gorrin, 1774), frontispiece.

[2] Michaud, IV, p. 184.

[3] J. Bertrand, 'Essai sur l'esprit de la législation, pour encourager l'agriculture et favoriser relativement à cet objet essentiel, la population, les manufactures, et le commerce', *Mémoires et observations recueillies par la Société Oeconomique de Berne, Année 1765*, pt 2 (Berne, 1765), p. 53.

[4] Bourde, p. 195 n. 5.

[5] *Ibid.*, p. 202.

[6] Fresnais de Beaumont, *La Noblesse cultivatrice, ou moyens d'élever en France la culture . . . au plus haut dégré de perfection* (Paris: B. Morin, 1778), p. 23.

[7] G.-J. Girard, *Traité des usemens ruraux de Basse-Brétagne, où l'on parle de tout ce qui peut favoriser les progrès de l'agriculture* (Quimper: M. Blot, 1774), p. xviii.

[8] *Ibid.*, p. aii.

grievance in Brittany. The *agronome* who came closest to making a general assessment of the effects on agriculture of feudal and seigniorial rights appears to be Ange Goudar. He was a prolific writer who later became a celebrity at the court in Naples, thanks to the effects of his wife's charms on King Ferdinand IV.[1] Even before these charms had begun to work on Goudar himself, he produced a treatise on agriculture that was both original and well-informed. *Les Intérêts de la France mal entendus, dans les branches de l'agriculture . . .*, according to Diderot, was a successful publication,[2] while it received high praise, for what it was worth, in Grimm's *Correspondance Littéraire*.[3] Goudar claimed that seigniorial rights reduced agricultural yield, although he excused himself from dealing with the matter at length on the grounds that the subject would have filled a separate treatise. However, despite lack of space he felt impelled to single out for special condemnation the right of *lods et ventes*. He held this seigniorial tax on the sale of property responsible for preventing land from passing into abler hands. He also considered that the holder of the property was deterred from undertaking improvements, as he knew that by the right of *lods et ventes* much of the benefit would later accrue to the seigneur. In France, through the existence of seigniorial rights and overlordship, he said, 'individuals are only the tenants of their own property; that fact throws discouragement everywhere'.[4] The rights of overlordship, in his words, 'today form a labyrinth for which our government has lost the thread'.[5] He saw no remedy short of resuscitating France's draconian *Chambres Ardentes* to suppress seigniorial dues that were levied improperly, and to lighten those which were lawful.[6] These remarks seem to represent the furthest limit to which an *agronome* pursued the political implications of his views on agriculture.

The reluctance of the *agronomes* to theorize about the social

[1] Michaud, XVII, p. 225.

[2] G. Weulersse, *Le Mouvement physiocratique en France, de 1756 à 1770* (Paris: F. Alcan, 1910), I, p. 52 n. 3.

[3] *Correspondance Littéraire*, III, pp. 207–8.

[4] A. Goudar, *Les Intérêts de la France mal entendus, dans les branches de l'agriculture, de la population, des finances, du commerce, de la marine et de l'industrie, par un citoyen* (Amsterdam: J. Coeur, 1756), I, pp. 55–6.

[5] *Ibid.*, p. 194.

[6] *Ibid.*, p. 196.

implications of their subject was more than offset by the readiness of the physiocrats and their supporters to do it for them. The clannish behaviour and moralizing tone of their writings earned for them from their contemporaries the sardonic title of 'the sect'. The view that they formed a recognizable 'movement', at least in their hey-day, has been confirmed by Georges Weulersse, the chief modern interpreter of the physiocrats in the title of his principal work about them.[1] Physiocratic ideas were so widespread that few writers on the economy and administration managed to escape their influence altogether. Indeed, the physiocrats had such a monopoly of economic theorizing that they were often referred to simply as 'the economists'.

The physiocrats and their disciples objected to feudal and seigniorial privileges principally on the grounds that they interfered with the rights of the holders of private property. It was their firm conviction that private property was a normal pre-condition for the existence of every society.[2] The government justified its existence, therefore, solely as an agent for the protection of property. In every other respect society was considered to be self-sufficient; the impetus for all activity within society was to be provided by the acquisitive instincts of the individual property-holders. If the physiocrats had simply been extollers of property rights, however, their voices would have been drowned by the rest of the chorus. In almost any age those who possess property have an instinctive reverence for it, even before the priest and the philosopher have added the seal of their approval. The physiocrats differed from their contemporaries in that they invested property itself with a new meaning. For others, property was equally a 'portmanteau' word that could cover everything from a right of seigniorial jurisdiction to begging as a livelihood.[3] Property in the fullest sense for the physiocrats took the form of land, which they considered to be the sole source of true wealth; in their eyes property also implied outright ownership by an individual. They disapproved of all sharing of property in the belief that individual incentive

---

[1] The title, which has been cited already, is: *Le Mouvement physiocratique en France, de 1756 à 1770*.

[2] Weulersse, *Le Mouvement physiocratique*, II, p. 3.

[3] A. Cobban, *Social interpretation of the French Revolution*, p. 136.

would suffer.[1] While they accepted the right of the State to own property, they wanted government to be an hereditary monarchy, so that the ruler himself would resemble as closely as possible a private property-holder.[2] In this scheme property practically conferred material existence on its owner. With social status determined in this way, feudal and seigniorial rights, together with the social hierarchy that they presupposed, were made to look irrelevant.

The first property right, according to the physiocrats, was the *propriété personnelle* or right of the individual to his own person. What was a lofty sentiment for the physiocrats, if a truism for others, was based on the conviction, which they claimed to derive from their own experience, that only the man who was free took pride in his work. For Quesnay, the founding father of the physiocrats, serfdom was condemned on the empirical grounds that 'it extinguishes all competition and all activity'.[3] In this way the disciples of a harsh economic code became the allies of the humanitarians in their campaign against serfdom. It was hardly surprising that physiocrats should sometimes be tempted to cloak the principles of their loveless creed in the more appealing language of humanitarian writers. This motive, perhaps, prompted a contributor to the *Éphémérides du Citoyen*, the official periodical of the physiocrats, to write: 'Servitude is repugnant to Natural Law; like every outrage against the personal property of men, it is a detestable crime, destructive of all law, all justice and all society.'[4] Conversely, humanitarian writers would often accompany their emotional appeal with arguments drawn from the physiocrats. The abbé Clerget, for instance, headed one chapter of *Le Cri de la raison*, 'Mortmain makes the feudatory cruel to no advantage'. 'The seigneur,' he explained, 'seduced by the hope of inheriting the possessions of the serf, is blind to his true interests.'[5] The incompatibility of the two partners in this strange alliance on behalf of the serf needs little comment. The view that social oppressors can be weaned from their cruel ways by trying to instil into them respect for the principles of a newly-devised

[1] Weulersse, *Le Mouvement physiocratique*, I, p. 408.
[2] *Ibid.*, II, pp. 48 ff.
[3] *Ibid.*, p. 5.
[4] *Ibid.*
[5] Clerget, *Le Cri de la raison*, p. 198.

economics was optimistic, even in *le siècle des lumières*. None the less, the edict which abolished serfdom on Crown lands in 1779 contained in the preamble traces of their influence, alongside that of Voltaire. One of the main arguments that was advanced in it for the abolition of serfdom could have come direct from the editorial staff of the *Éphémérides du Citoyen*: serfdom was condemned because 'it deprives society of the effects of that working energy, which the feeling of the freest proprietorship is alone capable of inspiring'.[1] This statement could go a long way towards mitigating their disapproval for an edict which had contradicted their principles by recognizing that serfs in private hands were a valid form of property, which the Crown should respect.[2]

Possession of personal freedom was the humblest qualification for entry into the physiocratic state; full citizenship was reserved for the owners of property. As already suggested, the physiocrats differed from their contemporaries in restricting 'property' in the fullest sense to land that was held in outright ownership by a single individual. They rejected, therefore, the widespread assumption that feudal dues and privileges constituted a perfectly legitimate form of property. It was against this attitude that a disciple of the school was protesting when he wrote that feudal rights were 'covered by the mask of property'.[3] Similarly, Letrosne considered that 'the greatest obstacle to the abolition of feudalism is that it is valued as property', and that 'under that title it is respectable'.[4] Conventional ideas about the nature of property, demanded, none the less, at least some display of outward respect on the part of these writers. Boncerf in *Les Inconvéniens des droits féodaux* described the situation with engaging frankness:[5]

Freedom of the land . . . has long been desired by all sensible people; writers, however, have omitted, as it were, to introduce the subject in public. They doubtless regard the mass of laws which protect the present form and character of property, as a wall of bronze against which they would shatter their opinions and endeavours in vain.

The safest course was doubtless that advocated by two abbés in their tract against serfdom. When 'the idol of property is

---

[1] Isambert, XXVI, p. 139.
[2] See pp. 128–9.
[3] *L'Esprit des Journaux, François et Étrangers,* XII (December 1784), p. 139.
[4] Letrosne, *De l'Administration provinciale* (1788), II, p. 359.
[5] Boncerf, *Les Inconvéniens des droits féodaux* (1776), p. 9.

deaf to the cries of reason,' they wrote, 'it is necessary to cense it with one hand, while undermining the altar surreptitiously with the other.'[1]

Feudal and seigniorial dues did not count as a form of property for the physiocrats, because they were not derived from the land, but were, on the contrary, an imposition on it. Letrosne expressed their view when he wrote that it 'would be to the interest of landed property to be delivered from the burden which is placed on it by this 'imitation property', by which he meant feudal and seigniorial dues.[2] The anonymous author of *De la Féodalité et de l'aristocratie française* equally described 'feudalism' as an 'imaginary property', in which all that was real were the expenses, cares and difficulties.[3] The virtue of *franc-alleu*, which was free of most feudal impositions, was, in Boncerf's view, that 'perfect properties' were best suited to the needs of agriculture.[4] Goudar, for all his battles with the physiocrats over the corn trade, expressed their viewpoint faithfully when he condemned seigniorial rights for undermining the economic drive which sprang, in his opinion, from the full ownership of property.[5] Such views were not confined to economists. Voltaire himself spoke of a feeling of ownership doubling man's strength,[6] while the abbé Clerget dubbed 'love of property', 'agriculture's most active stimulant'.[7]

The view that feudal dues were not a true form of property was so widespread that it was shared even by some of the commentators on feudal law. A distinction had long been made by jurists, as Professor Cobban remarked, between the *domaine direct* or the seigneur's overlordship and the *domaine utile* or use of the property by another.[8] By the eighteenth century the man who enjoyed the use of the property was called the real

---

[1] P.-F. Clerget and J. P. Baverel, *Coup d'oeil philosophique et politique sur la main-morte* (London, 1785), p. 69.

[2] Letrosne, *De l'administration provinciale* (1788), II, p. 464.

[3] (Anon.), *De la Féodalité et de l'aristocratie française, ou tableau des effets désastreux des droits féodaux: et réfutation des erreurs sur lesquelles la noblesse fonde ses prétentions* (n.p., date illegible on British Museum copy), p. 18.

[4] Boncerf, *La Plus importante et la plus pressante affaire*, pp. 37–8.

[5] See p. 138.

[6] Cit. A. and A. F. Bayet, *Les Écrivains politiques du XVIIIe. siècle* (Paris: Armand Colin, 1904), p. 87.

[7] Clerget, *Le Cri de la raison*, p. 199.

[8] Cobban, *Social Interpretation of the French Revolution*, p. 27.

owner, even in the *terriers* of the seigneur.[1] The *feudistes* of the eighteenth century, in the words of Karyeev, a pioneer of French agrarian history, 'made progress over their predecessors in only one point: by recognizing frankly that *dominium utile* was the real property, and that *dominium directum* was only a kind of servitude'.[2] This important development shows that even the *feudiste* could not altogether ignore the fact that he lived in *le siècle des lumières*. Yet these writers who were sometimes capable of enunciating radical principles were equally capable, as we have seen, of ignoring their implications. If use conferred 'true ownership', this did not deter *feudistes* from recognizing so many restrictions on their true ownership that it was far from complete.[3] Did the peasant, to take only one example, feel that he was the 'true owner' in any real sense when the seigneur was exercising the right to hunt on his land?

It is hard to believe, however, that the physiocrat, still less the *feudiste*, was the French peasant's best friend. As far as this role was filled, the credit belongs rather to some of the *agronomes*; for instance, to Beardé de L'Abbaye who argued that peasant prosperity was the best index of economic well-being.[4] Most of the physiocrats were preoccupied less with defending the interests of the peasants than with vaunting the merits of large-scale farming.[5] To benefit the latter, they showed particular eagerness in advocating the enclosure of the common lands that were an essential source of livelihood for the poorer peasantry.[6] Dupont de Nemours, one of their leading writers, who had the honour of being initiated into 'the sect' by the marquis de Mirabeau himself,[7] expressly reassured his readers that the new physiocratic order would increase, rather than diminish, inequality.[8]

It is, therefore, hardly surprising that the physiocrats directed their appeal mainly towards the seigneurs themselves. They knew this market for their ideas too well to cloud material

[1] *Ibid.*, p. 28.
[2] Karyeev, p. 256.
[3] M. Garaud, *La Révolution et la propriété foncière* (Paris: Recueil Sirey, 1958), p. 2.
[4] Weulersse, *Le Mouvement physiocratique en France*, I, p. 246.
[5] *Ibid.*, pp. 323 ff.
[6] *Ibid.*, II, pp. 172 ff.
[7] *Ibid.*, I, p. 87.
[8] *Ibid.*, II, p. 33.

interests with appeals to high-minded principles. Their basic argument was always the same; the high cost of levying feudal and seigniorial rights made them a source of financial loss for their owners.[1]

The seigneur, to gather and exercise these dues, [wrote Boncerf] is obliged to shoulder considerable expenses. He must have archives, *terriers*, that are immensely costly to draw up and renew, rolls, receivers, collectors, sergeants and very extensive accounts: often the right, the amount due or the manner of payment are contested; often the *mouvance* is disputed by other seigneurs who claim the right for themselves; the enormous law-suits which the disputes engender pass from father to sons, devour the seigneurs, the vassals and the land on which they are raised.

Most costly of all to the seigneur, according to Letrosne, was the drawing up of the *terriers*, which played an essential part in the levying of feudal and seigniorial dues. He spoke of one uncompleted *terrier* that had cost to date 25–30,000 livres, while another *terrier*, despite the services of some ten clerks over a period of more than twenty-five years, was still unfinished.[2] Writers also drew attention to the costs which the seigneurs incurred from the many law-suits which the levying of these rights provoked. The abbé Roubaud, prominent among the later physiocrats, claimed not only that feudal dues crushed the tenant, but also that 'the endless discussions, litigation, law-suits, abuses and injustices are sooner or later as fatal for the seigneurs themselves, as for the cultivators and the state'.[3] Turgot's attack on feudal and seigniorial rights was defended by one of the leaders of the physiocrats as the rendering of a service to the nobility by depriving them of 'rights which bring barely any profit to them'.[4] The physiocrats, if they believed their own propaganda, were, doubtless, disappointed to discover in 1776 that many nobles did not regard Turgot's aims in that light.[5]

The argument that feudal and seigniorial rights ran counter

[1] Boncerf, *Les Inconvéniens des droits féodaux* (1776), p. 17.

[2] Letrosne, *De l'Administration provinciale* (1788), II, p. 440.

[3] G. Weulersse, *La Physiocratie à la fin du règne de Louis XV, 1770–1774* (Paris: PUF, 1959), p. 41.

[4] G. Weulersse, *La Physiocratie sous les ministères de Turgot et de Necker, 1774–1781* (Paris: PUF, 1950), p. 58.

[5] See pp. 164 ff.

to the interests of their owners was publicized in the preamble of the edict in which they were abolished in Savoy by Charles-Emmanuel in 1771. The Crown, in that case, seems to have been prompted by purely practical considerations. Yet, if French writers had done nothing to bring about the promulgation of the edict, they could invoke it as a model for a similar reform in France. This theme was pursued with particular skill in a *Mémoire* by Clicquot de Blervache, who is an interesting example of one who was a prominent administrator as well as a man of letters. He was of sufficient importance as an inspector-general of manufactures and commerce and a notable of Reims to be given the order of Saint-Michel.[1] Social respectability, however, did not inhibit his originality and his concern for the poor, in which respect he put most of his fellow economists to shame. His *Mémoire* was guaranteed attention from the public by the fact that it had been crowned in 1783 by the Academy of Châlons-sur-Marne, which was renowned for its support for social reform. On the opening page Clicquot de Blervache singled out Charles-Emmanuel as one of the most enlightened of the century's rulers.[2] The king, he reported, had discovered in the existence of feudalism the reason why his people were abandoning their homes.[3] Although in this *Mémoire*, as its title suggests, he gave first place to the needs of the peasants, the edict was quoted at length to show that the owner of feudal and seigniorial dues was also the loser by levying them. 'We know,' Charles-Emmanuel was quoted as saying in the preamble of his edict, 'that these rights are onerous not only to those who pay them, but often to the owners, whether through disputes that are inseparable from exacting them privately, or through the difficulty and cost of renewals [of the *terriers*].'[4] The same passage was reproduced by another pamphleteer, a certain Boudin,[5] who was later to gain prominence as a member of a committee on agriculture during the Revolution.[6]

[1] J. de Vroil, *Étude sur Clicquot-Blervache, économiste du XVIIIe. siècle* (Paris: Guillaume, 1870), p. xxxi.

[2] Clicquot de Blervache, p. 1.

[3] *Ibid.*, p. 2.

[4] *Ibid.*, p. 60.

[5] J.-A. Boudin, *Nouvelles réflexions sur le rachat des droits féodaux* (Paris: Desenne, 1790), p. 7.

[6] Balteau, VI, p. 1260.

The owners of feudal and seigniorial rights were not, of course, expected by the economists to relinquish them for nothing. They were urged to commute them for a fixed sum, which, they were assured, would be to their profit.[1]

Up to the present, they [the seigneurs] have been dupes of habit [wrote Boncerf]. It is difficult to imagine how they have neglected to convert their overlordship into landed properties. There are no vassals who would not purchase exemption from all the *cens*, *surcens*, *corvées* etc. at 50, or 60, or more times, the annual rate; the rights of *lods*, of *relief*, of *champart*, the banalities more dearly still. A seigneur would draw from the sale of his rights more than if he sold his whole estate.

Other writers expressed similar views in more moderate terms. Clicquot de Blervache and an anonymous pamphleteer both claimed that the seigneur would be able to invest the money that was realized from the sale of feudal dues to greater profit.[2] All this eloquence had very little effect on the owners of feudal and seigniorial rights who knew their own interests better than the writers. A few seigneurs in Haute-Guyenne appear to have been almost alone in commuting their rights of *champart* for a fixed annual return.[3]

The concern of the physiocrats and their associates for the welfare of those other than peasants emerges very strongly in their criticisms of *franc-fief* and other levies on the sale of property that formed part of a fief. It might be thought that the nobles themselves would approve of an imposition that penalized the bourgeois propensity for buying up their lands. However, franc-fief had the practical disadvantage for them that, by lowering the value of land for non-nobles, it also reduced the price which they were willing to pay for them. Even Boulain-villiers, who had described 'feudalism' as 'the masterpiece of the human mind', disapproved of *franc-fief* on the grounds that it had swollen the coffers of French princes without any benefit to the nobles themselves.[4] This view was certainly shared by many in his own order. Out of all the *cahiers* of 1789 in the

---

[1] Weulersse, *La Physiocratie sous les ministères de Turgot et de Necker*, pp. 57–8.

[2] Clicquot de Blervache, *Mémoire sur les moyens d'améliorer en France la condition des laboureurs*, p. 69; (Anon.), *Mémoire sur les rentes et les droits féodaux*, p. 38.

[3] Weulersse, *La Physiocratie sous les ministères de Turgot et de Necker*, p. 272.

[4] Boulainvilliers, *Essais sur la noblesse de France*, p. 153.

Archives Parlementaires, in only two, those for the nobility of
Evreux and Rouen, was it requested that franc-fief should be
maintained,[1] while in over a dozen cases nobles asked for its
abolition.[2] D'Argenson, whose *Considérations sur le gouvernement
ancien et présent de la France* had existed in manuscript since
about 1739, had been one of the first in the country to criticize
taxes on the sale and inheritance of feudal property for essentially economic reasons. He condemned what he called 'the
considerable rights of *mutation* and *relief*', by which, he maintained, 'lands that are badly tended pass with greater difficulty
into hands which would cultivate them better'.[3] The same view
was spelt out in detail by Goudar in his work of 1756. 'The
majority of lands in France,' he wrote, 'stagnate under impoverished owners or small-holders who lack the means to
cultivate them, because the right of *lods et ventes* prevent them
passing into better hands, which would raise their value, with
greater benefit to the state.'[4] The interest of society itself
suffered, according to Letrosne, when land-holdings were not
sold freely and citizens invited to invest their capital in them.[5]
Boncerf likewise blamed *franc-fief* for hindering the sale of lands
and for reducing the investment of capital in the countryside.[6]
These arguments appear to have been widely diffused, as even
an obscure pamphleteer could write: 'It is impossible to protest
too much against the abuses of *francs-fiefs* which put so many
obstacles in the way of dealing in lands, and consequently
harm agriculture and the circulation of money.'[7]

The reiterated phrases about land passing into the hands of
those with capital, or of those who would cultivate them better,
suggest that the physiocrats made their appeal primarily to the
rich. Those references to the state and society which might
be taken to contradict this view can really be discounted as the
pious platitudes of writers who elsewhere unmistakably fashioned

---

[1] Mavidal and Laurent, III, p. 299 and V, p. 596, art. 51, respectively.

[2] *Ibid.*, I, p. 741, art. 25; II, p. 427; III, p. 177, art. 44; p. 392; p. 665, art. 7;
IV, p. 88, art. 12; p. 111, art. 50; V, p. 529, art. 82; p. 652, art. 10; p. 753;
VI, p. 78, art. 71; p. 142, art. 11; p. 168, art. 38.

[3] Argenson, p. 120.

[4] Goudar, *Les Intérêts de la France mal entendus*, I, p. 55.

[5] Letrosne, *De l'Administration provinciale* (1788), I, p. 362.

[6] Boncerf, *La Plus importante et la plus pressante affaire*, pp. 36–7.

[7] (Anon.), *Lettre à un plébéien au sujet de l'Assemblée des États Généraux*
(20 September 1788), p. 17.

their ideas around the egoism of the individual. While there were many nobles who had the means to be improving landlords, they normally possessed fiefs of their own. The purchasers of fiefs, as one would expect, were usually non-nobles. It is rather the vast number of these transactions that may cause surprise. 'The majority of lands conferring a title,' wrote Taine, 'are becoming the property of financiers, businessmen and their descendants, and fiefs fall into the hands of the bourgeoisie of the towns.'[1] As Professor George V. Taylor has shown, 'the aristocracy by tradition and the wealthy urban groups by emulation showed an incurable esteem for rural property'.[2]

Whatever the physiocrats felt about the 'unnatural' amassing of wealth in manufactures and trade, they appear to have had no difficulty in welcoming capital from those sources for the sake of carrying out agricultural improvements. This fact has encouraged the belief that the physiocrats consciously pioneered a new social and economic order. Lefebvre himself seems to have given some support to this view when he wrote: 'Towards the middle of the eighteenth century the example of England and the propaganda of the physiocrats had created a current of opinion in favour of the transformation of agriculture in a capitalist sense.'[3] The development of large-scale farming and the more systematic use of capital to increase agricultural yield should not, however, be interpreted as marking the advent of a Marxist type of capitalism in France. The physiocrats were 'capitalists' only in the sense that they wished the nature of society to be determined by the acquisitive instincts of the individual. They made no proper provision for a specially 'bourgeois' class of landowners, and failed to disavow the practice of purchasing land as a means of enhancing social status. This prejudice worked so clearly against the implementation of physiocratic ideas that these writers must take some reponsibility for neglecting to attack it. Those who disapproved so strongly of the industrial and commercial developments of their time can hardly be called heralds of modern capitalism. The price of bringing about an agricultural revolution in France was surely the making of some concessions to the 'bourgeois' world that

[1] Karyeev, p. 115.
[2] Taylor, p. 473.
[3] G. Lefebvre, *Études sur la Révolution française* (Paris: PUF, 1954), p. 255.

the physiocrats despised. The flaw in the project to turn nobles, and those who aped their ways, into model landlords was the strong prejudice among them against attending to humble matters of administration. In the interests of farming it was desirable that *roturiers* should continue to practise the celebrated 'bourgeois virtues' after they had purchased land. The physiocrats, however, offered them no real encouragement to do so. As a result, the seigneur, whether a noble or not, relied upon middlemen to do his work for him. Physiocracy made few converts from these business agents; they were too busy enriching themselves at the expense of the seigneur and his peasants to heed the guidance of the physiocrats. It is not surprising, therefore, that the entrepreneur, to whom the physiocrats did not deign to give a place in their system, helped to thwart its implementation.

The physiocrats and other economists were eloquent in their denunciation of these agents of the 'feudal reaction'. 'Unworthy and thrice stigmatized,' wrote the marquis de Mirabeau, precise even in his anger, 'let the owner or administrator of lands be, who disdaining essential relationships and rejecting the most sacred duties of property, sells and delivers his cultivators to the voracity of covetous men.'[1] The same point was made even more strongly by Boncerf, who was on the fringes of 'the Movement'. 'It is impossible to protect the vassal too much,' he wrote, 'from the over-frequent enterprises of these formidable "aggrandizers" who buy from the seigneurs the right to draw up their *terriers*; these then become in their hands instruments of pillage, that always goes unpunished because they are judges and parties in their own cause.'[2]

Yet the economists who fulminated against the *feudistes* were not as guiltless of bringing about the 'feudal reaction' as they liked to imagine. In their writings against the collective property-rights of the peasants they had lent respectability to some of the most rapacious acts of the very *feudistes* whom they denounced. Boncerf, at least, went further still: it was reported in *Mémoires Secrets*, one of the most informative of contemporary periodicals, that in draining marshes for the Prince de Conti he

[1] Weulersse, *Le Mouvement physiocratique en France*, I, p. 441.
[2] Boncerf, *La Plus importante et la plus pressante affaire*, p. 41.

had tried to drive out 400 poor families from land on which they were accustomed to pasture their cattle.[1] As the Prince de Conti had been conspicuous for his virulent attack on *Les Inconvéniens des droits féodaux*, Boncerf must be credited with carrying inconsistency to remarkable lengths. The physiocrats and other economists at worst served the interests of the eighteenth-century 'conman'; at best they stood for more efficient methods of cultivation, which usually worked in practice to the detriment of the peasants. In neither case did they attack the root of the feudal and seignioral regime.

The enforcement of the rights and dues depended in the first instance on the seigniorial courts. It was at this point, as I have suggested elsewhere, that the feudal and seigniorial regime was most vulnerable to attack from the Crown.[2] If the seigneur's judicial authority had been removed, the exactions of the *feudistes* could have been held in check by royal officials. The suppression of the seigniorial courts, therefore, was likely to be a principal objective of any determined attack on 'feudalism'. The good faith and purposefulness of those who criticized feudal and seigniorial rights can be gauged largely from how they wrote about seigniorial justice.

Seigniorial justice was criticized, in fact, more fiercely than almost any other aspect of 'feudalism'. It was common to call for the complete suppression of seigniorial jurisdiction. This request was even incorporated in the title of one pamphlet.[3] 'I hardly dare speak of the seigniorial justice,'[4] wrote another writer', before embarking on a lengthy account in which he called for their suppression.[5] Similarly, Besné de la Hauteville wrote in a memorandum to the Controller-General that the only remedy was the entire suppression of seigniorial jurisdiction.[6] 'The necessity for reforming the seigniorial justices,' announced Bucquet, 'is felt universally.' He said that he doubted whether there was anyone in his own day who would defend

---

[1] *Mémoires Secrets pour servir à l'Histoire de la République des Lettres en France, depuis MDCC LXII jusqu'à nos jours* (London, 1777–89), XIV, p. 27.

[2] See p. 66.

[3] Fouqueau de Pussy, *Idées sur l'administration de la justice dans les petites villes et bourgs de France, pour déterminer la suppression des jurisdictions seigneuriales* (Paris: Godefroy, 1789).

[4] Mézard, p. 41.

[5] *Ibid.*, p. 94.

[6] Giffard, p. 357.

seigniorial jurisdiction. The only writer whom he could remember having done so in the past had been an anonymous pamphleteer who had been answered effectively the following year.[1] The surprising fact about this forthright claim is that it appears to have been partly correct. The only writer of note who had defended seigniorial justice had been Montesquieu, who, as a holder of seigniorial jurisdiction, contrived to find it a necessary adjunct of a monarchy.[2] Otherwise, seigniorial justice seems to have been defended at length only in a work by a certain Doyen,[3] who was essentially a *feudiste*, despite the fact that he was an associate of Brissot de Warville.[4] It is true that most of his fellow commentators on feudal law, conservative in this respect as in so many others, usually accepted the legitimacy of seigniorial justice without comment. However, these 'technicians of feudalism' hardly had a direct influence on public opinion. Among the *cahiers* of 1789 seigniorial justice could on occasion be defended as a cheap and expeditious means of administering justice locally.[5] Yet these were the views of a minority. The Third Estate, disagreeing in the *cahiers* on so many points, showed a remarkable degree of unanimity in their desire to be rid of seigniorial justice. It seems significant that one conservative pamphleteer, who as late as 1789 still wished to preserve a reformed 'feudal regime',[6] was quite reconciled to the disappearance of seigniorial justice. 'The suppression of the seigniorial justices', he wrote, 'is doubtless a benefit for those under their jurisdiction, as it is for the seigneurs.'[7]

In the literary criticisms of seigniorial justice, as stated already, inspiration was derived far less from legal, than from utilitarian, principles.[8] The main concern of pamphleteers was that justice should be administered quickly and cheaply. In case these points should escape their readers they often put them in

---

[1] L.-J.-B. Bucquet, pp. 31–2.

[2] Montesquieu, *Oeuvres*, I, *De l'Esprit des Loix*, bk 2, chap. 4, p. 21.

[3] G. Doyen, *Recherches et observations sur les loix féodales, sur les anciennes conditions des habitans des villes et des campagnes, leurs possessions et leurs droits* (1779), pp. 60 ff.

[4] Balteau, fasc. LXIII, p. 717.

[5] P. Combe, *Mémoire inédit du Chancelier d'Aguesseau sur la réformation de la justice* (Grenoble: Valence, 1928), p. 51.

[6] Villemonney, p. 22.

[7] *Ibid.*, p. 25.

[8] See pp. 72 ff.

the title — a sensible precaution in an age that produced the recognizable forerunner of today's reviewer. Thus, the title of Bucquet's *Discours*, for which he won a prize from the Academy of Châlons-sur-Marne, ran, 'What are the means of dispensing justice in France with the greatest speed and least possible expense?'[1] Almost identical words had appeared already in the title of a work by Pétion de Villeneuve, a future mayor of Paris during the Revolution.[2]

In the eyes of these writers the seigniorial courts had virtually no redeeming features. The high costs and the interminable delays in the courts were the main themes of their criticism. There were complaints about the vast number of seigniorial officials. Letrosne wrote of the absurdity of having as many as twelve or fifteen judges in a single town.[3] No less than one hundred seigniorial jurisdictions, according to one writer, could be found within a radius of twelve or fifteen leagues.[4] Yet these ubiquitous officials were equally blamed for being absent from the area of their jurisdiction when their services were in demand.[5] Fouqueau de Pussy wrote wrathfully of the way in which judges would allow cases to accumulate until they had a fine day for the outing.[6] On the other hand, owing to the competition for cases among the many seigniorial officials, according to Pétion de Villeneuve, 'they grasp with all their strength those who fall into their claws; like certain voracious animals they do not let go of their prey, except when there is scarcely any more blood to suck'.[7] The marquis d'Argenson also denounced the operations of seigniorial justice which he said was 'exercised by a race of avid people' who were forever inciting the ordinary inhabitant to go to law.[8]

---

[1] The full title, already cited, is: *Discours qui a remporté le prix de l'Académie de Chaalons, en l'année M. DCC. LXXXIII sur cette question proposée par la même Académie: 'Quels seraient les moyens de rendre la justice en France avec le plus de célérité et le moins de frais possibles?'*.

[2] J. Pétion de Villeneuve, *Les Loix civiles et l'administration de la justice, ramenées à un ordre simple et uniforme: ou réflexions morales, politiques . . . sur la manière de rendre la justice en France, avec le plus de célérité et le moins de frais possible* (London, 1782).

[3] Letrosne, *De l'Administration provinciale* (1788), II, p. 361.

[4] (Anon.), *De l'Administration de la justice dans les campagnes*, p. 5.

[5] Boucher d'Argis, p. 18; Pétion de Villeneuve, pp. 8 and 236.

[6] Fouqueau de Pussy, p. 53.

[7] Pétion de Villeneuve, p. 238.

[8] Argenson, p. 120.

Challan accused the judges of even stirring up quarrels, so that they would have the opportunity of hearing more lawsuits.[1]

Accounts of the proceedings themselves read like the scripts of a comic opera. Justice, recounted Mézard, was often dispensed by 'an ignorant *laboureur*',[2] while Linguet spoke of peasants leaving their ploughs to become the spokesmen of Themis.[3] Even Renauldon, who was himself a commentator on feudal law, admitted that the seigniorial judges 'are for the most part only simple practitioners who have no knowledge of the laws nor of jurisprudence', and, he added with tactful understatement, 'often do not have the delicacy of feeling for which one could wish'.[4] Justice itself was described as being dispensed, along with a good deal of liquor, in the village pub. 'To secure an underhand settlement of the case,' wrote Fouqueau de Pussy, quoting Loyseau, 'it is necessary to inebriate the judge, the clerk of the court and the prosecutor of the case in a fine tavern . . . where cases are often settled in favour of whoever pays the bill.'[5] The judge, according to Linguet, was usually made drunk on arrival. He never showed any anxiety about payment of the bill because, Linguet assured his readers, 'he well knows that it is not he who will pay it'.[6] Such stories were apparently intended to be accepted at their face value. The Controller-General was solemnly informed in a *mémoire* by a senior official that seigniorial justice was administered 'in the tavern, where in the midst of drunkenness and debauchery the judge sells justice to whoever pays most'.[7]

Most of these writers would have agreed with Letrosne that the most obvious shortcoming of the seigniorial courts was their failure to maintain law and order.[8] It was stated as a fact in several standard works of reference that the seigneurs habitually shirked their basic responsibility to prosecute

---

[1] Challan, p. 14.

[2] Mézard, *Essai sur les réformes à faire dans l'administration de la justice en France*, p. 41.

[3] Linguet, *Nécessité*, p. 58.

[4] J. Renauldon, *Dictionnaire des fiefs et des droits seigneuriaux utiles et honorifiques* (Paris: Knapen, 1765), I, p. 27.

[5] Fouqueau de Pussy, p. 57.

[6] Linguet, *Nécessité*, p. 59.

[7] Giffard, p. 358.

[8] Letrosne, *Vues sur la justice criminelle*, p. 111.

criminals within the area of their jurisdiction.[1] Letrosne and Linguet wrote as if one of the chief tasks of the seigniorial judge was to ensure that criminals were induced to flee else-where.[2] This indignation, however, hardly became authors who benefited as a group from the administration's civilized practice of warning them in advance of the issue of warrants for their arrest.

In view of the condition of many seigniorial prisons it was, perhaps, just as well that so few suspects found their way into them. La Poix de Fréminville, who had shown that his sympathies lay with the seigneur by putting his professional skill at the service of the 'feudal reaction',[3] none the less felt constrained to deplore the fact that less than two prisons out of every hundred, on his own reckoning, met the requirements of the law. Despite the fact that prisons were supposed not to be injurious to health or below ground, he spoke of 'frightful cellars and subterranean places', where prisoners perished for want of fresh air.[4] Renauldon, who surely should have been one of the century's 'Gothic novelists' rather than a commentator on feudal law, described the majority of seigniorial prisons as being 'situated in the interior of the *châteaux*, at the base of towers, subterranean and humid places, where the unfortunate prisoners, without light, grow fetid in the water in the midst of animals that are aquatic and sometimes dangerous'.[5]

The shortcomings of the courts were attributed partly to the fact that their owners valued them largely as symbols of social status.[6] Linguet, who complained that the seigneur wished to have the honour of High Justice at no cost to himself, drew the conclusion that there would be no inconvenience in suppressing a prerogative which the nobility themselves feared to use.[7] A sardonic proposal for a compromise came from Bucquet. Seigniorial justice should be suppressed, but out of respect for the vanity of the seigneur, the gibbets, pillories and posts of

---

[1] A.-F. Prost de Royer, *Dictionnaire de jurisprudence et des arrêts, ou nouvelle édition du dictionnaire . . . de Brillon* (Lyons: A. de la Roche, 1781–8), I, p. 290; Renauldon, *Dictionnaire*, cited by Combe, p. 48.

[2] Letrosne, *Vues sur la justice criminelle*, p. 111; Linguet, *Nécessité*, p. 61.

[3] See pp. 63 ff.

[4] Fréminville, *Dictionnaire*, p. 485.

[5] Renauldon, *Dictionnaire*, II, p. 167.

[6] Letrosne, *Vues sur la justice criminelle*, p. 115.

[7] Linguet, *Nécessité*, pp. 61–2.

justice should remain as symbols of the rights which they no longer exercised.[1]

The literary criticism of seigniorial justice is hard to accept at its face value. The seigniorial courts, for all their failings, dealt with comparatively unimportant matters. The bucolic, or even Hogarthian, atmosphere in which sessions of the courts were held might well shock an urban pamphleteer, particularly one who was anxious to be shocked. It is safe to assume that the peasants themselves were made of sterner stuff. The stories about inebriating the judge in order to win the case prove little, except, perhaps, the gullibility of those who repeated them. Moreover, it was presumably only in suits between peasants, and in which the seigneur had no interest, that his judge was open to the influence of others. The stereotyped descriptions of the misdoings in the seigniorial courts are far from convincing. Anecdotes and information about the seigniorial courts are frequently drawn from Loyseau's brief, *Des Abus des justices de village*, which was already over a century and a half out of date on the eve of the Revolution, when most of these works appeared.[2] If conditions in the seigniorial courts had really remained unchanged throughout the centuries, the writers would have carried more conviction if they had illustrated their views from contemporary experience. The reader may well feel that few of the pamphleteers, despite their self-righteous indignation, had ever been inside a seigniorial court. Whatever first-hand experience these writers may have possessed, however, they certainly seldom saw matters from the viewpoint of the peasants, who were those who suffered most from the shortcomings of the courts. The seigniorial court for the peasant was essentially the place where payment of feudal and seigniorial dues was enforced. In these cases they could only have welcomed the inebriation of the judge, if it had led him to overlook the fact that he was the hireling of the seigneur. This fact, which was all-important to the peasant, receives only cursory treatment from the majority of the pamphleteers.[3] Bucquet, who in most respects was one of the most radical of these writers,

[1] Bucquet, *Discours*, pp. 53–4.

[2] See, for instance, Bucquet, *Discours*, p. 31; Fouqueau de Pussy, pp. 54 ff; Pétion de Villeneuve, p. 240; (Anon.), *De l'Administration de la justice dans les campagnes*, p. 6.

[3] For a partial exception, however, see Fouqueau de Pussy, pp. 58–9.

could even advocate that seigniorial courts should be confined to 'feudal cases and to those requiring despatch'.[1] As 'feudal cases belong in some sense to property,' he wrote, 'it does not appear that there are absolutely serious inconveniences in preserving the seigniorial justices to take cognisance of them.'[2] Yet, while the pamphleteers wanted all jurisdiction removed from the seigniorial courts, except what was an instrument for the exploitation of the fief, it was precisely that kind of justice which the peasants did not wish to remain.[3]

There is a certain artificiality about some of the literary criticisms of seigniorial justice. Trivial points tend to loom large, while some of the principal grievances are overlooked. The reader may wonder why these writers did not produce a more convincing case against seigniorial justice. The general standard of these pamphlets is sufficiently high for it to seem unlikely that their authors failed for want of literary skill. To accept this view of their proficiency, however, is to raise doubts about their seriousness of purpose in attacking seigniorial justice. What exactly were their motives in doing so? The writers themselves seemed to imply throughout that they were actuated solely by concern for humanity and the public good. Occasionally, they would state motives which were normally taken for granted. 'I have believed that each citizen owed to the fatherland,' wrote Boucher d'Argis, 'the tribute of his reflections and experience. I offer this tribute with all the more confidence', he modestly revealed, 'as my zeal is pure, and as it is impossible to believe me with views other than those for the public good.'[4] The more bashful Pétion de Villeneuve relied upon an anonymous editor to expound his motives. Besides having the ambition to merit the laurels of an academic crown, the author was described as being inspired by 'the still nobler desire to be useful'.[5]

Yet the purest intentions can sometimes be reinforced by

[1] Bucquet, p. 6.
[2] *Ibid.*, p. 51.
[3] R. Génestal, 'A. Giffard: Les Justices seigneuriales en Bretagne aux XVIIe. et XVIIIe. siècles, 1661–1791', *Nouvelle Revue Historique de Droit Français et Étranger*, XXVII (1963), p. 886.
[4] Boucher d'Argis, p. 1.
[5] Pétion de Villeneuve, *Les Loix civiles*, 'Avis de l'éditeur', second unpaginated page.

material interest. A clue may be provided by the fact that so many of the critics of seigniorial justice were officials in the royal administration.[1] One of the first to write, the marquis d'Argenson, as a minister of the Crown had been hostile to the privileges of the nobility and had fallen from power as a result of aristocratic intrigue; Letrosne practised for many years as an *avocat du roi* at the *bailliage* and *présidial* court of Orléans, while being closely associated with both Turgot and Necker; Mézard was president at the royal court at Ajaccio; Bucquet and Challan were the king's procurators at the *présidial* courts of Beauvais and Meulan, respectively. If Pétion de Villeneuve was the unswerving enemy of the monarchy during the Revolution, none the less his father had been the king's procurator in the *présidial* court at Chartres, where he himself had practised as a barrister. Boucher d'Argis was a *conseiller* at the court of the Châtelet where the overbearing attitude of the Parlement of Paris may have predisposed him to feel sympathetic towards the Crown in its own conflicts with the Parlement. Linguet was hostile to the Parlement for the more obvious reason that he had been struck off its rolls as a barrister. Although Besné de la Hauteville was employed in a legal capacity by the clergy, he made it clear to the Controller-General that his services were available to the Crown in the carrying out of the reforms which he himself suggested. Among those considered, the only pamphleteer who may not have been a royal official was Fouqueau de Pussy, whose life-history is so obscure that his name does not even grace the biographical dictionaries of Michaud, Hoeffer, Arnault, or Rabbe.

Why were critics of seigniorial justice so often officials in the royal administration? An obvious explanation is the government's own openness to proposals for reform. Judicial torture, serfdom on Crown lands, and discrimination against Protestants were all abolished by statute on the eve of the Revolution. When the Crown showed its enlightenment in this way, it was natural enough for its own officials to make proposals for reform. Yet it hardly seems likely that royal officials, whatever their claims, had a quasi-monopoly of zeal for the public good. Those who attack seigniorial justice are noticeably silent about

---

[1] A fuller statement of the careers of the writers mentioned above may be found in the author's article in *French Government and Society*, ed. J. F. Bosher.

the abuses in the royal courts. Arthur Young, none the less, in his travels in France immediately before and during the Revolution found that there was universal dissatisfaction with the administration of justice of all kinds.[1] Even if abuses were commoner in the seigniorial than in the royal courts, the reform of the latter was more pressing, if only because they dealt with more important matters. The fact that officials in the royal courts looked with so much disapproval at seigniorial jurisdiction can hardly have been unconnected with the intense rivalry between the two parallel judicial systems.[2] The more seigniorial jurisdiction was curtailed, the more the royal courts and those who served in them stood to gain in power and prestige.

The suspicion that the self-interest of royal officials supplied the real motive for the attack on seigniorial justice is confirmed by the nature of their criticisms. The day-to-day misconduct of the seigniorial officials in their courts was denounced by writers who seldom appear to have bothered to observe them, except through the eyes of a jurist of the preceding century. Although the writers professed themselves to be deeply concerned about the welfare of the peasants, they gave little consideration, and some of that unsympathetic, to the use of the courts as a means for the fiscal exploitation of the fief by the seigneur. Perhaps the neglect of the needs of nine-tenths of the population was excusable on the part of those who owed their primary allegiance to the Crown. Yet even the case for the administration of justice being a prerogative of royal sovereignty was presented in a stereotyped fashion which hardly served the Crown better than letting it go by default. It would be unfair, of course, to blame officials in the royal courts for failing to write about their subject as if they were jurists. As I tried to show in chapter III, it was largely because the government refused to patronize the jurists that the Crown received so little backing in the field of legal theory. None the less, it is hard not to conclude that even among the officials who criticized seigniorial justice the Crown lacked supporters who were really committed to its cause.

How far did the Crown heed the critics of seigniorial justice?

[1] A. Young, *Travels in France during the years 1787, 1788 and 1789*, ed. C. Maxwell (Cambridge University Press, 1929), p. 333.
[2] See pp. 67–8.

The fact that reforms were demanded and that some were carried out may suggest that the two were related as cause and effect. The dates of the two principal edicts, however, hardly support this view. The first appeared in 1771, long before anyone except Linguet had criticized seigniorial jurisdiction at any length. Although the second was promulgated as late as May 1788, it appears that the balance of pamphlets was still to come; if Linguet, d'Argenson, Letrosne and Pétion de Villeneuve wrote before 1789, works by Fouqueau de Pussy, Challan, Bucquet and Boucher d'Argis were published in that year. It is true that a pamphlet by Mézard and a reissue of Letrosne's *De l'Administration provinciale* appeared in the same year as the edict. Yet even if these works preceded its promulgation there can have been little time for them to influence those who drew it up. The wording of the preamble seems to owe nothing to their writings on seigniorial justice. On the contrary, the first remedy which the king was reported to have considered would not have been welcomed by most of them. The proposal had been 'to restrict the extent of the jurisdiction assigned to our courts'. It is clear from the context that 'our courts' comprised especially the parlements.[1] Quite apart from the fact that some of the writers who have been discussed were dependent on cases at the parlements for a living, there do not appear to have been any requests that the jurisdiction of the parlements should be circumscribed. It seems clear that the edict which, if it had been applied, would practically have abolished the criminal jurisdiction of the seigniorial courts and have made resort to them in civil suits purely voluntary, was largely a by-product of the Crown's quarrel with the parlements.[2] Not only did the critics of seigniorial justice have little effect on royal legislation, but many of them appear to have developed an interest in law reform only after the Crown had shown the way. The increase in the number of writings in the late 1780s probably also owed much to changes among the government's top legal officials, as well as to the growing revolutionary ferment. While the post of Advocate-General had been filled by Séguier, who could claim in 1786 that French laws had in some ways reached the highest degree

[1] Isambert, XXVIII, p. 535.
[2] See pp. 70-1.

of perfection of which human legislation was capable,[1] criticism of seigniorial justice was unlikely to receive official encouragement. However, the situation had altered in April 1787 when Miromesnil was replaced as Keeper of the Seals by Lamoignon, a keen supporter of legal reform.[2] Criticisms of seigniorial justice which were made after Lamoignon had taken office were not only more likely to have practical effect, but might also serve to advance the careers of their authors.

There is little evidence concerning the attitude of successive royal administrations towards the literary attacks on feudal and seigniorial rights. The government does not appear to have made a serious attempt to curb them, with the possible exception of Turgot's support for Boncerf in 1776. Weulersse, in his very thorough examination of the extent to which the ideas of the physiocrats were put into effect, could find little trace of their influence on government legislation. One of the few exceptions was an edict of 1762 by which *franc-fief* and similar rights were suspended partly as a means of encouraging longer leases, of which the physiocrats strongly approved. As *franc-fief* was a royal tax, however, its abrogation did not interfere with the feudal and seigniorial rights of individuals, who gained from it, as far as their tenants could afford to pay higher rents.[3]

The first sign that the government might undertake a frontal attack on the feudal and seigniorial regime came with the outbreak of the Boncerf affair in 1776. As the discussion of Boncerf's views may have suggested already, his pamphlet, *Les Inconvéniens des droits féodaux*, contained few original or daring proposals. It was dragged into political prominence by the Parlement of Paris, as a means of discrediting Turgot, who was supposed to have encouraged its publication while, in fact, he had tried to withdraw it from circulation.[4] As the Boncerf affair will be discussed in the light of peasant discontent in the next chapter, it is enough to note here that there is little reason to suppose that Turgot intended a serious attack on feudal and seigniorial rights at this point.

The only possible evidence to the contrary in his papers is

[1] Esmein, p. 376.

[2] J. Egret, *La Pré-révolution française, 1787–1788* (Paris: PUF, 1962), p. 122.

[3] Weulersse, *Le Mouvement physiocratique en France*, II, p. 171.

[4] D. Dakin, *Turgot and the 'ancien régime' in France* (London: Methuen, 1939), p. 247.

a project for legislation against the banalities which he attacked, however, almost exclusively, because he saw them as an obstacle to free trade in corn.[1] While Turgot gave loyal support to his protégé and clearly approved of his ideas, the pamphlet was more in the nature of an appeal to the privileged than a plan for political action by the Crown. Whatever Turgot's long-term plans, he retreated swiftly (while protecting Boncerf) before the storm of abuse which he had raised.

Did the abolition of serfdom on Crown lands in 1779 represent the first stage in a new and better planned attack on all feudal and seigniorial rights? As I suggested in the last chapter, the edict was regarded as an anti-climax by several of those who had written against serfdom.[2] The physiocrats, in particular, were dissatisfied because serfs in private hands had been recognized as a legitimate form of property in the edict. According to Condorcet in his *Vie de Monsieur Turgot*, the Minister had refrained from abolishing serfdom on Crown lands precisely because he did not wish even to appear by his silence to give support to the idea that serfs on seigniorial *terres* were a form of property. 'It is distressing that this view', wrote Condorcet, 'has been adopted for the first time by the government in the preamble of the Edict.'[3] By showing respect for the most disreputable institution of the *ancien régime*, as Monsieur Garaud has pointed out, the Crown announced that it would never undertake a serious agrarian reform.[4] The government had succeeded in advertising at the same time both the purity of its intentions and its inability to carry them out; surely, no one would deny it the role of heroic failure to which it aspired.

'Utilitarian' writers of every description would seem to have achieved by the eve of the Revolution almost nothing against the 'feudal regime'. The *agronomes* had wrought little change in French agriculture, and had hardly even considered in their writings how the levy on feudal and seigniorial dues affected farming. While the physiocrats denounced 'feudalism', their businesslike advice on the management of estates had probably served to encourage the 'feudal reaction'. The critics of seigniorial

---

[1] Turgot, *Oeuvres*, V, p. 321.
[2] See pp. 128 ff.
[3] J.-A.-N. Condorcet, *Vie de M. Turgot* (London, 1786), p. 186.
[4] Garaud, p. 164.

justice were scarcely more successful. The reforms which were carried out by the government seem to have owed little to their influence. Was the reason for their failure a lack of 'utilitarian' writers of stature? Perhaps if the abbé de Saint-Pierre had been alive he might have produced a *mémoire* on how such 'utilitarians' could be made useful, as he had done previously for dukes and peers. It can hardly be denied that there was no writer of outstanding ability in their ranks. Yet, it was so common for feudal and seigniorial privileges of various kinds to be criticized as harmful to agriculture or to society in general, that it seems safe to assume that they had at least succeeded in popularizing their views in France before the Revolution. The fact that the traditional defence of feudal and seigniorial rights on historic and legal grounds was seldom mentioned shows how far these 'rights' had been discredited. The feeble arguments of 'utilitarian' writers may itself reflect the lack of stimulus from their opponents. It was a measure of their influence that it became commonplace to judge not only feudal and seigniorial rights, but many other things as well, not on grounds of principle, but by their usefulness. Their attitude was shared by many revolutionaries. If the 'utilitarians' did not sow the seeds of revolution, they shaped the minds of many revolutionaries. If revolutions cannot be prevented, perhaps they can be made less harmful by ensuring that they will be led by 'utilitarians' and pragmatists who will keep dangerous matters of principle at bay.

VII

+++

Epilogue

+++

The literary attack on 'feudalism' was followed by the abolition of feudal and seigniorial rights during the Revolution. The writers might well seem, therefore, to have been the instigators of political events. Yet it is notoriously difficult to trace the diffusion of ideas among those who are largely illiterate. While few peasants can have read the philosophes, some of the latter's ideas in very diluted form were retailed in the poor man's *Bibliothèque Bleue*, which took its name from the cheap bluish paper that was used more often to wrap sugar loaves than to purvey ideas.[1] A fascinating study of this source has shown a real, if sluggish, movement of ideas away from the legendary tales of a primitive culture towards the practical self-help that was so characteristic of the eighteenth-century at higher intellectual levels.[2] An edge of social criticism can also be seen in the greater insistence in the popular literature on the equality of all before death, the imminence of which naturally filled the minds of the peasants who saw it so often around them.[3] Publicists left a still clearer mark on some of the broadsheets which circulated in and around Bordeaux, and other towns. They contained echoes of, among other works, Mably's *Observations sur l'histoire de France*, Voltaire's *L'Ingénu*, Raynal's *Histoire des établissements des Européens dans les deux Indes*, and even of Boncerf's *Les Inconvéniens des droits féodaux*, the possible

[1] G. Bollème, 'Littérature populaire et littérature de colportage au 18e. siècle', *Livre et société dans la France du XVIIIe. siècle*, by G. Bollème, F. Furet and others (Paris and The Hague: Mouton, 1965), pp. 64 and 89, respectively.

[2] *Ibid.*, esp. pp. 71–3.

[3] *Ibid.*, p. 78.

influence of which will be considered shortly.[1] The ideas of the publicists probably reached the peasants by word of mouth. It would, indeed, be surprising if the peasants on their frequent visits to their market-town did not pick up some of the more advanced ideas that were current there. Other possible disseminators were some of the curés whose obsession with the problem of improving their status in the Church was to lead at least some of them in 1789 to make common cause with the Third Estate.[2] Criticism of the administration of feudal and seigniorial rights was also likely to come from those curés who were engaged in feuds with their seigneurs.[3] Yet, whatever the possibility that the publicists reached the peasants, it must be admitted that there is practically no positive evidence. A few isolated events like the public rejoicings at Clermont-Ferrand over the signing of the American Declaration of Independence may show that the masses were not always entirely indifferent to politics, but they hardly provide convincing evidence for the diffusion of 'enlightened' ideas among them. The same must be said of the pilgrimage of a single 'philosophic' peasant who walked from Provence to Paris where he threw himself at the feet of a doubtless embarrassed Benjamin Franklin.[4] A surer indication of the inertia of peasant opinion is the fact that conservative writers showed little concern over the possible effects of 'philosophic' propaganda on them. Even those who were quick to condemn the ideas of the publicists seldom tried to strengthen their case by charging them with corrupting the peasantry.

It is the exceptional nature of such accusations against Boncerf that lends the incidents with which his name is associated particular interest. His pamphlet, *Les Inconvéniens des droits féodaux*, which appeared in 1776, was so moderate in tone that contemporaries themselves were surprised by the uproar it caused. 'It is inconceivable,' reported the well-informed *Mémoires Secrets*, how the *parlementaires* 'have censured this

[1] D. Mornet, *La Pensée française au XVIIIe. siècle* (Paris: Armand Colin, 1926), pp. 210–11.

[2] M. Hutt, 'The Curés and the third estate: the ideas of reform in the pamphlets of the French lower clergy in the period 1787–1789', *Journal of Ecclesiastical History*, VIII (1957), pp. 86–90.

[3] See p. 57.

[4] Mornet, *La Pensée française*, p. 210.

small work, which at most deserved to be suppressed, with laceration and burning.' The pamphlet was described as 'containing only very sensible arguments, reflections, opinions and a plan that were always submitted respectfully to the wisdom and enlightenment of the legislator, who is invoked incessantly. However dry and boring it is this event makes it fashionable and sought after, and bolsters the courage of the reader.'[1] None the less, the *parlementaires* professed themselves to be seriously concerned in case Boncerf's pamphlet would incite 'all vassals against their seigneurs, by representing to them all feudal and domanial rights as so many usurpations, vexations and acts of violence, that were equally odious and ridiculous, and by suggesting to them ways in which they could supposedly be abolished'. When Louis XVI, at Turgot's request, ordered them to stop judicial proceedings against Boncerf, the *parlementaires* practically accused the government of encouraging vassals to band together to force their seigneurs to relinquish their rights.[2]

The *parlementaires* were moderate in their views in comparison with the *Avocat-Général*, who reached a kind of oratorical climacteric in these words of his indictment:[3]

From the reading of new writings of all kinds with which the public is inundated, and especially from seeing this pamphlet, *Sur les inconvéniens des droits féodaux* it is tempting to credit the existence in the state of a secret faction, a hidden agency, which endeavours to shake its very foundations by blows from within, like those volcanoes which after being heralded by subterranean sounds and repeated tremors reach their climax in a sudden eruption, covering all that surrounds them in a burning torrent of debris, ashes and larva which spring from fire that is trapped in the entrails of the earth.

Even after the pamphlet had been duly lacerated and burnt at the foot of the main staircase of the *palais* of the parlement, the *Avocat-Général* secured it further free publicity by repeating

---

[1] *Mémoires Secrets*, IX (1776), p. 55.

[2] J. Flammermont, *Remontrances du Parlement de Paris au XVIIIe. siècle* (Paris, 1888–98), III, p. 357.

[3] *Arrest de la cour de Parlement*, 23 February 1776, p. 2, in the Despatches of Lord Stormont, the British Ambassador at Paris (Public Record Office, State Papers Foreign 78.298). It was typical that the *Avocat-Général* should be so certain of the harmfulness of Boncerf's pamphlet while misquoting the title.

his accusations. The king was solemnly informed that the work contained a programme which, besides endangering the laws and very constitution of the monarchy, threatened to set peasants against their lords and to foment civil war.[1] About a month later the parlement again warned the king of the direct effect which writings had on public opinion, and reinforced their point by recalling earlier *jacqueries* in the course of which 'peasants caused torrents of the most illustrious blood to flow'.[2]

Vague declamatory rhetoric is, of course, the legal profession's own argot: an *avocat-général* who refused to produce reassuring clichés when they were expected of him could be accused of failing in his duty to society. However, his speech differed from the usual fulminations of the bench in one important respect: his warnings were soon fulfilled. Twelve days later a contemporary periodical reported:[3]

The pamphlet condemned by the Parlement on the *Inconvéniens des droits féodaux* has just brought about the disorders which M. Séguier predicted in his indictment.

When the marquis de Vibraye wished to force one of his peasants to pay arrears of the *cens* he refused, and when his seigneur imprisoned him, thirty or forty peasants rebelled and came to reclaim their comrade. On the refusal to surrender him, they went home, armed themselves, and returned in force to besiege the château, where everything was sacked with such effect that M. de Vibraye had to yield and even take flight to save his life. This event, which the Parlement will seize upon, will cause M. Turgot further trouble. A copy of the pamphlet which was read in the village gave rise to this disorder. And everywhere this work is read, people may be expected to agree with the author, just as they would second the view of whoever proposed that royal taxes should not be paid.

A very similar incident was reported shortly afterwards in the same periodical:[4]

A parliamentary decree of the 30th. of last month created more of a sensation than might have been anticipated. The affair which gave

---

[1] J. Flammermont, III, p. 358.

[2] *Ibid.*, pp. 361–5.

[3] *Correspondance secrète, politique et littéraire, ou mémoires pour servir à l'historie des cours, des sociétés et de la littérature en France, depuis la mort de Louis XV* (London, reprinted 1787–90), II, p. 421.

[4] *Ibid.*, III, p. 23.

rise to it, or which served as the pretext, resembles the one that I described earlier. A relative of the Duc de Mortemart who was hunting on his lands was attacked by peasants who tried to prevent him. They were very rude and even shot at him and his party, while claiming to be the true owners of their lands. The Duc de Mortemart at once rushed to Versailles and lodged his complaints with the ministers, and attributed what happened to the 'system' of M. Turgot and to the works that he has hatched out. Reading them and the opinions which are disseminated among the people may, indeed, stir up unruly minds. The matter has been brought before the Parlement and the decree with which it has intervened bears indirectly on the Minister and his principles, as well as on the pamphlet, *Les Inconvéniens des droits féodaux.*

The accusations of the *parlementaires* were unconvincing even by their own standards. If they really wished to cast Boncerf and Turgot convincingly as architects of peasant revolution they should have provided, or manufactured with their usual skill, the evidence against them. It is surely significant that when the duc de Mortemart went hotfoot to Versailles he did not complain apparently of the effect which *Les Inconvéniens des droits féodaux* had had on his vassals, but instead denounced Turgot's 'system' and inveighed in general terms against 'the works that he has hatched out'. In both cases it was Turgot's policies rather than Boncerf's pamphlet that came under attack. In neither instance was a serious attempt made to establish the actual effect of the work in promoting disturbance. The *Avocat-Général* revealed his prejudices when he admitted that he had barely managed to read the brief pamphlet which he considered so harmful.[1] Far from being typical examples of their class, the seigneurs in question seem to have been so rigid in outlook that this fact alone may largely account for the discontent among their vassals. The duc de Mortemart was an active member of the Parlement of Paris, and was to crown a career of political protest in the Constituent Assembly by his denunciation of the decisions of 4 August in which the 'feudal regime' was declared to be abolished.[2] The marquis de Vibraye showed himself to be in other ways equally intransigent. He was reported to have resigned his post as French Ambassador in Copenhagen rather

[1] *Mémoires Secrets*, IX (1776), p. 57.
[2] *Réimpression de l'ancien Moniteur* (1843–63), III, p. 570.

than appear to condone the removal of the king's right of absolute veto.[1] In the context of the endemic rural violence of eighteenth-century France incidents like the ones described hardly required a literary catalyst to set them off. It was common, for example, for vendettas between seigneur and curé to reduce the *grandes et petites honneurs* in the parish church to the level of a slapstick farce.[2] If the occasional fracas between a seigneur and his vassals had imperilled the 'feudal regime' as a whole, contemporaries would surely have drawn attention to it in their writings. There seems little reason, on the contrary, to suppose that the undercurrent of violence in the countryside greatly disturbed them.

In 1789 the views of the peasants cease to be a matter for speculation and become a subject for research. The peasants who took the lead in abolishing the 'feudal regime' in the summer of 1789 recorded their views about it in their *cahiers* during the previous spring. Could they have done more to ensure that historians would interpret their motives correctly? They could hardly have foreseen that their testimony in the *cahiers* would often be dismissed as too good to be true as source material for the study of public opinion. Sometimes there are, indeed, grounds for scepticism. The seigneur's interference is very apparent in *cahiers* like that of the *tiers* of Quercy who actually defended the feudal system. These *cahiers*, however, stand out so clearly against the uninhibited criticism in the remainder, that there is little risk of their authenticity going unchallenged.[3] Peasant *cahiers* were also shaped occasionally by the models with which enterprising publicists tried to guide them. Yet, even in these cases it was rare for indiscriminate borrowing to take place. The model might add tone to a *cahier* by setting parochial concerns in a wider context, but it seldom obscured them. Even the least original *cahiers* were never entirely derivative.[4] In any case, some publicists, like the economist Véron de Forbonnais in his *cahier* for Champaissant, showed real understanding of peasant problems.[5] With more

---

[1] *Ibid.*, XIV, p. 125.

[2] See p. 57.

[3] S. Herbert, *The Fall of feudalism in France* (London: Methuen, 1921), p. 75.

[4] H. Sée, 'La Rédaction et la valeur historique des cahiers de paroisses pour les États-Généraux de 1789', *Revue Historique*, CIII (1910), p. 297.

[5] Bois, *Paysans de l'Ouest*, p. 183.

justification the *notaire* has also been suspected of influencing the content of the *cahier* to which he gave the legal form. It is likely that requests for reforms of the administration, with which few peasants can have been familiar, were inspired by the notary. Similarly, the occasional references to Natural law may reflect concern for the tone of the *cahier* by the man who drew it up. The articles that bear the influence of either publicists or lawyers are almost always peripheral to the statement of peasant grievances. Complaints about local conditions figure far more prominently than general statements of principle, or matters of wider public concern. In the case of the banalities, for instance, peasants were mainly preoccupied with the particular inconveniences and expense of resorting to the mill and oven of their own seigneur. It is impossible to read many *cahiers* without being impressed by the frank and rustic character of the overwhelming proportion of those from peasant communities. Grievances were nearly always voiced openly, and the overall tone itself usually carries conviction, down to the quaint French that is so often poorly concealed behind the legal jargon of the notary.

Perhaps it may be objected that the peasants had no intention of setting down a true account of their conditions, but on the contrary wished to air grievances, if not to exaggerate them. The *cahiers de doléances*, as their title suggests, were, indeed, intended to contain complaints. As the French experience showed, any government that asks for complaints is likely to get more than it bargains for. The difficulty of distinguishing the real grievance from the immemorial grumble, however, can be exaggerated. Few historians, for example, would accept at face value all that the Third Estate in the small village of Louzes say about their misfortunes. 'If they are to be believed,' writes Professor Bois, 'these poor people live in "precipitous mountains where the snow and hoar-frost begin in October and disappear only at the end of March". That is saying a good deal for a hill of 340 meters at a time when the touristic formula for the Mancelles Alps had not yet been invented!'[1] The simple exaggerations of eighteenth-century peasants should be easily discounted by any reader who can cope with the more complex prejudices of the twentieth-century historians who claim to interpret them. A more serious reason for suspecting that the

[1] *Ibid.,* pp. 177–8.

cahiers fail to reflect the views of the peasantry as a whole is evidence which shows that the *coqs de village* often allowed the poorer peasants little or no part in drawing up the *cahier*.[1] If allowance is made for the fact that a few of the more well-to-do peasants actually owned feudal and seigniorial rights themselves, or benefited from administering those of the seigneur, it remains true that the vast majority of peasants both rich and poor bore most of the weight of the seigniorial regime. The *cahiers* of the peasants, whatever their defects, are invaluable in illuminating their attitudes towards feudal and seigniorial rights. This fact is underlined by the reactions of their urban contemporaries. As Professor Cobban showed, it was usual for the complaints against feudal and seigniorial rights to be toned down, if not edited out of existence altogether, when the general *cahier* was drawn up for the whole electoral area.[2] The owners of feudal and seigniorial rights in the towns naturally resented criticism from peasants, whom they claimed as vassals. The very anxiety to suppress the objections of the peasants is itself a tribute to their outspokenness.

The peasants in their *cahiers* seldom spoke of either 'feudalism' or 'the feudal regime'. As I have suggested already, they were less concerned to trace the origins of feudal rights and dues than to record the particular hardships to which they were subjected. In itemizing grievances they often failed to describe the rights as either 'feudal' or 'seigniorial'. They appear to have seen them in isolation, rather than as part of an oppressive system. Their frequent use of the two terms as if they were interchangeable reflects the same attitude. The peasants should not be criticized, of course, for failing to make this distinction when educated contemporaries were equally at a loss. The reports of Merlin de Douai and the Feudal Committee illustrate the extent of the confusion among France's leading lawyers. The conception of feudalism among the peasants, however, was closer to that of the publicists than might have been expected. Echoes of what I called 'the myth of the feudal anarchy' occurred quite frequently. Rights were condemned sometimes on the grounds that they had been acquired during times of 'feudal anarchy', or of 'feudal despotism', while rights were often

[1] Davies, p. 34.
[2] Cobban, *Social Interpretation of the French Revolution*, pp. 37–8.

declared to be so 'exorbitant', 'outrageous', 'hateful' etc., as to be unmistakably usurped. Contemporary historiography left its mark still more clearly on a few *cahiers*. As fiefs had originally belonged to the State and as official posts had been held for life, declared the Third Estate of Saint-Julien-le-Montagnier, the nation should abolish feudal and seigniorial rights, especially as it had never agreed to their becoming hereditary in the first place.[1] In another *cahier* the government was even treated to a brief lecture on the history of the Franks. It was doubtless from these military assemblies on the Champ de Mars, concluded the *tiers*, 'that the feudal regime, so contrary to nature, had been derived'.[2] It was argued that, irrespective of whether feudal rights had been usurped, altered circumstances had removed the justification for them.[3] It was even suggested in one *cahier*, already cited, that of Saint-Julien-le-Montagnier, that owners of fiefs should be freed completely from all obligations to undertake military service and administer justice, so that there could be no possible objection to the complete abolition of all privileges and exemptions that were attached to fiefs.[4] Although the peasants were concerned mainly with specific grievances, there appears to have been a widespread feeling among them that their ancestors had been cheated in an earlier period of feudal oppression.

As feudal dues and privileges were upheld by law, any serious attack on them was a challenge to the legal system. Even a cursory review of the *cahiers* shows that this attack was hardly ever pressed to the point of questioning the legitimacy of feudal and seigniorial rights themselves. They were usually accepted in principle, while objections were directed against the ways in which they were levied in practice. Similarly, the peasants usually reserved their criticism, not for the seigneur, but for his *feudiste*. Again, the 'renovation', rather than the existence itself, of *terriers* was condemned.[5] Although protests were mainly against the new ways in which rights were being exploited, the peasants showed some understanding of the legal apparatus by

[1] Mavidal and Laurent, VI, p. 416.

[2] *Ibid.*, IV, p. 525.

[3] M. Godard and L. Abensour (eds.), *Cahiers de doléances du bailliage d'Amont* (Besançon, 1918–27), I, p. 88.

[4] Mavidal and Laurent, VI, p. 416.

[5] Bois, *Paysans de l'Ouest*, pp. 191–7.

which this end was achieved. They could argue their case on occasion with more skill than lawyers had ever been accustomed to expend on their behalf. The Third Estate of Colombotte, for instance, showed that it was against the terms of a deed of 1683 that the Chapter of Vesoul had reduced them to serfdom.[1] At Beaudean they complained that 'feudal administration carried to excess for about twenty-five years has let loose a deluge of evils on this unfortunate community', and pointed out that the original charter of 1326 provided for one mill only, while in their own time there were three.[2] Although such references to particular charters and title deeds were rather rare, there was a deep-rooted suspicion among communities of peasants concerning the authenticity of the feudal charters. A common refrain in their *cahiers* was the demand that the seigneur should produce the *titre primordial* or original title-deed.[3]

As these rights were enforced in the seigniorial courts, the intentions of the peasants must be evaluated largely in terms of their attack on seigniorial justice. There was undoubtedly widespread hostility to seigniorial jurisdiction. Yet the motives behind the many curt demands for the suppression of the courts are far from clear. There is a noticeable lack of references to the use of the seigniorial courts for the enforcement of the seigneur's claims. The inadequate functioning and poor distribution of the courts was criticized, Professor Bois found, without the seigneur himself coming under attack. The demands for the improvement or even for the suppression of the courts, in his view, was part of a wider demand for law reform, rather than the reflection of a social conflict.[4] As the seigniorial courts are known to have been particularly strongly entrenched in Brittany, which falls within the area of his study, it is likely that his conclusions have still greater application to the rest of France. Another reason for doubting that the seigniorial courts were denounced because of their part in upholding the 'feudal regime' is the almost complete failure to press the attack home against the appeal courts in the form of the local parlements. No attack on the rights themselves stood much chance of success as long as the ultimate

[1] Godard and Abensour, I, p. 375.

[2] G. Balencie (ed.), *Cahiers de doléances de la sénéchaussée de Bigorre* (Tarbes: Lesbordes, 1925), pp. 147–8.

[3] Aulard, p. 112.

[4] Bois, *Paysans de l'Ouest*, p. 167.

appeal was to a court whose members were almost invariably
seigneurs themselves.

It was scarcely to be expected that the peasants would have
much to say about the more literary objections to feudalism in
commercial, humanitarian and utilitarian writings. As already
suggested, the nobles were more anxious than the Third Estate
to secure permission to engage in trade without loss of caste.
It was only in the towns where some of the richer inhabitants
might hope to enter the nobility that a motive for making this
demand existed. Similarly, the peasants as a whole were unaffected by the writings of the *agronomes*, physiocrats and other
writers whom I classified as 'utilitarians'. This fact emerges
particularly clearly in the case of *franc-fief*, which so many of
the 'utilitarian' writers criticized severely. Requests for the
abolition of *franc-fief* are largely absent from the *cahiers* of the
peasants; they occur much more frequently in the general
cahiers, which were drawn up in the principal town of each
bailliage and *sénéchaussée*.[1] Finally, in the case of humanitarian
objections to serfdom and to feudal and seigniorial rights in
general, the views of the *cahiers* seem to owe little to outside
influences. It is even possible that the peasant sometimes knew
that he was receiving inhuman treatment from his seigneur
without waiting to be informed of the fact by a contemporary
pamphleteer. The publicists were moved by the picturesque
plight of an insignificant and dwindling number of serfs; the
peasants were more concerned with the hardships of a whole
variety of feudal and seigniorial rights. Serfdom is set in a
truer perspective by the peasants themselves. Their attitude is
reflected in the *Archives Parlementaires*, where out of an enormous collection of *cahiers*, there are only a score or so of
requests for the abolition of serfdom.

Although the peasants took the initiative in overthrowing
the 'feudal regime', historians have tended to focus their attention on the deputies in the National Assembly. This fact is all
the more remarkable because it is no longer seriously disputed
that the Assembly 'abolished feudalism' on 4 August in order
to pacify the countryside. About a hundred moderate deputies
had agreed in the Club Breton the night before that it would be
better to concede some of their rights in order to safeguard the

[1] See under *franc-fief* the *cahiers* listed in Mavidal and Laurent, VII, pp. 340–2.

rest.[1] However, it has obviously been difficult for many Frenchmen to accept that one of the main reforms of the Revolution was secured by peasants—a group whose conservatism in the nineteenth century is still widely deplored. Distaste has been reinforced by historians who adopt the methodology of Marxism, if not its ideas.[2] The Marxist view that the Revolution saw both the overthrow of feudalism and the advent of capitalism to France hardly squares, among other facts, with the important part that the peasants took in overthrowing 'feudalism'.

It is worth looking more closely at the 'reluctant revolutionaries' in the National Assembly. The night of 4 August was long hailed as a corner-stone of the Revolution. Although the deputies in the Assembly claimed to have destroyed the feudal regime entirely, like the shrewd businessman of today who nullifies his guarantee in 'the small print at the bottom', they undid most of their concessions in their subsequent decrees. Even before the pronouncements of 4 August, the Archbishop of Aix, 'energetically depicting the evils of feudalism', warned the Assembly of the need to prohibit in advance all contracts that could lead to its revival.[3] As this was precisely what many members secretly wanted, they established a Feudal Committee to ensure that the warning had no effect. The inclusion among its members of one bishop, four nobles, three landowners, one lieutenant-general and an overwhelming preponderance of conservative-minded lawyers practically guaranteed that it would take no precipitate measures against the holders of fiefs.[4] The Assembly's confidence in the Committee was shown to be well-placed when it achieved the rare distinction in a revolution of postponing its proposals for an unwelcome decree for six months. Merlin de Douai, who was mainly responsible for drafting it, managed to construct an elaborate defence of the rights to which his Committee had been publicly instructed to abolish. In the report he produced on 18 February 1790 he practically admitted, as Professor Cobban pointed out, that he was trying to consolidate the former dues under the name of freehold property.[5] It is impossible to remain unimpressed by

[1] M. Garaud, p. 176.

[2] Cobban, *Social Interpretation of the French Revolution*, pp. 169 ff.

[3] *Réimpression de l'ancien Moniteur*, I, p. 285.

[4] Garaud, p. 183.

[5] Cobban, *Social Interpretation of the French Revolution*, p. 42.

the deft way in which Merlin de Douai rehabilitated 'feudalism' by removing from it all that could be of no use to the landlord. He split 'feudalism' into two halves; a fictitious 'feudalism' which embraced rights that bore on the person of the vassal and which had no contractual basis; and on the other hand 'feudalism' proper which comprised property rights that issued from a contract.[1] In this way, he introduced a new criterion which had no place in the decrees of August 1789: feudal rights were to be acceptable provided they were the result of a contract. This rule was applied in March 1790 even to the hated banalities which had earlier been declared abolished without compensation. At the same time the owners of fiefs were invited to resume claims that they had abandoned since January 1789 through fear of peasant reprisals.[2] As Buzot in the Assembly told the Feudal Committee, 'You have concerned yourselves greatly with the interests of the creditor and very little with those of the payer of the *cens*.'[3] The situation is supposed to have been remedied eventually when further pressure from the peasants forced the Convention to pass the law of 17 July 1793. At first sight this law might seem, in the words of one historian, to have 'completed the destruction of feudalism'. The first article ran: 'All dues formerly seigneurial, feudal rights whether fixed or casual . . . are suppressed without indemnity.' The title deeds were to be burnt publicly, and those who failed to comply with the order were to be punished for their carelessness by spending five years in irons.[4] The reader will hardly be surprised to learn that even this act promised more than it performed: it can hardly be denied that the defrauding of the peasants had become one of the traditions of the Revolution. The provision to burn the title deeds was the final insult. Not only were many deeds not burnt in practice,[5] but the rights themselves often continued in force under other names. If legislative sanction were needed for those who could usually be relied upon to help themselves, it was

[1] These distinctions are borrowed from a recent article by Mlle R. Robin in which the rich ambiguities of the subject are pursued with exquisite linguistic subtlety. See her 'Fief et seigneurie dans le droit et l'idéologie juridique à la fin du XVIIIe siècle' in *Annales Historiques de la Révolution Française*, XLIII (1971), 592.

[2] M. Garaud, pp. 185–7.

[3] *Réimpression de l'ancien Moniteur*, IV, p. 218.

[4] Herbert, p. 196.

[5] Garaud, pp. 228 ff.

given by a decree of November in the same year. While denouncing the reintroduction of feudal rights in the preamble, the Convention legitimized them in the most explicit terms in the text.[1]

The present decree [it was declared] does not prejudice the right which owners, tenants, small-holders and *métayers* have to make by mutual agreement, *all pacts that they consider suitable*, whether regarding the sharing of the produce, or the payment of taxes, provided, however, these agreements have no connection, neither in name nor reality with the rights mentioned [and confirmed] by the first article.

Once the names were dropped, therefore, feudal and seigniorial rights became respectable. All that the Convention insisted was that 'a spade should not be called a spade'. The owner was perfectly free, except when there was no lease or it predated 1789, to add to the rent a sum equivalent to the former yield of the 'abolished' rights. The procedure could be described as a form of fiscal consolidation for the owner's benefit. Even contemporaries, who should have been accustomed to the hypocrisy of revolutionary governments, were baffled by the law of 14 June 1794, by which the defence of the former feudal rights was again undertaken. At least one local *tribunal* asked the Convention incredulously if the abolition of the various rights was really meant to be to the sole advantage of the owner without any benefit to the leaseholder. The Convention characteristically considered the owner was so obviously the more deserving party that, after recalling earlier decrees in his favour, they pronounced further debate to be pointless. They showed more interest in regaining ground that had been lost earlier by the *ci-devant* seigneurs.[2] The cause of reaction was championed still more openly under the Directory in the *Conseil des Anciens*, where in August 1797 a report was introduced to secure the re-establishment of ground-rent, 'which a false interpretation has caused to be considered suppressed on the grounds that it bordered on feudalism'.[3]

Far from being legislated out of existence by the many

[1] A. Soboul, 'Survivances "féodales" dans la société rurale française au XIXe. siècle', *Annales. Économies. Sociétés. Civilisations*, XXIII (1968), p. 968.
[2] *Ibid.*, p. 969.
[3] *Réimpression de l'ancien Moniteur*, XXVIII, p. 759.

revolutionary decrees, some feudal rights survived the Revolution to carry the spirit of the *ancien régime* deep into the nineteenth century. Successive governments were only too eager to hasten the assimilation of former dues to property rights. Feudal rights in their new form did not so much survive as prosper. A closely documented account for the west of France shows that there, at least, rights were seldom challenged successfully in the courts and lasted sometimes until the dawn of the twentieth century. For instance, a *terrage* that dated from the late sixteenth century was upheld in the courts in the years V and X of the Revolution, was rescinded in 1809 only to be upheld again the following year, and lasted down till the 1880s.[1]

While feudal dues were being transformed into property rights the ghost of a long-deceased feudalism continued to haunt France. Seldom has a spectre been so overworked. The legislature was tireless in producing decrees against 'feudalism' in which displays of verbal violence were innocent of almost all effect, except, perhaps, to bring catharsis to the deputies themselves. Not content with limiting legislation to feudal and seigniorial rights, they aspired to banish the very memory of 'feudalism'. In June 1793 a member of the Convention reminded his colleagues that they had established his committee to scrutinize the list of all the communes in France with a view to the elimination of names that recalled feudal institutions. 'You thought,' he reminded them, 'that everything which may perpetuate that hateful memory sullies the language of free Frenchmen, and should disappear along with their tyrants.' By way of implementing these revolutionary sentiments he suggested, among a few immediate changes, that Mont-Louis should be renamed Mont-Libre, and Carla-le-Comte be known as Carla-le-Peuple.[2] Even greater concern appears to have been caused by the number of symbols of 'feudalism' which were still to be found in the capital. Urgent representations were made by members of the Convention to the civic authorities to remove 'all monuments and symbols of feudalism which have not yet fallen under the hammer of patriotism'.[3] A few months later the

---

[1] P. Massé, 'Survivances des droits féodaux dans l'Ouest (1793–1902)', *Annales Historiques de la Révolution Française*, no. 181 (1965), pp. 275–6.
[2] *Réimpression de l'ancien Moniteur*, XVI, pp. 538–9.
[3] *Ibid.*, XVII, p. 169.

same deputies were doubtless shocked to learn from the indignant Louchet at Le Havre that in the Department of Seine-Inférieure there were still what he called, without specifying them, 'signs of feudalism', the destruction of which he had at once ordered.[1] Shortly afterwards, the indefatigable *conventionnels* in Paris were threatening to confiscate buildings that sported armorial bearings. Churches and other public buildings, it was also decreed, should be purged of any taint of royalism and feudalism. When a virtuous member expressed concern over the deleterious influence of the royal and feudal insignia on playing cards, even that possible source of corruption was legislated out of existence.[2] If the perils of picture cards were apparent, the legislators could hardly overlook the far greater danger from books and prints. Accordingly, the political purity of citizens was protected by patriotic holocausts of the vestiges of 'feudalism' and royalty. When private sources appear to have been exhausted, the Parisian authorities offered generously to purge the contents of the Bibliothèque Nationale.[3] The enthusiasm to destroy these emblems 'of pride or folly' was so great, in fact, that the leaders felt obliged to restrain their followers.[4] Yet their anxiety to remove all traces of 'feudalism' appears to have remained as strong as ever. Early in 1794 legal officials were strictly enjoined to avoid all expressions that tended to recall, directly or even indirectly, 'the feudal or noble regime, or royalty itself'.[5]

Why should the protectors of feudal dues be the assailants of 'feudalism'? It may seem surprising that successive legislatures tried so hard to preserve the substance of 'feudalism' while fighting its shadow. The cynic might see it as an elaborate manœuvre by which those who had profited from the Revolution tried to sell it to the countryside. According to this view the peasants were given to understand that 'feudalism' lay essentially in the trappings which had been surrendered, while profitable 'rights' continued to be paid as before under other

[1] *Ibid.*, XVIII, p. 158.
[2] V. A. D. and P. A. Dalloz, *Jurisprudence générale: répertoire méthodique et alphabétique de législation, de doctrine et de jurisprudence* (Paris, 1845–70), XXXVIII, p. 349.
[3] *Réimpression de l'ancien Moniteur*, XVIII, p. 194.
[4] *Ibid.*, XVIII, pp. 223–4.
[5] *Ibid.*, XIX, p. 325.

names. Such an explanation leaves out of account the native shrewdness of the peasants for which there is ample evidence in the *cahiers* and elsewhere. It would also be mistaken to place much weight on the supposition that the revolutionary politicians were unusually self-seeking. In terms of corruption and graft it is likely that the legislatures of the Revolution have been outstripped by most of their successors. The demonstrations against the 'feudal regime' among the politicians were too spontaneous to be fully credible as purely propagandist exercises. If the attack on 'feudalism' was designed to divert attention from the rights themselves, it had the opposite effect. From the owner's viewpoint, the less said about 'feudalism' the better. The contents of the *Moniteur*, which supplied the official record of events, does not really support the view that feudal dues were guarded from criticism by a barrage of invective against a fictitious 'feudalism'. The *Moniteur*, for instance, carried a letter in March 1790 from a man whose claim to a political hearing could easily have been ignored. Contemporaries, indeed, had such a low opinion of the marquis de Villette that they found it hard to decide whether he deserved more ridicule for his sexual exploits or his literary pretensions.[1] Villette's exhibitionism in this case took the form of stripping himself publicly of various feudal rights. Among others he renounced the banalities because 'they have always appeared to me to be the most revolting privilege'.[2] That was strong language to apply to rights which would be given a new basis for respectability in a decree of a few weeks later. Outspoken criticism of the decrees of the majority from other sources also appears in the columns of the *Moniteur*.[3] These expressions of opinion were doubtless tolerated because they were not felt to be dangerous. Politicians were surely right during the Revolution if they felt that the defence of feudal dues could be left safely to hand-picked committees, while views and propaganda one way or the other would be of little account.

The attacks in so many revolutionary decrees on symbols of 'feudalism', from the marks of deference paid to the seigneur in his parish church to the names of towns, is barely explicable if

---

[1] Hoefer, XLVI, pp. 218–19.
[2] *Réimpression de l'ancien Moniteur*, III, p. 494.
[3] *Ibid.*, IV, p. 218 and XI, pp. 59–60.

the meaning of the term is limited to certain rights and dues. 'Feudalism' in the eighteenth-century writings that were considered in earlier chapters stood for a wide range of attitudes, as well as the privileges with which they were associated. The idea of social deference was particularly strongly tied to 'feudalism'. Participants in the controversy over whether the nobility should engage in trade could seldom argue their case, for instance, without referring to 'feudalism' in some form.[1] It seems equally clear that historical writings on the Franks and early history of France had a direct bearing on the nobility's claims to privileged social status.[2] However, it was probably by being measured against the criterion of 'utility' that ideas of social prestige based on a feudal past received the hardest knock.[3] If 'feudalism' meant for many bourgeois landowners exaggerated claims to social deference, the attack on 'feudalism', while feudal dues were protected, becomes all the more understandable. Fiefs fulfilled two roles in the society of the time: they bolstered family pride and ensured a safe return on capital invested. Allowing for the need to acquire social status through the ownership of fiefs which was still seen as a mark of nobility, the main concern of the aspiring bourgeois was to secure his capital. However much the prestige of the nobility was coveted, that, like almost everything else in eighteenth-century France, could be bought. It made good social as well as economic sense to prize the 'useful' right above the 'honorific'. The same rule applied to many nobles as well as bourgeois. The most likely to cling to their 'honorific' rights were those who lacked the money to buy their way up the social scale: for the impecunious country gentleman the right to hunt over the lands of others, or erect a weather-vane above his *château*, or have his own pew in the parish church and receive separate censing at mass on Sundays, was all-important, because such rights underlined his social superiority to peasants who might not be much poorer than himself. In the elections to the Estates General in 1789 it was these backwoodsmen rather than the liberal nobles who triumphed. Thus, although rich nobles and commoners had been tending to draw together, except perhaps in the immediate past,

[1] See p. 85 ff.
[2] See esp. pp. 24–5.
[3] See pp. 133 ff..

the gap between them was again widened. The sharp antagonism between nobles and commoners reflected in the virulent hatred for armorial bearings and other marks of social status which the majority in the Assembly expressed in their decrees. To call the various status symbols 'feudal' was little more than a convenient means of denigration.

If 'feudalism' symbolized no more than claims to inflated social status, it is surprising that the word 'noble' did not replace it in simple pejorative use. Yet, not only was 'noble' used rather rarely in this sense, but the word 'aristocrat' suddenly came into common use on the eve of the Revolution to take its place. This is all the more surprising as *les aristocrates* meant not so much nobles by blood as the political enemies of the regime.[1] An impoverished Chouan in revolt against the Republic, therefore, was numbered among the hated *aristocrates*, while the former noble who worked his passage in the Convention was spared the label. 'Noble' was also unsuitable as a comprehensive term of abuse as it excluded the clergy who at that time received more than their usual share of unpopularity. 'Feudalism', on the other hand, was admirably fitted as a vehicle for expressing abhorrence of the clergy, as their misdoings were lovingly chronicled by their critics, especially in descriptions of 'the feudal anarchy'.[2]

'Aristocracy' and 'feudalism' were so often bracketed together that their meaning for contemporaries almost certainly overlapped. As 'aristocrat' had connotations that were primarily political, it is likely that the political connotations of 'feudalism' during the Revolution were at least as important as the social ones. In the historical works where 'feudalism' was discussed most fully writers almost always had a form of government, 'the feudal regime', in mind. It was characterized, in their view, by the usurpation of the sovereign power by the magnates. 'Feudalism' came by extension to mean any infringement, particularly by the nobility, of royal sovereignty. There was a tendency to draw a sharp contrast between a strong, efficient government on the one side, and an anarchical 'feudal system' on the other.[3] In the historical accounts much stress was laid on the sheer 'anarchy' inherent in feudalism, while much of the

[1] Brunot, IX, pt II, pp. 646–8.
[2] See pp. 31–4.
[3] See pp. 38 ff.

literary objection to feudal dues concentrated on the inefficient and wasteful methods for their collection.[1] Feudalism, therefore, came to be associated with the administrative chaos of the *ancien régime*. It represented precisely those qualities which the Republic had to suppress if it were to forge a nation and repel the invader. In these circumstances the political connotations of 'feudalism' could be expected to outweigh the social.

The political implications of 'feudalism' are all the easier to overlook, as they changed radically during the Revolution. Under the *ancien régime* 'feudalism' had been the very antithesis of monarchical power. Almost all the publicists had urged the French Crown to assert its authority against the privileged and, by implication at least, to side with the Third Estate. Yet in many of the revolutionary decrees, as we have seen, 'feudalism' and 'royalism' were coupled in condemnation.[2] That development would almost certainly not have come about, however, if the Crown had heeded the publicists. Yet Louis XVI, who had once led the assault against 'feudalism' by abolishing serfdom on Crown lands, chose to declare his express support for feudal and seigniorial rights shortly before 4 August. The Assembly's decrees, instead of bringing him to his senses, only called forth from him capricious arguments in favour of the status quo.[3] By going against a long-established tradition, the monarchy had become associated in the minds of the revolutionaries with the hated 'feudal regime', of which earlier writers had considered it the first victim. They wrote more truly than they could have known.

Those who create myths are often the first victims. While the bogey of 'feudalism' may have served a useful political purpose in welding the French people together, the upper classes certainly did not wish to encourage peasants to deprive them of their feudal and seigniorial rights. Did their propaganda have this effect? The question is almost unanswerable because historians have failed to chart the change in the conditions of the peasants during the Revolutionary period. Setting aside the fact that different classes of peasants fared very differently, and that there were important regional variations, all that can be said with any assurance is that the peasants often gained less

[1] See pp. 144 ff.
[2] See p. 178.
[3] Garaud, pp 164–5 and 181, respectively.

than might have been expected. Many, though not all, feudal dues were given a new lease of life through being transformed into property rights. On the other hand, the peasants clearly won a moral victory by forcing first the Assembly and afterwards the Convention to pronounce the total abolition of feudal rights. The success of the peasants, such as it was, can be attributed to many causes. It probably owed much to the stolid determination of the peasants themselves. Events also showed that the peasants made headway with their demands, however just, only when the forces of repression were weak. If the peasants owed any of their success to the politicians, it was in the purely negative sense of learning to distrust them and to take the law into their own hands. The pronouncement of 4 August that 'the feudal regime is destroyed' in particular served the peasants, against the wishes of the Assembly, with a rallying-point for their discontent. Otherwise, the attitude of the peasants towards 'feudalism' appears to have been of little political consequence. Their attitude is all-important, however, if the atmosphere of the times and the mentality of the peasants themselves is to be understood.

The thoughts of the peasants about 'feudalism' can be read in their *cahiers*; their feelings are expressed more freely in their actions during the Revolution. However faithful to their outlook in other respects, the *cahiers* seldom convey that deep sense of outrage which broke out intermittently among peasant communities both during and after the Revolution. These feelings cannot be measured, of course, statistically, and peasant unrest itself is poorly documented. There are indications—but little positive proof—of how the peasants felt towards the 'feudal regime'. Small wonder that 'serious' historians pass over these questions in silence. It is only those for whom the feelings of even peasants matter, who will insist on trying to interpret the scanty evidence available.

The most characteristic feature of almost all peasant protest was the absence of violence. Sicilian peasants might like to eat the roasted livers of their gentry, but those in France preferred to make their point with greater human dignity.[1] An investigation

---

[1] They added this item to their culinary repertoire during the revolt of 1860. See D. Mack Smith, *A History of Sicily* (New York: Viking Press, 1968), II, p. 439.

of the uprisings around Quercy, for instance, revealed that the only blood shed was that of a sheep.[1] Needless to say, the owners of fiefs made the most of the few sanguinary incidents. The assertion in the *Moniteur* that during the first wave of unrest 'it was a crime to be a gentleman and sex itself was no guarantee against the vengeance of the multitude' was wide of the truth.[2] The same can be said with even greater assurance of the bitter complaint by two brothers that they had been assassinated. [*sic!*]. The reader may be interested to learn that poetic justice was done, however, when the Balud brothers, who were the aggressors, provoked an attack which led to the suicide of the one and the hanging of the other.[3]

When peasants rose against their seigneurs in the summer of 1789, their chief ambition was to destroy the charters and *terriers* which were used in the exaction of feudal and seigniorial dues. Violence hardly ever occurred except when they met resistance. The restraint shown by the peasants seems to bear witness to their own belief in the justice of their cause. At Chapelle-Grézignac the peasants demanded the repayment of the dues which had just been levied and, in their view, abolished on 4 August. When the *châtelaine* refused to comply with their demands, they broke into the granary and removed exactly what they said was theirs.[4] At Aynac, where they claimed that the dues had been three times the proper amount, they took no reprisals beyond taking possession of a meadow which they said had been seized forcibly from them.[5] In another form of protest they planted a *mai*, a kind of maypole, in front of the *château* as a symbol of their independence. This simple demonstration was occasionally given added relevance for the seigneur by hanging on the *mai* grain sieves used in the collection of feudal dues.[6] To bring the point home further at the *château* of the comte de Durfort-Lêobard they chanted 'victory' as they danced around the *mai*.[7] At Saint-Alvère the peasants put on a demon-

---

[1] J. Viguier, 'Les Émeutes populaires dans le Quercy en 1789 et 1790', *La Révolution Française: revue d'histoire moderne et contemporaine*, XXI (1891), p. 39.
[2] *Réimpression de l'ancien Moniteur*, I, p. 275.
[3] Aulard, p. 136.
[4] *Ibid.*, pp. 147–8.
[5] Herbert, p. 166.
[6] Aulard, p. 129, and Viguier, p. 42.
[7] Viguier, p. 38.

stration that would have done credit to the French symbolists of the next century. 'Today,' the marquis de Lostanges was informed by his bailiff, 'they planted a tall tree which they call a *mai* in the middle of the square, and they attached to the top of this *mai* a mill-stone for grinding corn and measures for the dues, which they broke, as well as a hen and a cat to stand for the *acapte*; they call the *acapte* in patois *la catte*, which means the cat.'[1] In rare cases the peasants would also erect a gallows. There was never any question of hanging the seigneur: it was intended rather to deter the irresolute from breaking the solidarity of the village by continuing to meet their 'feudal' obligations.[2]

The attack on the weather-vanes may seem too reminiscent of the adventures of Don Quixote to call for serious study. Yet these incidents illumine the mentality of both nobles and peasants. The *girouettes* were reminders of an age when almost all authority in the countryside was wielded by the local seigneur. It was probably for this reason that they were condemned so forcefully in the *Encyclopédie* for being in appearance 'entirely Gothic and barbarous', two epithets which were sure to bring to mind for contemporaries the despised 'feudal regime'.[3] The fact that no less than fourteen were seized by the peasants from a single *château* certainly suggests that their owner prized them for other reasons as well as their use in indicating the direction of the wind.[4] Their emotional significance for the peasants, as Aulard showed, was greater still.[5]

These weather-vanes to which the seigneurs in certain provinces had, or claimed to have, the exclusive right, in the eyes of the peasants were a symbol of feudalism, of an insolent supremacy over them. When the *châtelain* did not remove them willingly they were knocked down with musket shots, or the peasants themselves invaded the house and climbed the tower to tear down these hated emblems.

Reports in the Assembly seem to show that attacks on the weather-vanes were widespread early in 1790. They were the

[1] Aulard, p. 142.
[2] *Ibid.*, pp. 147–8.
[3] Diderot, VII, p. 674.
[4] Viguier, p. 38.
[5] Aulard, pp. 167–8.

occasion a year later of troubles that were sufficiently serious for the departmental authorities in Corrèze to write to the Assembly for advice. There was unrest, it was explained, because people thought that 'the weather-cocks, having always served as the exterior sign of a fief, and consequently of feudal power, ought to be torn down'.[1] It is likely that the peasants were moved by the same sort of feelings when they burnt the seigneur's pew in the parish church. Although both kinds of demonstrations were the exception rather than the rule, they seem to underline the peasant's concern for his self-respect. It was not just the financial burden of the various dues that he resented, it was also the social inferiority that went with his subjection to them. While the *cahiers* alone might convey the impression that the peasants seldom saw beyond the individual feudal dues to the 'feudal regime' itself, the events of the Revolutionary period broadened their understanding in this and other areas. References to the 'feudal regime' from 1789 onwards appear to have been common, while the preoccupation with symbols of 'feudalism' suggests that they had come to see the system as a whole. Addresses like the following to the Constituent Assembly in December 1791 show a political maturity that would hardly have been conceivable two years earlier.[2]

We announce to you with peaceful joy [wrote the Commune of Lourmarin] that the destruction of the feudal regime will bring death to aristocrats. It is in the hope of re-establishing it that they emigrate, conspire and bestir themselves in all directions . . . When you have banished the monster of feudalism, the aristocracy will be destroyed for ever and the fields that are so desolate today will become the firmest rampart of the Republic.

Few politicians could fix the price for their political support more eloquently. The same message in less coherent form came from enough of the rural communes for the Convention to feel the need to purchase the support of the countryside by the final decree of July 1793, which, however incomplete, became 'the symbol of peasant emancipation' for future generations.[3]

If 'feudalism' in the eighteenth century was an anachronism,

---

[1] Herbert, pp. 161–2.
[2] Sagnac, pp. 401–2.
[3] Garaud, p. 238.

in the nineteenth fears of 'feudalism' became a neurosis. It were as if the 'regime' itself were followed by delayed shock. The fear that the whole apparatus of 'feudalism' would one day be resuscitated appears to have lain deep in the peasants' collective unconscious. Periodically, these fears would be precipitated to the surface by some rumour or chance event and the otherwise inert peasants would be impelled into political action.

One of the first to exploit these fears was Napoleon on his return from Elba when he appealed for help in overthrowing the Bourbons. 'You have allowed yourselves,' he rebuked the Mayor of Autun, 'to be led by the priests and nobles who hankered after the tithes and the feudal dues.'[1] With a view to regaining control of France, one of his first public acts was to decree at Lyons the abolition of nobility and the suppression of feudal titles.[2] Once he had recaptured power, it became official policy to equate Bourbon rule with attempts to reintroduce feudal and seigniorial rights. As befitted an intelligent despot, Napoleon left the more inane propaganda to the National Assembly. That body announced a few days after Napoleon's re-entry to Paris that it abolished the 'feudal monarchy' of the Bourbons, who were also accused of preparing the ground for the re-establishment of feudal dues and the tithes.[3] The same message came with greater propriety from Grenoble which had befriended Napoleon during the first critical days of his return. The Academy, in its address to Napoleon, after reminding him of the city's services to him, recalled how feudalism under the restored Bourbons had gained a new lease of life.[4]

Despite the shrewdness of Napoleon's propaganda, the Bourbons had more to fear from their own supporters. With such friends, Louis XVIII could congratulate himself that he had no need of enemies. The king's attempts to bridge the divisions in French society were frequently jeopardized by ultras who felt that the government's only obligations were to themselves. Even a leading ultra theorist in Toulouse, which was one of the chief centres of their support, admitted that there were many

[1] Soboul, *Annales. Économies. Sociétés. Civilisations*, XXIII (1968), p. 971.
[2] *Le Moniteur Universel* (Paris, 1 January 1811–29 June 1901), 21 March 1815, p. 325.
[3] *Ibid.*, 27 March 1815, p. 348.
[4] *Ibid.*, 1 April 1815, p. 369.

among the local aristocracy who hoped for a counter-revolution that would enable them to regain property lost during the Revolution.[1] The groundswell of this new 'feudal reaction' reached such a pitch that there was even an attempt in 1829 to restore one of the hated seigniorial pews, which an earlier generation had delighted to burn as symbols of feudal oppression.[2] The pretensions of the ultras, therefore, even lent a certain credibility to the charge that they were scheming to restore the feudal regime itself. The strength of the liberal backlash can be gauged from works such as the *Dictionnaire de l'ancien régime et des abus féodaux*. It was so successful when it appeared in 1820 that its editor was complaining that his material had already been plagiarized in a rival *Dictionnaire féodal*.[3] The tone of the first work was set by the opening words: 'When the waters are low work on the dikes; it is with the intention of following this prudent advice that the present work is published. The partisans of feudalism cry out that feudalism is no more and will never be reborn; but, if its ghost terrifies us, it must be fought and above all chased away.'[4] The editor went on to say that the best way of laying the ghost was to unveil the crimes into which the spirit of feudalism had breathed life. Feudalism might appear to be dead, the reader was warned, but like a vampire still wished to gorge itself on blood.[5] In this 'Gothic' atmosphere one of the most effective polemicists was the abbé Grégoire. As a former priest and bishop of the Constitutional Church he had all the advantages of inside knowledge when abusing the Church for its part in the politics of reaction. Grégoire drew much of his material from the contents of diocesan catechisms, which appear to have rivalled even episcopal pastorals as compendia of clerical folly. In one case he denounced 'the affection with which the vicar-generals and bishops in their catechism instigate the return of the feudal regime by inculcating obedience *to the parochial seigneurs*, as if

[1] D. C. Higgs, 'The Ultra-royalist movement at Toulouse under the Second Restoration (1815–1830)' (unpublished Ph.D. thesis London University, 1964), p. 257. This important work by an eminent Canadian scholar will be published shortly.

[2] Soboul, *Annales. Économies. Sociétés. Civilisations*, XXIII (1968), p. 974n.

[3] *Dictionnaire de l'ancien régime et des abus féodaux, par P.D.XXX de P.XXX* (Paris, 1820), pp. ii–iii.

[4] *Ibid.*, p. i.

[5] *Ibid.*, p. x.

they still existed . . .' 'Thus,' he continued, 'prelates in revolt
against the fundamental laws of the state wish in the name of
heaven to re-establish the feudal regime,' while dragging after
it, perhaps, he added, all sorts of dues, including mortmain, the
banalities, and the *corvées*.[1] In the hysterical atmosphere under
the restored Bourbons it was understandable for the peasants,
especially around Toulouse, to fear the restoration of the feudal
regime.[2] At the same time, past successes seem to have given
them enough confidence to lend their fears a truculent edge.
During the famine of 1816 a citizen of Toulouse was to assure
the prefect of their loyalty to the king, while declaring that 'if
the gentry wish to regain their former rights, and to make us
crawl on our bellies, I give my word, they will regret it!'[3] Some
villagers in the Pyrenees in 1822 were equally emphatic. 'The
undersigned', the prefect was informed in a petition, 'regard
M. de Fleury only as their mayor . . . and not as their former
seigneur armed with feudal power and the arbitrary dispenser of
the product of their sweat.'[4]

'Feudalism' might have been expected to lose its hold over
the popular imagination after the Indemnity Law of 1825. The
passing of the law in the Chamber of Deputies had served to
sharpen social antagonisms. In a speech that made a great impression, General Foy argued that the payment in compensation
of a million francs, which he claimed was twenty times the size
of the deficit that 'caused the outbreak of the Revolution', would
only serve to whet the appetite of the *émigrés*. The indemnity,
he said, would exacerbate the divisions in society and would
arouse the apprehensions of all the holders of the former *biens
nationaux*.[5] Once the law had been passed, however, it con-
founded the prophets of doom. Almost everywhere it was taken
to mark the culmination of ultra ambitions and the limits of
popular forbearance. Far from its making the fortunes of the
émigrés, the law's real beneficiaries were their creditors. It was
actually decreed in the act that the indemnified should pay their
debts, which was a provision that was hardly in keeping with the

[1] Soboul, *Annales, Économies. Sociétés. Civilisations*, XXIII (1968), p. 972.
[2] Higgs, p. 258n.
[3] *Ibid.*, p. 97.
[4] R. Forster, 'The Survival of the nobility during the French Revolution',
Past and Present, XXXVII (July 1967), p. 85.
[5] *Le Moniteur Universel*, 22 February 1825, p. 238.

traditions of the *ancien régime*, still less those of a feudal reaction.[1] Nevertheless, peasant fears continued. There are tantalizing hints in the official records of a kind of collective uneasiness that appears to have lain behind much of the agrarian unrest of the early nineteenth century. On occasion it would even drive the peasants to adopt radical views that were at variance with their traditional conservatism. The success of the 'Socialists' in the Dordogne in 1840 was ascribed by the Procurator-General at Bordeaux, for instance, to fears of the re-establishment of the tithes and the *corvées*.[2] In 1849 a left-wing candidate warned the peasants in his electoral manifesto of the seigneur's ambition to rebuild his 'feudal dovecote', which had been one of the most hated features, as well as itself a symbol, of the *ancien régime*.[3] As late as 1868 at Charente and elsewhere there were riots which were ascribed to 'rumours in the countryside of the re-establishment of the tithes and the feudal dues'.[4] Until recently the fragmentary evidence from documents bore no comparison with the rich oral tradition among the peasants themselves.[5]

In the nineteen-twenties [relates Professor Goubert] in the country-side where modern life had made few inroads, it was not unusual to meet old men, born under the Second Empire or earlier still, who through their own ancestors had made living contact with the Revolution and the period that had gone before it, and called it unhesitatingly 'the age of the seigneurs', an expression which the historical text-books of the Third Republic would often repeat.

The peasant world with its exaggerated fears of a return to the *ancien régime* has aroused little interest among historians. They probably feel that French society in the nineteenth century suffered from enough ills without adding a fictitious feudalism to the list. Yet the historian commands a very limited field if he restricts his attention to the few rational acts of his fellows. As the wars, revolutions and ideologies of the last few hundred years have shown, man's irrational behaviour has shaped much

---

[1] Forster, *Past and Present*, XXXVII (July 1967), p. 81.

[2] Soboul, *Annales. Économies. Sociétés. Civilisations*, XXIII (1968), p. 978.

[3] R. Rémond, *La Vie politique en France depuis* 1789 (Paris: Armand Colin, 1968–9), II, p. 95.

[4] Soboul, *Annales. Économies. Sociétés. Civilisations*, XXIII (1968), p. 978.

[5] P. Goubert, *L'Ancien Régime* (1969), I, p. 17.

of his history. The attitude of the peasants towards 'feudalism', though less important, clearly belongs to this category. While few would deny that the fears of the peasants were largely imaginary, it is equally certain that they left their mark on the politics of the period. The real problem is surely not to explain away these fears, but to discover why they had such a hold over the peasantry. As early as 1856 de Tocqueville pondered this very question, which has received too little attention since. 'Why,' he asked, 'have feudal dues excited such strong hatred in the heart of the people in France that it survived the object itself and for this very reason appears to be unquenchable?'[1]

De Tocqueville's immediate reaction was to explain the motives of the peasants in purely rational terms. When the peasant became the owner of his land and escaped from the control of his seigneur, argued de Tocqueville, he resented the seigneur's remaining claims over him all the more, as an infringement of his independence. While de Tocqueville's explanation appears convincing at first — especially when he applies it to the breakdown of feudalism before the Revolution — he himself sensed its inadequacy. Alongside the thoughts of the peasants he reconstructed their feelings with that warmth of sympathy which marked the victory of the historian over the political scientist. De Tocqueville by his own powers of empathy made it easy for the reader also to experience at second hand the hopes and frustrations of the peasant under the *ancien régime*: his lust for his own piece of land in which he buried his heart along with the grain; his resentment of the troublesome neighbours — the seigneur and the priest — who spoilt his pleasures, hampered his work and ate his produce. 'Imagine,' de Tocqueville concluded, 'the needs, the character, the passions of this man, and calculate if you are able the treasures of hate and envy that are piled up in his heart.'[2]

De Tocqueville's invitation was taken up by politicians who made 'the treasures of hate and envy' their own political capital. The exploitation of the peasants under the *ancien régime* had prepared the ground for those who wished to prey upon them further in the nineteenth century. Frequent betrayal had soured

[1] Soboul, *Annales. Économies. Sociétés. Civilisations*, XXIII (1968), p. 976.
[2] A. de Tocqueville, *L'Ancien Régime*, ed. G. W. Headlam (London: Oxford University Press, 1904), pp. 39–41.

them and had caused them to withdraw sullenly into a world of their own, which they were in no position to defend. Those who sought their votes soon learnt that they wanted nothing in return but to be left alone. Under the *ancien régime* they had been cheated of their produce; during the Revolution they were cheated of many of the gains from their supposed emancipation from feudal and seigniorial obligations; subsequently they were cheated of the economic and social reforms that could have improved their lot. If the peasant continued to live in the past, it was largely because that was where his social superiors wanted him to live. The peasant who continued to see an oppressive feudal seigneur behind an extortionate landlord was shrewd rather than alarmist. The tragedy for the peasants was that the attack on 'feudalism' came too late to save them. In the early years of Louis XVI's reign it looked as if the royal administration might carry out reforms that would have improved the lot of the peasant at the expense of the privileged.

The peasants benefited from the Revolution more in the short than in the long term. In 1789 there was a vogue for engravings in which peasants were depicted bent under the weight of the other two orders. It was the achievement of the upper classes that the peasants continued to bear their weight upon their backs, while there were no longer engravings to tell the tale.

Bibliography

Primary Sources

1. Manuscripts

Archives Nationales, AD XI 9, *Arrest du Conseil d'Estat du Roy*, 25 April 1716.

Public Record Office, State Papers Foreign, 78.298, Despatches of Lord Stormont, British Ambassador in Paris.

2. Books and pamphlets

ACADÉMIE FRANÇAISE, *Dictionnaire*, 1st ed., 4 vols (Paris: J.-B. Coignard, 1694).

— *Grand Dictionnaire des arts et des sciences*, 2nd ed., 4 vols (Amsterdam: J.-B. Coignard, 1696).

— *Nouveau Dictionnaire*, 3rd ed., 2 vols (Paris: J.-B. Coignard, 1718).

— *Dictionnaire*, 4th ed., 2 vols (Paris: Brunet, 1762).

ACADÉMIE ROYALE DES SCIENCES, *Description des arts et métiers, faites ou approuvées par Messieurs de l'Académie Royale des Sciences* (Paris: Desaint et Saillant, 1761–88).

ALÈS DE CORBET, P.-A. (vicomte d'), *Nouvelles observations sur les deux systèmes de la noblesse commerçante ou militaire* (Amsterdam, 1758).

ARCQ, P.-A. DE SAINTE-FOIX (chevalier d'), *La Noblesse militaire, ou le patriote françois* (n.p., 1756).

ARGENSON, R.-L. DE VOYER (marquis d'), *Considérations sur le gouvernement ancien et présent de la France* (Amsterdam: M. M. Rey, 1764).

BARTHOUL, ABBÉ, *Lettre à l'auteur de 'La Noblesse Commerçante'* (Bordeaux, 1756).

BELLAMI (avocat fiscal au bailliage et marquisat-pairie d'Herbault),

Traité de la perfection et confection des papiers terriers généraux du Roy (Paris: Paulus du Mesnil, 1746).

BELLONI, G. (marchese de), *Dissertation sur le commerce, traduit de l'Italien par M.A.**** (The Hague, 1755).

BERTRAND, J., 'Essai sur l'esprit de la législation, pour encourager l'agriculture, et favoriser relativement à cet objet essentiel, la population, les manufactures et le commerce', *Mémoires et observations recueillies par la Société Oeconomique de Berne*, 1765, pt 2 (Berne, 1765).

BILLARDON DE SAUVIGNY, E.-L., *L'Une ou l'autre ou la noblesse commerçante et militaire, avec des réflexions sur le commerce et les moyens de l'encourager* (Mahon, 1756).

BONCERF, P.-F., *Les Inconvéniens des droits féodaux. Nouvelle édition, augmentée de fragmens sur l'origine des droits féodaux, et de l'examen de la règle, nulle terre sans seigneur, par M. Francaleu* (London, 1776), B.M. ref.: FR 237 no. 8.

— *Les Inconvéniens des droits féodaux* (n.p., 1791), B.N. ref.: Lb³⁹ 203D.

— *La Plus importante et la plus pressante affaire, ou la nécessité et les moyens de restaurer l'agriculture et le commerce* (n.p., n.d.).

BOUCHER D'ARGIS, A. J.-B., *Cahier d'un magistrat du Châtelet de Paris, sur les justices seigneuriales et l'administration de la justice dans les campagnes* (Paris: Clousier, 1789).

BOUDIN, J. A., *Nouvelles réflexions sur le rachat des droits féodaux* (Paris: Desenne, 1790).

BOUHIER, J., *Observations sur les coutumes du Duché de Bourgogne*, 2 vols (Dijon: Arnauld Jean-Baptiste Augé, 1742-6).

BOULAINVILLIERS, H. (comte de), *Essais sur la noblesse de France, contenant une dissertation sur son origine et abaissement* (Amsterdam, 1732).

— *État de la France*, 3 vols (London: T. Wood, S. Palmer and W. Roberts, 1727-8).

— *Mémoire pour la noblesse de France contre les ducs et pairs* (n.p., 1717).

BRÉQUIGNY, L. G. O. F. DE, 'Recherches sur les communes' and 'Recherches sur les bourgeoisies', *Collection des meilleures dissertations notices et traités particulières relatifs à l'histoire de France*, ed. C. J. Leber, 20 vols (Paris: J.-G. Dentu, 1826-38), XX, pp. 42-144 and 145-211, respectively.

BRISSOT DE WARVILLE, J.-P., *Bibliothèque philosophique du législateur, du politique, du jurisconsulte*, 10 vols (Berlin, 1782-5).

BUCQUET, L.-J.-B., *Discours qui a remporté le prix de l'Académie de Chaalons (sic.) en l'année M. DCC. LXXXIII sur cette question proposée par la même Académie: 'Quels seraient les moyens de rendre la*

justice en France avec le plus de célérité et le moins de frais possibles?'
(Beauvais: Desjardins, 1789).

CHALLAN, A.-D.-J.-B., *Réflexions sur l'administration de la justice, sur la formation de tribunaux ordinaires et municipaux, afin de rendre la justice gratuite, et d'éviter les abus qui règnent spécialement dans les justices seigneuriales* (1789).

CHALLINE, P., *Méthode générale pour l'intelligence des coustumes de France* (Paris: Bobin et Le Gras, 1666).

CHÉRIN, L. N. H., *La Noblesse considérée sous ses divers rapports dans les assemblées générales et particulières de la nation* (Paris: Boyez, 1788).

CLERGET, P.-F., *Le Cri de la raison, ou examen approfondi des loix et des coutumes qui tiennent dans la servitude main-mortable quinze cent mille sujets du Roi* (Besançon: Simard, 1789).

— and BAVEREL, ABBÉ J. P., *Coup d'oeil philosophique et politique sur la main-morte* (London, 1785).

CLICQUOT DE BLERVACHE, S., *Mémoire sur les moyens d'améliorer en France la condition des laboureurs, des journaliers, des hommes de peine vivans dans les campagnes, et celle de leurs femmes et de leurs enfans* (Paris: Delalain Paîné, 1789).

CONDORCET, J.-A.-N. (marquis de Caritat), *Vie de M. Turgot* (London, 1786).

COSTA DE BEAUREGARD, J.-H. (marquis), *Essai sur l'amélioration de l'agriculture dans le pays monteux, et en particulier dans la Savoye* (Chambéry: Gorrin, 1774).

COURTÉPÉE, C., and BEGUILLET, E., *Description générale et particulière du duché de Bourgogne, précédée de l'abrégé historique de cette province,* 6 vols (Dijon: L.-N. Frantin, 1774–85).

COYER, G.-F., *La Noblesse Commerçante* (London and Paris: Duchesne, 1756).

— *La Noblesse Militaire et Commerçante; en réponse aux objections faites par l'auteur de la Noblesse Militaire* (Amsterdam, 1756).

— *Développement et défense du système de La Noblesse Commerçante* (Amsterdam and Paris: Duchesne, 1757).

DANIEL, G., *Histoire de France, depuis l'établissement de la monarchie françoise dans les Gaules,* 7 vols, 2nd ed. (Amsterdam, 1720–5).

— *Histoire de la milice françoise,* 2 vols (Paris: Coignard, 1721).

DELANDINE, A.-F., *Couronnes académiques, ou recueil des prix proposés par les sociétés savantes,* 2 vols (Paris: Cuchet, 1787).

DÉMEUNIER, J.-N., *Encyclopédie méthodique. Économie politique et diplomatique,* 4 vols (Paris and Liège: Pancoucke, 1784–8).

DÉNISART, J.-B., *Collection de décisions nouvelles et de notions relatives à la jurisprudence actuelle,* 3 vols, 6th ed. (1768).

DIDEROT, D. (ed.), *Encyclopédie ou dictionnaire raisonné des sciences, des arts et des métiers*, 17 vols (Paris, 1751–65).

DOYEN, G., *Recherches et observations sur les loix féodales, sur les anciennes conditions des habitans des villes et des campagnes, leurs possessions et leurs droits* (Paris: Valade, 1779).

DUBOS, J.-B., *Histoire critique de l'établissement de la monarchie françoise dans les Gaules*, 3 vols (Amsterdam: Osmont, 1734).

DULAURE, J.-A., *Crimes et forfaits de la noblesse, et du clergé, depuis le commencement de la monarchie jusqu'à nos jours* (Paris, n.d.).

— *Histoire critique de la noblesse depuis le commencement de la monarchie jusqu'à nos jours* (Paris: Guillot, 1790).

DUNOD DE CHARNAGE, F.-I., *Traités de la mainmorte et des retraits* (Dijon, 1733).

— *Traités de la mainmorte et des retraits*, new ed. (Paris: Depuis, 1760).

DU REY DE MEYNIÈRES, O. G. (Dame Belot), *Observations sur la noblesse et le tiers-état* (Amsterdam: Arkstee et Merkus, 1758).

DUTOT, *Réflexions politiques sur les finances et le commerce: où l'on examine quelles ont été sur les revenus, les denrées, le change étranger, et conséquement sur notre commerce, les influences des augmentations et des diminutions des valeurs numéraires des monnoyes*, 2 vols (The Hague: Vaillant et Prevost, 1738).

EON, J., *Le Commerce honorable, ou considérations politiques, contenant les motifs de nécéssité, d'honneur et de profit, qui se treuvent à former des compagnies de personnes de toutes conditions pour l'entretien du négoce de mer en France* (Nantes, 1646).

FILANGIERI, G., *La Science de la législation . . . ouvrage traduit de l'italien d'après l'édition de Naples, de* 1784 *(par J.-Ant. Gouvain Gallois)*, 6 vols (Paris: Cuchot, 1786–91).

FLEURY, C., *Droit public de France, ouvrage posthume de M.l'abbé Fleury, composé pour l'éducation des princes, et publié avec des notes par J.-B. Daragon*, 2 vols (Paris: Pierre, 1769).

— FABRE, J.-C., and GOUJET, G. P., *Histoire Écclésiastique*, 36 vols (Paris: Manette et Guerin, 1722–04–38).

FLORIAN, J.-P. CLARIS DE, *Fables de Florian, précédées d'une notice sur sa vie et ses ouvrages (par L.-F. Jauffret), Nouvelle édition augmentée de fables inédites* (Paris: Pouthieu, 1825).

FOUQUEAU DE PUSSY (avocat), *Idées sur l'administration de la justice dans les petites villes et bourgs de France, pour déterminer la suppression des jurisdictions seigneuriales* (Paris: Godefroy, 1789).

FRÉMINVILLE, E. DE LA POIX DE, *Dictionnaire ou traité de la police générale des villes, bourgs, paroisses et seigneuries de la campagne* (Paris: Gissey, 1758).

— *La Pratique universelle pour la rénovation des terriers et des droits seigneuriaux*, 5 vols (Paris: Morel et Gissey, 1746–57).

FRESNAIS DE BEAUMONT, *La Noblesse cultivatrice, ou moyens d'élever en France la culture . . . au plus haut degré de perfection* (Paris: B. Morin, 1778).

GARNIER, J.-J., *Le Commerce remis à sa place: réponse d'un pédant de collège aux novateurs politiques, addressée à l'auteur de la 'Lettre à M.F.'* (n.p., 1756).

GIN P.-L.-C., *Les Vrais principes du gouvernement français, démontrés par la raison et par les faits* (Geneva and Paris: Servière, 1782).

GIRARD, G.-J., *Traité des usemens ruraux de Basse-Brétagne, où, l'on parle de tout ce qui peut favoriser les progrès de l'agriculture* (Quimper: M. Blot, 1774).

GLATIGNY, G. DE, *Oeuvres posthumes de Monsieur de ***, contenant ses harangues au Palais, ses discours académiques* (Lyons: Duplain, 1757).

GOUDAR, A., *Les Intérêts de la France mal entendus, dans les branches de l'agriculture, de la population, des finances, du commerce, de la marine et de l'industrie*, 3 vols (Amsterdam: J. Coeur, 1756).

GRAPPIN, P.-P., *Quelle est l'origine des droits de main-morte dans les provinces qui ont composé le premier royaume de Bourgogne . . .?* (Besançon: J. M. Couché, 1779).

GUYOT, G.-A., *Observations sur le droit des patrons et des seigneurs de paroisse aux honneurs dans l'église* (Paris: B. Brunet, 1751).

— *Traité des fiefs tant pour le pays coutumier que pour les pays de droit écrit*, 7 vols (Paris: Saugrain, 1746–58).

HÉNAULT, C. J. F., *Nouvel abrégé chronologique de l'histoire de France*, 3 vols, new ed. (Paris: Prault, 1768).

HENRION DE PANSEY, P. P. N. (baron), *Traité des fiefs de Dumoulin, analysé et conferé avec les autres feudistes* (Paris: Valade, 1773).

HERVÉ, F., *Théorie des matières féodales et censuelles*, 7 vols (Paris: Knapen, 1785–8).

HOTMAN, F., *La Gaule françoise* (Cologne: H. Bertuphe, 1574).

JOLLIVET (frères et commissaires aux droits seigneuriaux), *Méthode des terriers, ou traités des préparatifs et de la confection des terriers* (Paris: Musier, 1776).

LA GARDE, F. DE P., *Traité historique de la souveraineté du roi et des droits en dépendans, de commencer à l'établissement de la monarchie*, 2 vols (Paris: Durand, 1754).

LA HAUSSE, DE, *La Noblesse telle qu'elle doit être, ou moyen de l'employer utilement pour elle-même et pour la patrie* (Amsterdam and Paris: A. M. Lottin, 1758).

LAURENT (avocat en Parlement), *Lettre d'un franc-comtois aux députés de sa province* (n.p., n.d.).

LEFÈVRE DE BEAUVRAY, P., *Dictionnaire social et patriotique* (Amsterdam, 1770).

LE LABOUREUR, J., *Histoire de la pairie de France et du Parlement de Paris* (London: S. Harding, 1740).

LESCÈNE-DESMAISONS, J., *Histoire politique de la Révolution en France, ou correspondance entre Lord D*** et Lord T**** (London, 1789).

LETROSNE, G.-F., *De l'Administration provinciale, et de la réforme de l'impôt*, ed. in 1 vol. in 1779, ed. in 2 vols in 1788 (Basle and Paris: P.-J. Duplain).

— *Vues sur la justice criminelle. Discours prononcé au bailliage d'Orléans* (Paris: Debure, 1777).

LE VASSOR, M., *Les Soupirs de la France esclave, qui aspire après la liberté* (Amsterdam, 1689–90).

LINGUET, S. N. H., *Nécessité d'une réforme dans l'administration de la justice et dans les loix civiles en France, avec la réfutation de quelques passages de 'L'Esprit des Loix'* (Amsterdam, 1764).

— *Théorie des loix civiles, ou principes fondamentaux de la société*, 2 vols (London, 1767).

MARCHAND, J.-H., *La Noblesse commerçable ou ubiquiste* (Amsterdam, 1756).

MARÉCHAL, M., *Traité des droits honorifiques des patrons et des seigneurs dans les églises*, ed. J. A. Sérieux (Paris: Barrois, 1772).

MELON, J.-F., *Essai politique sur le commerce* (n.p., 1734).

MÉZARD (chevalier et Président de la Cour Royale d'Ajaccio), *Essai sur les réformes à faire dans l'administration de la justice en France. Dédié aux États-Généraux* (n.p., 1788).

MÉZERAY, F. EUDES DE, *Histoire de France depuis Faramond jusqu'à maintenant*, 3 vols (Paris: M. Guillemot, 1643–51).

MIRABEAU, V. RIQUETTI (marquis de), *L'Ami des hommes, ou traité de la population*, 3 vols (The Hague: Benjamin Gibert, 1758).

MONTESQUIEU, C.-L. (baron de La Brède et de Secondat), *Oeuvres complètes publiées sous la direction de M. André Masson*, 3 vols. (Paris: Nagel, 1950–5).

MURAT-MONTFERRAND (comte de), *Qu'est-ce que la noblesse, et que sont ses privilèges?* (Amsterdam, 1789).

NÉE DE LA ROCHELLE, J.-B., *Mémoires pour servir à l'histoire du Nivernois et Donziois, avec des dissertations* (Paris: Moreau, 1747).

PERRECIOT, C.-J. DE, *De l'État civil des personnes et de la condition des terres dans les Gaules, dès les temps celtiques jusqu'à la rédaction des coutumes*, 2 vols (Switzerland, 1786).

PÉTION DE VILLENEUVE, J., *Les Loix civiles et l'administration de la justice, ramenées à un ordre simple et uniforme: ou réflexions morales, politiques . . . sur la manière de rendre la justice en France, avec le plus de célébrité et le moins de frais possible* (London, 1782).

PÉZEROLES (abbé de), *Le Conciliateur ou la noblesse militaire et commer-çante; en réponse aux objections faites par l'auteur de 'La Noblesse Militaire'* (Amsterdam and Paris: Duchesne, 1756).

POULLAIN DE SAINT-FOIX, G.-F., *Essais historiques sur Paris*, 3 vols, new ed. (London and Paris: Duchesne, 1759).

PROST DE ROYER, A.-F., *Dictionnaire de jurisprudence et des arrêts, ou nouvelle édition du Dictionnaire . . . de Brillon*, 7 vols (Lyons: A. de la Roche, 1781–8).

RENAULDON, J., *Dictionnaire des fiefs et des droits seigneuriaux utiles et honorifiques*, 2 vols (Paris: Knapen, 1765).

— *Traité historique et pratique des droits seigneuriaux* (Paris: Despilly, 1765).

ROCHON DE CHABANNES, M.-A.-J., *La Noblesse oisive* (n.p., 1756).

ROZET (Libraire), *Véritables origines des biens écclésiastiques* (Paris: Desenne, 1790).

SAINT-PIERRE, ABBÉ C.-I. CASTEL DE, *Ouvrajes* (sic) *de politique*, 16 vols, (Rotterdam: J.-D. Beman; Paris: Briasson, 1733–41).

SAINT-SIMON, L. ROUVROY (duc de), *Mémoires*, 45 vols, ed. A. de Boislisle (Paris: Hachette, 1879–1928).

SAPT, ABBÉ DE, *L'Ami du prince et de la patrie, ou le bon citoyen* (Paris: J.-P. Costard, 1769).

SEDAINE, M.-J., *Le Philosophe sans le savoir, comédie en prose et en 5 actes*, ed. C. Brereton (London: Blackie, 1907).

SÉRAS, *Le Commerce Ennobli* (Brussels, 1756).

SIEYÈS, E.-J. (comte and abbé), *Qu'est-ce que le tiers état?* (n.p., 1789).

SIMMONEL, D., *Dissertation sur l'origine, les droits, et les prérogatives des pairs de France* (n.p., 1753).

TRÉVOUX, *Dictionnaire universel françois et latin, vulgairement appelé Dictionnaire de Trévoux*, 7 vols, ed. P. C. Berthelin (1752).

— *Dictionnaire universel françois et latin, vulgairement appelé Diction-naire de Trévoux*, 8 vols, ed. abbé Brillant (Paris, 1771).

TURGOT, A.-R.-J. (baron de l'Aulne), *Oeuvres de Turgot et documents le concernant, avec biographie et notes par Gustave Schelle*, 5 vols (Paris: F. Alcan, 1913–23).

VELLY, P.-F., VILLARET, C., and GARNIER, J.-J., *Histoire de France, depuis l'établissement de la monarchie jusqu'au règne de Louis XIV*, 33 vols, new ed. (Paris: Desaint, Nyon et Saillant, 1769–63–99). B.M. ref.: 283 d 6.

VENTE DE PENNES (marquis de), *La Noblesse ramenée à ses vrais principes, ou examen du développement de 'La Noblesse Commerçante'* (Amsterdam, 1759).

VÉRON DE FORBONNAIS, F. DE, *Élémens du commerce*, new ed. (Leyden, 1754).

— *Lettre à M.F., ou examen politique des prétendus inconvéniens de la faculté de commercer en gros, sans déroger à sa noblesse* (n.p., 1756).

VILLEMONNEY (avocat en Parlement), *Considérations sur la destruction du régime féodal* (Paris: Laurens, 1789).

VILLETTE, C. M. (marquis de), *Lettre de M. de Villette à M. Necker* (n.p., 17 May 1789).

— *Protestation d'un serf du Mont-Jura* (n.p., 1789).

VOLTAIRE, F. M. AROUET DE, *Correspondance*, 107 vols, ed. T. Besterman (Geneva: Institut et Musée Voltaire, 1953–65).

— *Oeuvres*, 52 vols, ed. L. E. D. Moland and G. Bengesco (Paris: Garnier, 1883–5).

YOUNG, A., *Travels in France during the years 1787, 1788 and 1789*, ed. C. Maxwell (Cambridge University Press, 1929).

3. *Anonymous works*

De l'Administration de la justice dans les campagnes (n.p., n.d.), B.N. ref.: Lf²³ 54.

Le Citoyen philosophe, ou examen critique de 'La Noblesse Militaire' (n.p., 1756), B.N. ref.: Ll³ 219.

Considérations sur l'injustice des prétentions du clergé et de la noblesse (n.p., 1789), B.M. ref.: F 13 no. 2.

Dictionnaire de l'ancien régime et des abus féodaux, par P.D.*** de P*** (Paris: de P. Mongie, 1820), B.M. ref.: 1195 g 26.

De la Féodalité et de l'aristocratie française, ou tableau des effets désastreux des droits féodaux; et réfutation des erreurs sur lesquelles la noblesse fonde ses prétentions (n.p., date of B.M. copy illegible), B.M. ref.: R 451 no. 3.

Lettre à un plébéien au sujet de l'Assemblée des États-Généraux (n.p., 20 September 1788), B.M. ref.: R 50 no. 8.

Mémoire des avocats du Parlement de Bretagne sur les moyens d'entretenir l'union entre les différens ordres de l'état (Rennes, 1788), B.M. ref.: FR 24 no. 14.

Mémoire sur les rentes et les droits féodaux . . . par un dauphinois (Paris, 1789), B.M. ref.: R 485 no. 3.

Nouveau plan d'administration de la justice civile dans lequel on propose les moyens d'assurer au mérite seul tous les offices ou places de judicature, d'accélérer le jugement des procès, et d'en diminuer les frais (Paris, 1789), B.N. ref.: Lf²³ 59.

Réflexions patriotiques, sur l'arrêté de quelques nobles de Bretagne . . . du 25 octobre 1788 (n.p., n.d.), B.M. ref.: FR 24 no. 8.

Réformes dans l'ordre social et particulièrement dans le commerce (n.p., n.d.), B.M. ref.: FR 580 no. 13.

BIBLIOGRAPHY

4. Periodicals and newspapers

Année Littéraire ou suite des lettres sur quelques écrits de ce temps, 292 vols (Amsterdam, 1754–90).

Bibliothèque Françoise, ou histoire littéraire de la France, 42 vols (Amsterdam, 1723–46).

Bibliothèque des Sciences et des Beaux-Arts, 50 vols (The Hague, 1754–80).

Correspondance Littéraire, Philosophique et Critique, 16 vols, ed. M. Tourneux (Paris, 1877–82).

Correspondance Secrète, Politique et Littéraire, ou mémoires pour servir à l'histoire des cours, des sociétés et de la littérature en France, depuis la mort de Louis XV, 18 vols (London, reprinted 1787–90).

Esprit des Journaux, François et Étrangers, 487 vols (Paris and Liège, 1772–1818).

Journal Encyclopédique, 306 vols (Liège, then Bouillon, 1756–93).

Journal des Sçavans, 128 vols (Paris, 1665–1792).

Journal des Sçavans, augmenté de divers articles qui ne se treuvent point dans l'édition de Paris, c.170 vols (Amsterdam, 1685–1753).

Journal des Sçavans, combiné avec les Mémoires de Trévoux, 79 vols Amsterdam, 1754–63).

Journal des Sciences et des Beaux-Arts, 50 vols (Paris, 1768–78).

Mémoires pour l'Histoire des Sciences et des Beaux-Arts, 265 vols (Trévoux, 1701–67).

Mémoires Secrets pour servir à l'histoire de la République des Lettres en France, depuis MDCC LXII jusqu'à nos jours, 36 vols (London, 1777–89).

Mercure de France, 974 vols (Paris, 1724–91).

Moniteur Universel (Paris, 1 January 1811–29 June 1901).

Nouvelles Éphémérides Économiques ou bibliothèque raisonnée de l'histoire de la morale et de la politique, 19 vols (Paris, 1774–6).

Observations sur les Écrits Modernes, 33 vols (Amsterdam, 1735–43).

Réimpression de l'ancien Moniteur, 31 vols (Paris, 1843–63).

Suite de la Clef, ou journal historique sur les matières du temps, 120 vols (Paris, 1717–76).

Supplément de la Clef . . . contenant ce qui s'est passé en Europe d'intéressant pour l'histoire depuis la Paix de Ryswick, 2 vols (Verdun, 1713).

5. Collections of documents

BALENCIE, G. (ed.), *Cahiers de doléances de la sénéchaussée de Bigorre* (Tarbes: Lesbordes, 1925).

BOIS, P. (ed.), *Cahiers de doléances du tiers-état de la sénéchaussée de Château-du-Loir* (Gap, 1960).

CHASSIN, C.-L. (ed.), *Les Élections et les cahiers de Paris en* 1789, 4 vols (Paris: Jouaust et Sigaux, 1888–9).

DALLOZ, V. A. D. and P. A. (eds.), *Jurisprudence générale: répertoire méthodique et alphabétique de législation, de doctrine et de jurisprudence,* 44 vols (Paris, 1846–73).

FLAMMERMONT, J., *Remontrances du Parlement de Paris au XVIIIe. siècle,* 3 vols (Paris: Imprimerie Nationale, 1888–98).

GODARD, M., and ABENSOUR, L. (eds), *Cahiers de doléances du bailliage d'Amont,* 2 vols (Besançon, 1918–27).

ISAMBERT, F. A., and others (eds), *Recueil général des anciennes lois françaises,* 29 vols (Paris: Et Imbert, 1822–8).

MAVIDAL, J. M., and LAURENT, E. (eds), *Archives parlementaires de 1787 à 1860,* 7 vols, 1st ser. (1789–99), 2nd ed. (1879).

PROST, F., *Les Remontrances du Parlement de Franche-Comté au XVIIIe. siècle* (Lyons: Boscfrères, M. and L. Riou, 1936).

Secondary Sources

1. *Reference works*

ARNAULT, A. V., JAY, A., and others, *Biographie nouvelle des contemporains,* 20 vols (Paris: 1820–5).

BALTEAU, J., and others, *Dictionnaire de biographie française* (Paris: Letouzey et Ané, 1933 onwards).

BRUNOT, F., *Histoire de la langue française dès origines à nos jours,* 13 vols (Paris: Armand Colin, 1924–53).

DAUZAT, A., *Dictionnaire étymologique de la langue française,* 7th ed. (Paris: Larousse, 1947).

HATIN, E., *Bibliographie historique et critique de la presse périodique française* (Paris: Firmin-Didot, 1866).

HATZFIELD, A., and DARMESTETER, A., *Dictionnaire général de la langue française du commencement du XVIIe. siècle jusqu'à nos jours,* 7th ed. (1924).

HOEFER, F., *Nouvelle biographie générale,* 46 vols (1857–66).

HYSLOP, B., *A Guide to the general cahiers of* 1789 (New York: Columbia University Press, 1936).

MARION, M., *Dictionnaire des institutions de la France aux XVIIe. et XVIIIe. siècles* (Paris: A. Picard, 1923).

MICHAUD, L.-G., *Biographie universelle ancienne et moderne,* 45 vols, new ed. (Paris: C. Desplaces et Michaud, 1843–65).

RABBE, A., *Biographie universelle et portative des contemporains,* 5 vols (Paris: F.-G. Levrault, 1834).

2. Other works

AULARD, F. V. A., *La Révolution française et le régime féodal* (Paris: F. Alcan, 1919).

BARRIÈRE, P., *L'Académie de Bordeaux: centre de culture internationale au XVIIIe. siècle*, 1712–1792 (Bordeaux and Paris: Bière, 1951).

BARTHÉLEMY, A. DE, *Le Droit de Seigneur* (Paris: Auguste Aubry, 1866).

BAYET, A. and A. F., *Les Écrivains politiques du XVIIIe. siècle* (Paris: Armand Colin, 1904).

BIRN, R. F., 'Pierre Rousseau and the Philosophes of Bouillon', vol. 29 of *Studies on Voltaire and the Eighteenth Century*, ed. T. Besterman (Geneva: Institut et Musée Voltaire, 1964).

BOIS, P., *Paysans de l'Ouest. Des Structures économiques et sociales aux options politiques depuis l'époque révolutionnaire dans la Sarthe* (Le Mans: M. Vilaire, 1960).

BOLLEME, G., FURET, F. and others, *Livre et société dans la France du XVIIIe. siècle* (Paris and The Hague: Mouton, 1965).

BOURDE, A. J., *The Influence of England on the French agronomes, 1750–1789* (Cambridge University Press, 1953).

BRINTON, C. C., *The Lives of Talleyrand* (New York: Norton, 1937).

BRUCHET, M., *L'Abolition des droits seigneuriaux en Savoie, 1761–1793* (Annecy: Hérisson, 1908).

CAHEN, L., *Condorcet et la Révolution française* (Paris: F. Alcan, 1904).

CARCASSONNE, E., *Fénelon. L'homme et l'oeuvre* (Paris: Boivin, 1946).

— *Montesquieu et le problème de la constitution française au XVIIIe. siècle* (Paris: PUF, 1927).

CARRÉ, H., *La Noblesse de France et l'opinion publique au XVIIIe. siècle* (Paris: Édouard Champion, 1920).

CASSIRER, E., *The Philosophy of the Enlightenment*, trans. F. C. A. Koelln and J. P. Pettegrove (Boston: Beacon Press, 1955).

CAUSSY, F., *Voltaire, seigneur de village* (Paris: Hachette, 1912).

CHASSIN, C.-L., *L'Église et les derniers serfs* (Paris: E. Dentu, 1880).

CHÉREST, A., *La Chute de l'ancien régime*, 3 vols (Paris: Hachette and H. Joly, 1884–6).

CHURCH, W. F., *Constitutional thought in sixteenth-century France* (Cambridge, Mass.: Harvard University Press, 1941).

— 'The Decline of the French jurists as political theorists, 1660–1789', *French Historical Studies*, V (1967), pp. 1–40.

COBBAN, A., *Aspects of the French Revolution* (London: Jonathan Cape, 1968).

— *The Social interpretation of the French Revolution* (Cambridge University Press, 1964).

COMBE, P., *Mémoire inédit du Chancelier d'Aguesseau sur la réformation de la justice* (Grenoble: Valence, 1928).

COMBIER, E. A., *Les Justices seigneuriales du bailliage de Vermandois sous l'ancien régime* (Paris: A. Fontemoing, 1898).

COUSIN, J., *L'Académie des Sciences, Belles Lettres et Arts de Besançon: deux cents ans de vie comtoise, 1752–1952. Essai de synthèse* (Besançon: Jean Ledoux, 1954).

CRUPPI, J., *Un Avocat journaliste au XVIIIe. siècle, Linguet* (Paris: Hachette, 1895).

DAKIN, D., *Turgot and the 'ancien régime' in France* (London: Methuen, 1939).

DAVIES, A., 'The Origins of the French Peasant Revolution of 1789', *History*, XLIX (1964), pp. 24–41.

DEMANTE, G., *Étude historique sur les gens de condition mainmortable en France, au XVIIIe. siècle* (Paris: A. Picard, 1894).

DEPITRE, E., 'Le Système et la querelle de la *Noblesse Commerçante* (1756–59)', *Revue d'Histoire Économique et Sociale* (VI, 1913), 137–76.

EGRET, J., *La Pré-Révolution française, 1787–1788* (Paris: PUF, 1962).

ESMEIN, A., *Histoire de la prôcedure criminelle en France* (Paris: Larose et Forcel, 1882).

EVANS, W. H., *L'Historien Mézeray et la conception de l'histoire en France au XVIIe. siècle* (Paris: J. Gamber, 1930).

FORD, F. L., *Robe and sword: the regrouping of the French aristocracy after Louis XIV* (Cambridge, Mass.: Harvard University Press, 1953).

FORSTER, R., 'The Provincial noble: a reappraisal', *American Historical Review*, LXVIII (1963), pp. 680–91.

— 'The Survival of the nobility during the French Revolution', *Past and Present*, XXXVII (July 1967), pp. 71–86.

GARAUD, M., *La Révolution et la propriété foncière* (Paris: Recueil Sirey, 1958).

GAY, P., *Voltaire's politics, the poet as realist* (Princeton University Press, 1959).

GÉNESTAL, R., 'A. Giffard: les justices seigneuriales en Bretagne aux XVIIe. et XVIIIe. siècles, 1661–1791', *Nouvelle Revue Historique de Droit Français et Étranger*, XXVII (1903), pp. 879–87.

GIFFARD, A., *Les Justices seigneuriales en Bretagne aux XVIIe. et XVIIIe. siècles (1661–1791)* (Paris: A. Rousseau, 1903).

GOUBERT, P., *L'Ancien régime* vol. 1 (Paris: Armand Colin, 1969).

GREAVES, H. R. G., 'The Political ideas of Linguet', *Economica*, XXVIII (March 1930), pp. 40–55.

GRUDER, V. R., *The Royal provincial intendants: a governing elite in eighteenth-century France* (Ithaca, New York: Cornell University Press, 1968).

HAMPSON, N., *The Enlightenment* (Harmondsworth: Penguin Books, 1968).

HARSIN, P. (ed.), *Dutot: 'Réflexions politiques sur les finances et le commerce*, 2 vols (Paris and Liège: E. Droz, 1935).

HECHT, J., 'Un Problème de population active au XVIIIe. siècle, en France: la querelle de la noblesse commerçante', *Population: Revue de l'Institut National d'Études Démographiques*, XIX (1964), pp. 267–89.

HECKSCHER, E. F., *Mercantilism*, 2 vols, ed. E. F. Söderlund, 2nd rev. ed. (London: Allen & Unwin, 1955).

HERBERT, S., *The Fall of feudalism in France* (London: Methuen, 1921).

HIGGS, D. C., 'The Ultra-royalist movement at Toulouse under the Second Restoration (1815–1830), unpublished Ph.D. thesis, London University (1964).

HUBERT, R., *Les Sciences sociales dans l'Encyclopédie* (Paris: F. Alcan, 1923).

HUTT, M., 'The Curés and the third estate: the ideas of reform in the pamphlets of the French lower clergy in the period 1787–1789', *Journal of Ecclesiastical History*, VIII (1957), pp. 74–95.

KARYEEV, N. I., *Les Paysans et la question paysanne en France dans le dernier quart du XVIIIe. siècle*, trans. from the Russian by C. W. Woynarowska (Paris: V. Giard et E. Brière, 1899).

LACOUR-GAYET, G., *L'Éducation politique de Louis XIV* (Paris: Hachette, 1898).

LA HARPE, J. DE, *Le Journal des Savants et l'Angleterre, 1702–89* (Berkeley: University of California Press, 1941).

LEFEBVRE, G., *Études sur la Révolution française* (Paris, PUF, 1954).

LEMARCHAND, G., 'Sur la société française en 1789', *Revue d'Histoire Moderne et Contemporaine* XIX (1972), pp. 73–91.

LEMERCIER, P. *Les Justices seigneuriales de la région parisienne de 1580 à 1789* (Paris: Domat-Montchrestien, 1933).

LÉVY-BRUHL, H., 'La Noblesse de France et le commerce à la fin de l'ancien régime', *Revue d'Histoire Moderne*, VIII (1933), pp. 209–235.

LÉVY-BRUHL, L., 'The Cartesian spirit and history', *Philosophy and history: essays presented to Ernst Cassirer*, ed. R. Klibansky and H. J. Paton (New York: Harper & Row, 1963), pp. 191–6.

LICHTEMBERGER, A., *Le Socialisme au XVIIIe. siècle* (Paris: F. Alcan, 1895).

LOUGH, J., *The 'Encyclopédie' in eighteenth-century England and other studies* (Newcastle: Oriel Press, 1970).

LUCAS-CHAMPIONNIÈRE, P., *De la Propriété des eaux courantes, du droit des riverains, et la valeur actuelle des concessions féodales* (Paris: C. Hingray, 1846).

MARION, M., *La Garde des Sceaux, Lamoignon et la réforme judiciaire de 1788* (Paris: Hachette, 1905).

MASSÉ, P., 'Survivances des droits féodaux dans l'Ouest (1793–1902)', *Annales Historiques de la Révolution Française*, no. 181 (1965), pp. 270–98.

MÉTHIVIER, H., *L'Ancien Régime* (Paris: PUF, 1961).

MONSELET, C., *Les Originaux du siècle dernier: les oubliés et les dédaignés* (Paris: Michel-Lévy, 1864).

MORNET, D., 'L'Enseignement des bibliothèques privées, 1750–1780', *Revue d'Histoire Littéraire de la France*, XVII (1910), pp. 449–96.

— *Les Origines intellectuelles de la Révolution française, 1715–1787* (Paris: Armand Colin, 1933).

— *La Pensée française au XVIIIe. siècle* (Paris: Armand Colin, 1926).

MOUSNIER, R., *Les XVIe. et XVIIe. siècles: les progrès de la civilisation européenne et le déclin de l'Orient (1492–1715)*, vol. IV of *Histoire générale des civilisations*, ed. H. Crouzet (Paris: PUF, 1954).

— *État et société sous François Ier. et pendant le gouvernement personnel de Louis XIV*, 2 vols (Paris, n.d.).

PALMER, R. R., *Catholics and unbelievers in eighteenth-century France* (Princeton University Press, 1939).

PAPPAS, J. N., 'Berthier's *Journal de Trévoux* and the philosophes', Vol. 3 of *Studies on Voltaire and the Eighteenth Century*, ed. T. Besterman (Geneva: Institut et Musée Voltaire, 1957).

POITRINEAU, A., 'Aspects de la crise des justices seigneuriales dans l'Auvergne du dix-huitième siècle', *Revue Historique de Droit Français et Étranger*, 4th ser., XXXIX (1961), pp. 552–70.

REESINK, H. J., *L'Angleterre et la littérature anglaise dans les trois plus anciens périodiques français de Hollande de 1684 à 1709* (Zutphen: W. J. Thieme, 1931).

REINHARD, M., 'Sur l'histoire de la Révolution française: travaux récents et perspectives', *Annales. Économies. Sociétés. Civilisations*, XIV (1959), pp. 553–70.

RÉMOND, R., *La Vie politique en France depuis 1789*, 2 vols (Paris: Armand Colin, 1968–9).

RICHARD, G., 'La Noblesse de France et les sociétés par actions à la fin du XVIIIe. siècle', *Revue d'Histoire Économique et Sociale*, XL 1962), pp. 484–523.

ROBIN, R., 'Fief et seigneurie dans le droit et l'idéologie juridique à la fin du XVIIIe. siècle', *Annales Historiques de la Révolution Française* XLIII (1971), 554–602.

SAGNAC, P., *La Législation civile de la Révolution française, 1789–1804* (Paris: Hachette, 1898).

sée, h., 'La Rédaction et la valeur historique des cahiers de paroisses pour les États-Généraux de 1789', *Revue Historique*, CIII (1910), pp. 292–306.

shackleton, r., *Montesquieu: a critical biography* (London: Oxford University Press, 1961).

shennan, j. h., *The Parlement of Paris* (London: Eyre & Spottiswoode, 1968).

simon, r., *Henry de Boulainviller: historien, politique, philosophe, astrologue, 1658–1722* (Paris: Boivin, 1942).

smith, d. mack, *A History of Sicily*, 2 vols (New York: Viking Press, 1968).

soboul, a., *La France à la veille de la Révolution*, vol. 1 (Paris: La Société d'Édition d'Enseignement Supérieur, 1966).

— 'De la Pratique des terriers à la veille de la Révolution', *Annales. Économies. Sociétés. Civilisations*, XIX (1964), pp. 1049–65.

— 'La Révolution française et la "féodalité". Notes sur le prélèvement féodal', *Revue Historique*, CCXL (July–September 1968), pp. 33–56.

— 'Survivances "féodales" dans la société rurale française au XIXe. siècle', *Annales. Économies. Sociétés. Civilisations*, XXIII (1968), pp. 965–86.

soreau, e., *La Chute de l'ancien régime* (Paris: Les Belles Lettres, 1937).

taylor, g. v., 'Noncapitalist wealth and the origins of the French Revolution', *American Historical Review*, LXXII (1967), pp. 469–496.

tieghem, p. van, *L'Année Littéraire, 1754–1790, comme intermédiaire en France des littératures étrangères* (Paris: F. Rieder, 1917).

tocqueville, a. de, *L'Ancien Régime*, ed. G. W. Headlam (London: Oxford University Press, 1904).

vaissière, p. de, *Gentilhommes campagnards de l'ancienne France* (Paris: Perrin, 1903).

viguier, j., 'Les Émeutes populaires dans le Quercy en 1789 et 1790', *La Révolution Française: revue d'histoire moderne et contemporaine*, XXI (1891).

vroil, j. de, *Étude sur Clicquot-Blervache, économiste du XVIIIe. siècle* (Paris: Guillaumin, 1870).

weil, g., *Le Journal: origines, évolution et rôle de la presse périodique* (Paris: La Rennaissance du livre, 1934).

weulersse, g., *Le Mouvement physiocratique en France de 1756 à 1770*, 2 vols (Paris: F. Alcan, 1910).

— *La Physiocratie à la fin du règne de Louis XV, 1770–1774* (Paris: PUF, 1959).

— *La Physiocratie sous les ministères de Turgot et de Necker, 1774–1781* (Paris: PUF, 1950).

WILSON, A. M., 'Why did the political theory of the Encyclopedists not prevail?', *French Historical Studies*, I (1960), pp. 283–94.

Index

academies, 105–6, 134; *Académie Française*, 6, 66–7, 107, 187; *Académie Royale des Sciences*, 131; Angers, 134; Besançon, 122; Châlons-sur-Marne, 106, 110, 134, 145, 152; Lyons, 106; Nancy, 105; Orléans, 106; Rouen, 106; Soissons, 106
acapte, droit d', 185
agriculture: feudal dues interference, 14, 136–8, 142–7; serfdom's effect, 122, 140–1
agronomes, 136–9, 143, 161, 173
Aix, archbishop of, 174
Alençon, nobles of, 101–2
Alès de Corbet, vicomte, 89–90
American Independence, Declaration of, 164
Anjou, nobles of, 102
Année Littéraire, periodical, 93; history in, 28; law, 74–5; trade, 93, 95, 96, 97
anti-clericalism, 31–4, 111, 119–20, 127, 181
Arcq, chevalier d', 87–8, 90–1, 94, 95–6
Argenson, marquis d', 41, 46, 94, 147, 157; on feudalism, 30, 39, 40, 43, 135; on seigniorial justice, 72–3, 152, 159
Argis, Boucher d', 6, 156, 157, 159
aristocrates, during Revolution, 181–2, 186
Aubry de Saint-Vibert, 64
Autun, mayor of, 187
Avesne, *tiers* of, 121
Aynac, peasants of, 184

Babeuf, 66
Balud brothers, 184
ban and *arrière-ban*, 2, 44, 102, 135
banalité, droit de, 5, 57–9, 131, 146, 160–1, 169, 175, 179, 189
Barthoul, abbé, 89
Bastille, 107
Baverel, abbé, 116, 141–2
Bayle, Pierre, 124
Beardé de L'Abbaye, 143
Beaudean, *tiers* of, 172
Beaumont, Fresnais de, 137
Beauvray, Lefèvre de, 42, 110
Bellami, *avocat*, 71
Bellicart, 105
Belloni, marchese de, 77
Benedictines, 123
Berne, Economic Society of, 137
Bertrand, Jean, 137
Besné de La Hauteville, 150, 157
Bibliothèque Bleue, 163
Bibliothèque Françoise, periodical, 63–4
Bibliothèque Nationale, purge of, 178
Bibliothèque des Sciences et des Beaux-Arts, periodical, 96, 97
bienfaisance, use of word, 104, 106
biens nationaux, 189
Billardon de Sauvigny, 89
Blervache, Clicquot de, 44, 129, 145, 146
Boncerf, 134, 149–50, 160, 161, 163–4; Affair, 164–7; on feudal dues, 135–6, 144, 146, 149; on ownership of property, 141, 142, 147; on serfdom, 108, 112–13, 129
Bordeaux, procurator-general at, 190
Bossuet, bishop, 10, 49